It's Another Ace Book from CGP

This book is for 14-16 year olds.

First we stick in all the really important stuff you need to do well in the Key Stage Four Physics Higher Paper.

Then we have a really good stab at making it funny — so you'll actually use it.

Simple as that.

CGP are just the best

The central aim of Coordination Group Publications is to produce top quality books that are carefully written, immaculately presented and marvellously funny — whilst always making sure they exactly cover the National Curriculum for each subject.

And then we supply them to as many people as we possibly can, as cheaply as we possibly can.

Buy our books — they're ace

	Quantity	Symbol	Standard Units	Formula
1	Potential Difference	V	volt, V	$V = I \times R$
2	Current	I	ampere, A	$I = V / R$
3	Resistance	R	ohm, Ω	$R = V / I$
4	Charge	Q	coulomb, C	$Q = I \times t$
5	Power	P	watt, W	$P = V \times I$ or $P = I^2R$
6	Energy	E	joule, J	$E = QV$ or $V = E/Q$
7	Time	t	second, s	$E = P \times t$ or $E = IVt$
8	Force	F	newton, N	$F = ma$
9	Mass	m	kilogram, kg	
10	Weight (a force)	W	newton, N	$W = mg$
11	Density	D	kg per m^3, kg/m^3	$D = m/V$
12	Moment	M	newton-metre, Nm	$M = F \times r$
13	Velocity or Speed	v or s	metre/sec, m/s	$s = d/t$
14	Acceleration	a	metre/sec^2, m/s^2	$a = \Delta v/t$ or $a = F/m$
15	Pressure	P	pascal, Pa (N/m^2)	$P = F/A$ $P_1V_1 = P_2V_2$
16	Area	A	$metre^2$, m^2	
17	Volume	V	$metre^3$, m^3	
18	Frequency	f	hertz, Hz	$f = 1/T$ (T=time period)
19	Wavelength (a distance)	λ or d	metre, m	$v = f \times \lambda$ (wave formula)
20	Work done	Wd	joule, J	$Wd = F \times d$
21	Potential Energy	PE	joule, J	$PE = m \times g \times h$
22	Kinetic Energy	KE	joule, J	$KE = \frac{1}{2}mv^2$

$$\text{Efficiency} = \frac{\text{Useful work output}}{\text{Total energy input}}$$

$$\frac{\text{Primary Coil Voltage}}{\text{Secondary Voltage}} = \frac{\text{No. of turns on Primary Coil}}{\text{No. of turns on Secondary}}$$

You should be pretty familiar with the 34 elements shown shaded.

You don't really need to know anything about the others.

Mass number (top of each box) — Atomic number (bottom of each box)

Periods	Group I	Group II											Group III	Group IV	Group V	Group VI	Group VII	Group O
1								1 H Hydrogen 1										4 He Helium 2
2	7 Li Lithium 3	9 Be Beryllium 4											11 B Boron 5	12 C Carbon 6	14 N Nitrogen 7	16 O Oxygen 8	19 F Fluorine 9	20 Ne Neon 10
3	23 Na Sodium 11	24 Mg Magnesium 12											27 Al Aluminium 13	28 Si Silicon 14	31 P Phosphorus 15	32 S Sulphur 16	35.5 Cl Chlorine 17	40 Ar Argon 18
4	39 K Potassium 19	40 Ca Calcium 20	45 Sc Scandium 21	48 Ti Titanium 22	51 V Vanadium 23	52 Cr Chromium 24	55 Mn Manganese 25	56 Fe Iron 26	59 Co Cobalt 27	59 Ni Nickel 28	64 Cu Copper 29	65 Zn Zinc 30	70 Ga Gallium 31	73 Ge Germanium 32	75 As Arsenic 33	79 Se Selenium 34	80 Br Bromine 35	84 Kr Krypton 36
5	85.5 Rb Rubidium 37	88 Sr Strontium 38	89 Y Yttrium 39	91 Zr Zirconium 40	93 Nb Niobium 41	96 Mo Molybdenum 42	98 Tc Technetium 43	101 Ru Ruthenium 44	103 Rh Rhodium 45	106 Pd Palladium 46	108 Ag Silver 47	112 Cd Cadmium 48	115 In Indium 49	119 Sn Tin 50	122 Sb Antimony 51	128 Te Tellurium 52	127 I Iodine 53	131 Xe Xenon 54
6	133 Cs Caesium 55	137 Ba Barium 56	139 La Lanthanum 57	178.5 Hf Hafnium 72	181 Ta Tantalum 73	184 W Tungsten 74	186 Re Rhenium 75	190 Os Osmium 76	192 Ir Iridium 77	195 Pt Platinum 78	197 Au Gold 79	201 Hg Mercury 80	204 Tl Thallium 81	207 Pb Lead 82	209 Bi Bismuth 83	210 Po Polonium 84	210 At Astatine 85	222 Rn Radon 86
7	223 Fr Francium 87	226 Ra Radium 88	227 Ac Actinium 89															

The Lanthanides	140 Ce Cerium 58	141 Pr Praseodymium 59	144 Nd Neodymium 60	147 Pm Promethium 61	150 Sm Samarium 62	152 Eu Europium 63	157 Gd Gadolinium 64	159 Tb Terbium 65	162 Dy Dysprosium 66	165 Ho Holmium 67	167 Er Erbium 68	169 Tm Thulium 69	173 Yb Ytterbium 70	175 Lu Lutetium 71
The Actinides	232 Th Thorium 90	231 Pa Protactinium 91	238 U Uranium 92	237 Np Neptunium 93	242 Pu Plutonium 94	243 Am Americium 95	247 Cm Curium 96	247 Bk Berkelium 97	251 Cf Californium 98	254 Es Einsteinium 99	253 Fm Fermium 100	256 Md Mendelevium 101 ...the old rogue	254 No Nobelium 102	257 Lr Lawrencium 103

Contents

Published by Coordination Group Publications Ltd.
Typesetting and layout by The Science Coordination Group

Coordinated by Paddy Gannon BSc MA

Contributors:
Bill Dolling
Jane Cartwright
Alex Kizildas

Design Editor: Ed Lacey BSc PGCE

With thanks to Colin Wells for the proof-reading

ISBN 1-84146-409-0

Groovy website: www.cgpbooks.co.uk

Printed by Elanders Hindson, Newcastle upon Tyne.

0701

Common Physics Apparatus

Know your Instruments

1) Write the *name* of each piece of apparatus shown below.

a) 

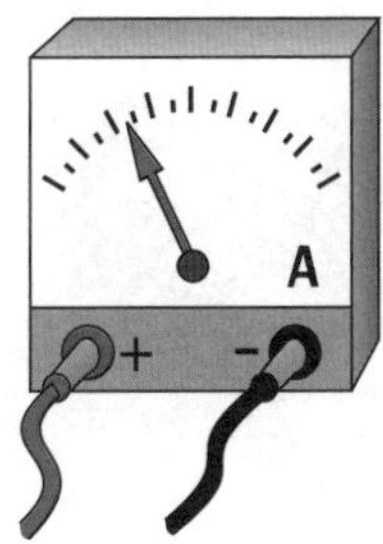

b)

c)

d)

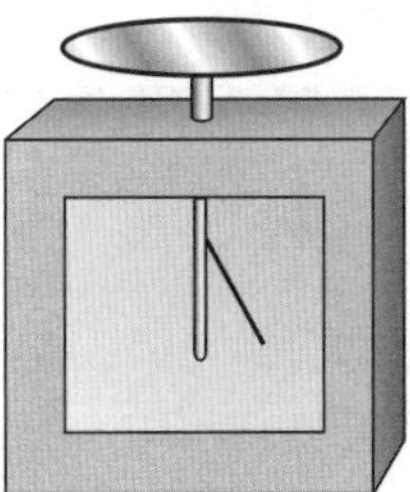

e)

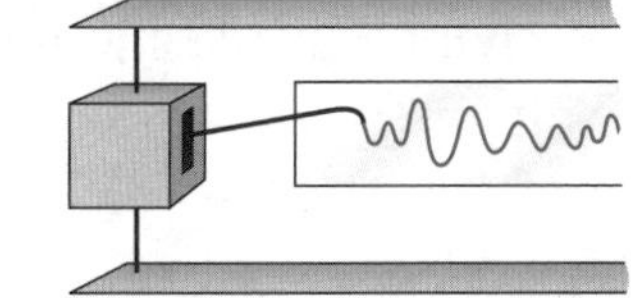

f)

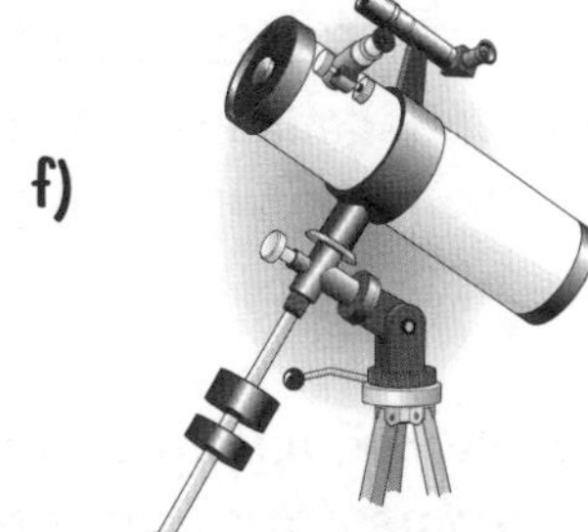

g)

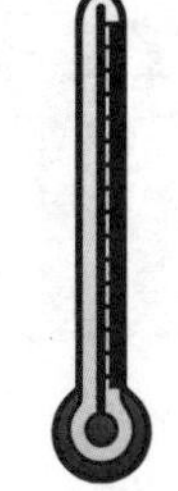

h)

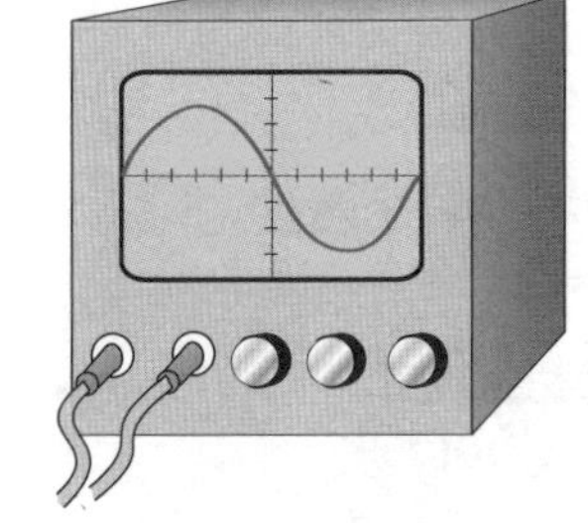

i)

j)

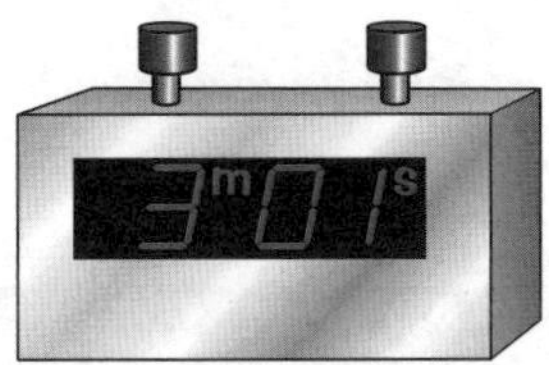

k)

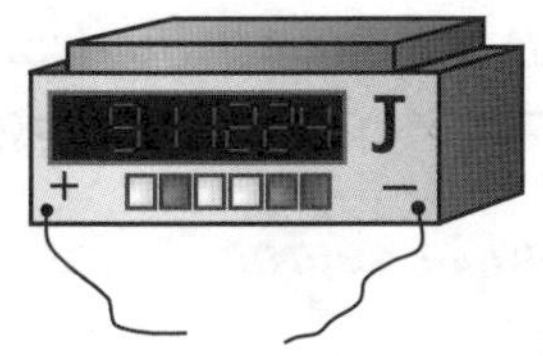

l)

2) Which piece of apparatus shown above is used to:

a) measure force?
b) measure radioactivity?
c) measure the current in an electric circuit?
d) detect the presence of electric charges?
e) measure time?
f) measure pressure?
g) measure the amount of electrical energy?
h) measure potential difference?
i) detect and measure seismic waves?
j) collect light from distant objects?
k) measure temperature?
l) display electrical signals?

Top Tip We've all spent lots of time staring at physics apparatus and wondering why it won't work. Just try to work out what it's supposed to do, even if there's little chance of it actually behaving. Look at the pictures and work out what each one is measuring, and remember the name.

Reading Scales

Making Sense of your Readings

1) *A student carries out an experiment with a resistor. An ammeter and voltmeter are used to measure the current through the resistor and the voltage across it.*

The meter reading taken in the experiment is shown opposite.

a) What *current* does the meter read?
b) What *voltage* does the meter read?
c) Calculate the *resistance* of the resistor using your answers to parts a) and b).
d) If the voltage is kept constant, what change would the meter show if the resistor is replaced with another one with *twice* the resistance?

2) *Angela carries out an experiment to find the electrical energy used by a light bulb. She ran the experiment for 2 minutes.*

The reading on the joulemeter she used is shown opposite.

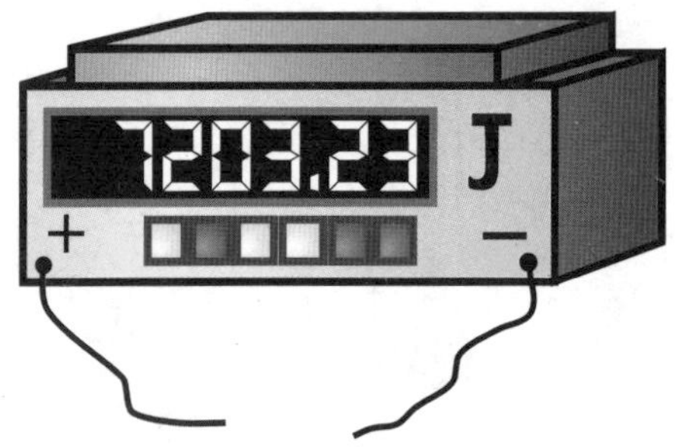

a) *Round* the reading to the nearest joule.
b) Use the rounded figure to calculate the *power* of the light bulb to the nearest watt.
c) What should she do to be *more confident* of her result for the power of the light bulb?

3) *Neville is part of a group carrying out a radioactivity experiment. They take several readings of background count and the average count rate is found to be 14 counts/min.*

They place a detector near a radioactive source (which they know emits beta particles).

The counter is switched on for 30 seconds and the counter reading is shown in the picture opposite.

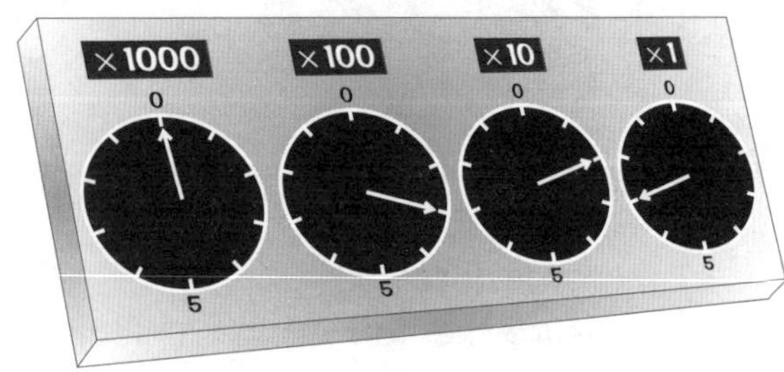

a) What *reading* does the counter show?
b) What is the count rate in *counts per minute*?
c) What is the *corrected* count rate due to the source alone?

They are told that the half-life of the source is 45 minutes.

d) How many counts per minute would you expect them to record 3 hours later?
e) Describe the likely *effect* of wrapping the detector in tissue paper.
f) Why is it necessary to take *several* measurements to work out the background count?

Reading Scales

Making Sense of your Readings

4) *A group of students is carrying out an experiment on pressure. They use a Bourdon gauge to measure the pressures.*

a) What is the reading on the Bourdon gauge (shown opposite)? Give your answer in kilopascals.

b) The pointer on the gauge does not return to zero when they disconnect the gauge from the apparatus. Explain this observation.

5) *An old forcemeter is being used to measure weights.*

Abbie looks at the scale of the forcemeter (shown opposite) before any weights have been hung on.

Before any weights on

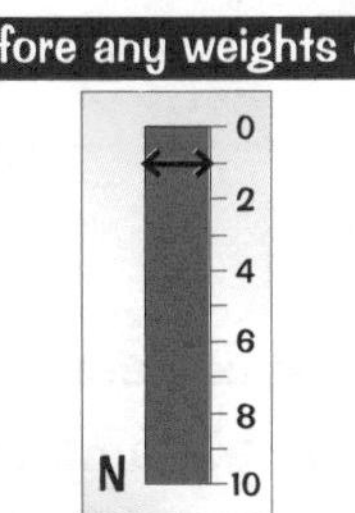

Then the first weight is attached...

With first weight on

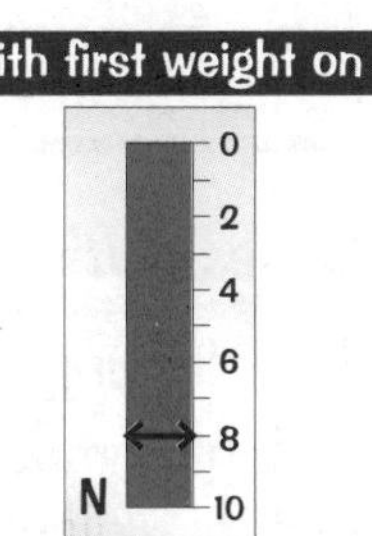

a) Calculate the force pulling the weight downwards.

b) What is the cause of this downward force?

c) How would the reading change if the weight was lowered gently into a beaker of water?

Rounding Off

6) Round the following numbers up or down:

a) 3645N to the nearest kN.

b) 195 seconds to the nearest minute.

c) 13.27 cm to the nearest mm.

d) 2493 kW to the nearest MW.

e) 12.56 Nm to the nearest joule.

f) 9854399 amps to the nearest kiloamp.

7) *Work out the answers to the following calculations.*

a) Calculate the resistance of a resistor if a potential difference of 5.5V drives a current of 2.1A through it. Give your answer to 3 significant figures.

b) Calculate the volume of a cylindrical barrel if it has a height of 1m and a radius of 0.32m. Give your answer to 2 significant figures.

c) Calculate the speed of a skier if he travels a distance of 35.7 metres through two slalom gates in a time of 5.2 seconds. Give your answer to 1 decimal place.

d) Find the work done when a tractor winch pulls a weight of 34.6N a distance of 9.1m vertically upwards. Give your answer to 2 significant figures.

e) An engine has an efficiency of 45%. What is the output of useful energy for the engine if the energy input is 98.4J? Give your answer to 2 significant figures.

f) Initially there is 39.6g of a radioactive element. It has a half-life of 2 days. What mass of the original element will remain after 10 days? Give your answer 2 significant figures.

g) Calculate the kinetic energy (in joules) of a cricket ball, mass 0.31 kg, travelling at a speed of 13 m/s. Give your answer to 1 decimal place.

Top Tip Reading a number from a scale, it couldn't be easier. Look carefully to see if the scale goes up in ones, tens, twos or fives, or even "point ones" or "point twos" — otherwise you'll be writing down completely the wrong number in your answers. Don't forget, you will be asked to read from a scale in the Exam, not just in practical assessments. One last thing: If you're asked to read from a scale, don't forget to include the correct unit with the measurement.

Units

Standard Units

1) In the table below, write down the standard unit for each of the quantities.

Quantity	Potential Difference	Power	Force	Velocity	Frequency	Current
Standard Unit						

2) In the table below, write down the quantity for each of the standard units.

Standard Unit	ohms	joules	kilograms	pascals	coulombs	seconds
Quantity						

3) *Physics units can be combined to give new units.*

For the following combinations a) to j), write down the correct unit if we:

a) multiply amps by ohms.
b) multiply amps by seconds.
c) multiply kilograms by metres/(sec)^2.
d) divide newtons by (metres)^2.
e) multiply hertz by metres.
f) multiply coulombs by volts.
g) divide volts by amps.
h) multiply newtons by metres.
i) multiply pascals by (metres)^2.
j) divide joules by seconds.

Derived Units

A derived unit is just a multiple or sub-multiple of a unit, and it can sometimes be written by adding a prefix before the unit.

4) In the following, calculate how many:

a) seconds in 3 minutes.
b) hours in 23 days.
c) metres in 3.2 km.
d) kilograms in 7200g.
e) newtons in 0.034 kilonewtons.
f) watts in 1.2 MW.
g) milliohms in 32 ohms.
h) coulombs in 6200000 microcoulombs.
i) milliseconds in 9.6 seconds.
j) watts in 33 kilowatts.
k) metres in 456 centimetres.

5) Write down the name and symbol of the derived unit for:

a) one thousand metres.
b) one thousandth of a watt.
c) one million joules.
d) one millionth of an ohm.
e) one millionth of a kilonewton.
f) one million millivolts.

6) Give the *prefix* we would put in front of a unit if we wanted to multiply it by the following numbers:

a) 10^3
b) 10^6
c) 10^{-3}
d) 10^{-6}
e) 0.000 000 000 1
f) $\frac{1}{10}$
g) $\frac{1}{1\,000\,000}$
h) 10^9
i) 0.000 000 000 001

Top Tip Way too many people lose way too many marks in the Exam just because they forget to *include the units* in their answers. It really doesn't take you long to put them in, so get into the habit of including the units *now*, and you won't be losing marks later.

Using Formulae

Rearranging Formulae

1) Draw *formula triangles* for the following equations a) to h):

a) V = I x R b) I = Q / t c) P = V x I
d) D = m / V e) d = s x t f) Wd = F x d
g) f = 1 / T h) P = F / A

2) Referring to the equations in Qu.1, *express*:

a) R in terms of V and I b) t in terms of d and s c) T in terms of f
d) V in terms of m and D e) Q in terms of I and t f) I in terms of V and P
g) F in terms of Wd and d h) I in terms of V and R i) t in terms of Q and I
j) m in terms of D and V k) s in terms of d and t l) F in terms of P and A

3) Using formula triangles or otherwise, *work out* the following:

a) Calculate a weasel's *speed* if it travels 8 metres along a tunnel in 2.5 seconds.
b) Calculate the circuit *resistance* if a voltage of 12V drives a current of 2A.
c) What is the *volume* of a washer with a mass of 0.08 kg and a density of 4000 kg /m^3?
d) How much *work* is done if a weightlifter lifts a weight of 400 newtons through a distance of 0.6 metres?
e) What *current* flows if a charge of 0.05 coulombs passes a fixed point in 0.001 seconds?

4) Use the formula triangles below to answer the following questions:

Write down the *equation* for:

a) f in terms of v and λ
b) M in terms of F and r
c) V in terms of E and Q
d) a in terms of F and m
e) P in terms of E and t
f) m in terms of W and g
g) E in terms of Q and V
h) F in terms of a and m
i) F in terms of M and r j) W in terms of m and g k) λ in terms of v and f

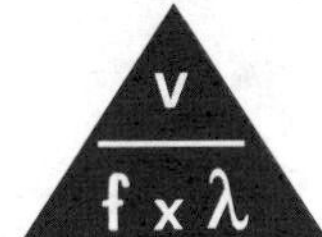

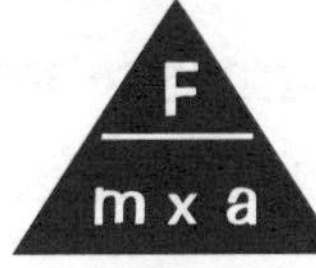

5) Use the formulae triangles in Qu.4 to help answer the following questions.

a) What is the *energy* transformed when a charge of 3C flows through a potential difference of 6V?
b) What is the *weight* of a 2.5 kg mass (g = 10 N/kg)?
c) A force of 300 newtons is used to slow a 4500 kg car. What is the *acceleration* of the car?
d) What is the *velocity* of a wave if it has a frequency of 6 Hz and a wavelength of 1.5m?
e) What is the *moment* on a lever if a 36 newton force acts 1.2 metres from the pivot?
f) How much *energy* does a 60 watt light bulb consume in 1 minute?
g) A rocket motor accelerates a 2 kg mass at 2.2 m/s^2. What *force* is the motor producing?
h) A wave of frequency 0.5 Hz travels at a velocity of 20 m/s. What is its *wavelength*?

Top Tip OK, it's a page full of boring, repetitive formulae, I admit — but if you plough through them all you'll get plenty of practice in using formulae and formula triangles. When it's like second nature, then it'll be easy. *Formula triangles* can make questions really straightforward. You stick in the numbers *(in SI units)*, you work out the *answer*, and you write it down with the *correct units*. That's all there is to it.

Current, Voltage, Resistance

These questions are about electric current: what it is, what makes it move and what tries to stop it.

Current and Voltage

1) *Fill the gaps* in the following paragraph about electric current.
Words to use: free electrons, charge, positive, metal, circuit

Current is a flow of __________ around the __________. Electric current can only flow if there are __________ __________ like in a __________, where electrons flow throughout the structure of __________ charged ions.

2) *Copy* the circuit diagram and mark on the (+) and (–) on the cell.
Mark the direction of the current, ⟶, and the direction of the moving electrons, ·········· .

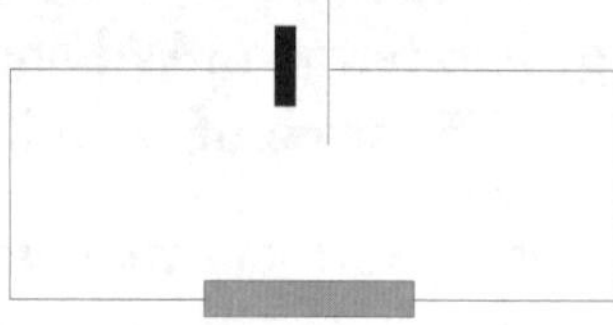

3) *Copy* these sentences using the correct underlined words.

The *current / voltage / resistance* in a circuit flows from *positive / negative* to *positive / negative*. Electrons flow in the *same direction as / opposite direction to* the flow of "conventional current".

Electrolysis

4) *Copy the diagram* on the right.
Label the electrodes positive (+) and negative (–) .
Draw arrows to show the movement of ions (⊕⟶ , ⟵⊖).

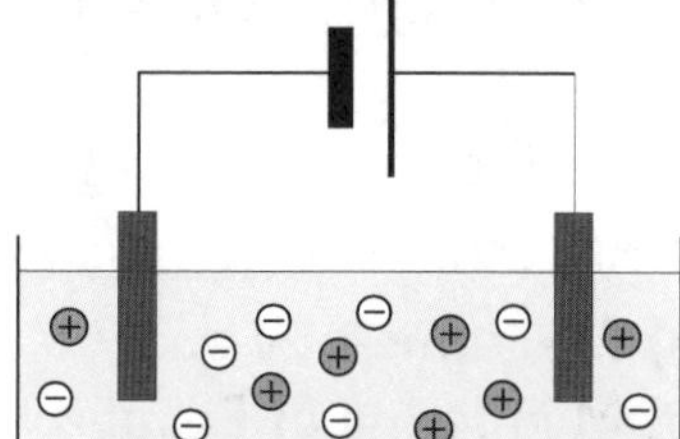

5) *Copy and complete* the following paragraph about electrolysis.
Use these words: sodium chloride, sodium chloride solution, liquids, positive, negative, charges, dissolved

Electrolytes are __________ which contain freely moving __________. They are either ions __________ in water like __________ or molten ionic liquids like __________. When the current is switched on, the __________ charges move towards the positive electrode and the __________ charges move towards the negative electrode.

Resistance

Resistance is anything that reduces the flow of current. Electrical components and household electrical appliances all have some resistance.

6) A kettle is plugged into a 230V mains socket and a current of 10A flows through its element. *Calculate* the resistance of the element.
7) Find the current that flows when a resistance of 18Ω is connected to a 9V battery.
8) What is the voltage of the battery that supplies a 3A current through a 5Ω resistor?
9) Complete the table on the right:

Voltage(V)	Current(A)	Resistance(Ω)
	2.0	6.0
230		23.0
6	3.0	
1.5		15.0
12	4.0	
	1.5	5.0

10) *The table shows measurements of voltage across and current through a component.*
a) *Plot a graph* of voltage (volts) against current (amps).
b) *Find* the component's resistance.
c) Is the component a resistor, a filament lamp or a diode?
d) *Explain* your answer to part c).

Voltage(V)	Current(A)
0	0
0.75	1.0
1.50	2.0
2.25	3.0
3.00	4.0
3.75	5.0

Current, Voltage, Resistance

Resistance

11) Answer the questions for the circuits a) to f).

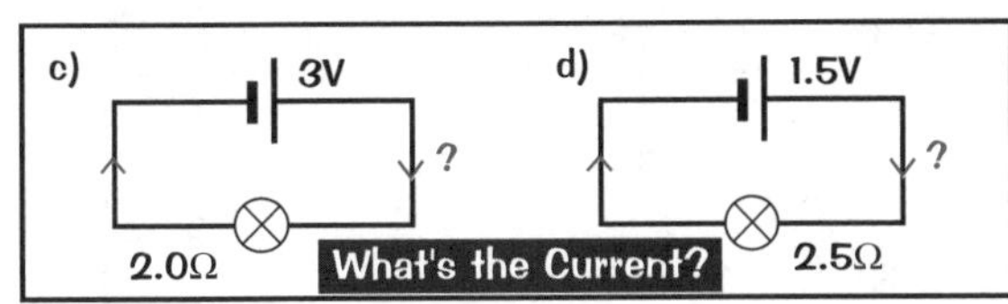

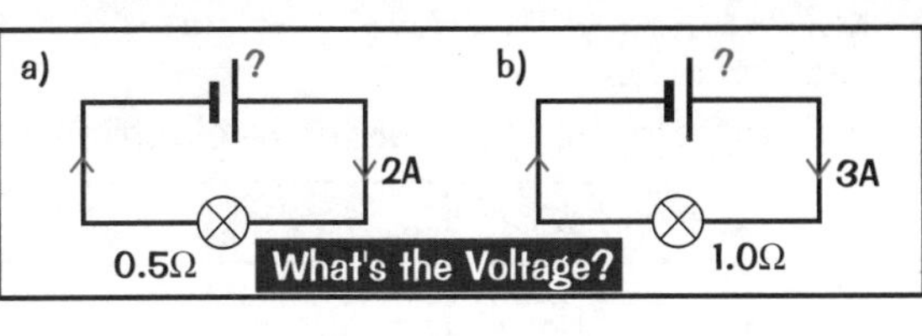

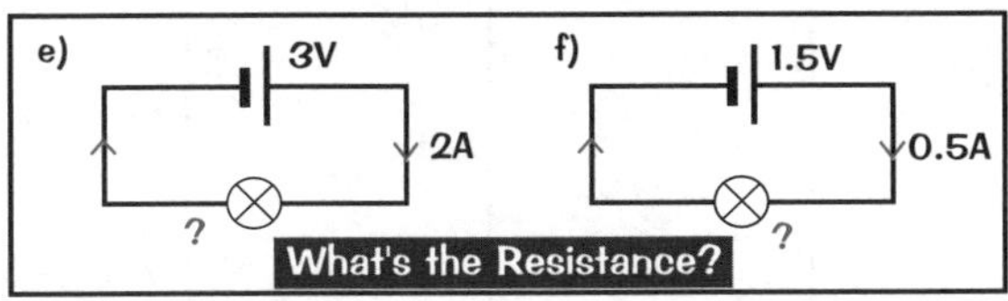

12) *Fill in the gaps* (or circle) the correct answer:

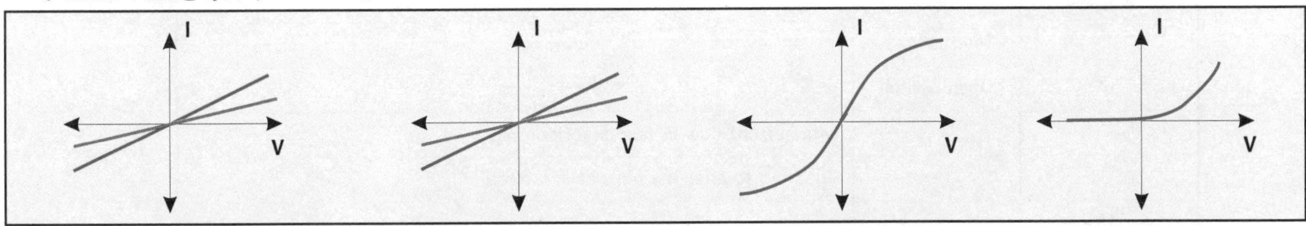

LONG AND SHORT WIRE
The graph with the steeper slope is the *longer/shorter* wire of the same material as it has a *higher/lower* resistance.

THIN AND THICK WIRE
The graph with the steeper slope is the *thick / thin* wire of the same material as it has a *higher / lower* resistance.

FILAMENT LAMP
As the ___________ of the filament ___________, the resistance increases.

DIODE
Current only flows through a diode in ______ __________.

Summary

13) *Match the words with their correct description on the right:*

- a) current
- b) resistance
- c) coulomb
- d) diode
- e) watt (W)
- f) electrolyte
- g) voltage increase
- h) amp (A)
- i) ammeter
- j) nichrome
- k) voltmeter
- l) increase the resistance
- m) copper
- n) volt (V)

- . Unit of charge
- . Measures voltage
- . More current will flow
- . Reduces current flow
- . Metal wire of high resistance
- . Measures current
- . Flow of electrons
- . Ions dissolved in water
- . Allows current flow in one direction only
- . Unit of voltage
- . Unit of current
- . Unit of power
- . Metal wire of low resistance
- . Less current will flow

Top Tips

This is the background to all the stuff on electricity. You need to understand *what it is*, *what makes it move* and *what tries* to stop it, otherwise you won't really understand any of the questions about electricity in this section. You do need to *learn* the four graphs of current/voltage in question 12. They come up in the Exam pretty often, and it'd be a shame to miss out on the marks.

Circuit Symbols and Devices

Symbols

1) *Complete the table* for these electrical components. You need to know these for your exam.

CIRCUIT SYMBOL	NAME FOR CIRCUIT SYMBOL	WHAT IT DOES
—||—		
	LDR	
		Converts electrical energy into sound energy.
—(V)—		
		Wire inside it breaks if the current is too high, protecting the appliance.
—▭—		
	Thermistor	
	Open Switch	
		Lets current flow in one direction only
		Adjusted to alter the current in a circuit
—(M)—		
	Ammeter	

Using Components

2) a) *Design a circuit* using these electrical components that would allow the speed of the motor to be varied.

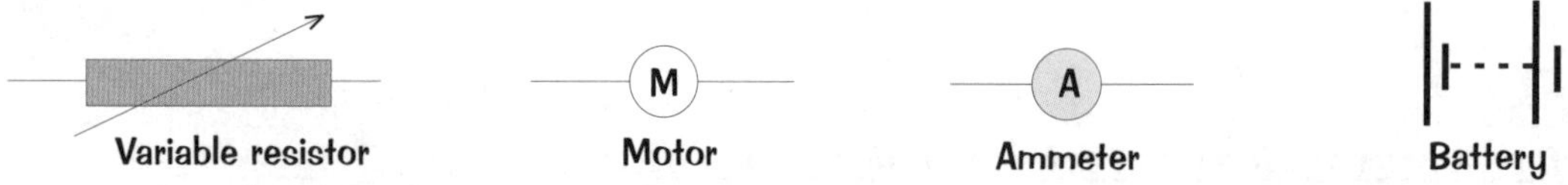

b) *The variable resistor can be adjusted to slow the motor down.* *Explain* this using the words *resistance* and *current*.

c) When the motor is *slowed down*, what happens to the reading on the ammeter?

d) *Suggest* how you could slow down the motor even more by changing one of the components.

3) *A dimmer switch controls the brightness of a light: turn it clockwise to increase the brightness, or anti-clockwise to decrease it. It works by using a variable resistor to control the current that the bulb receives.*

— It is illustrated in the diagram opposite.

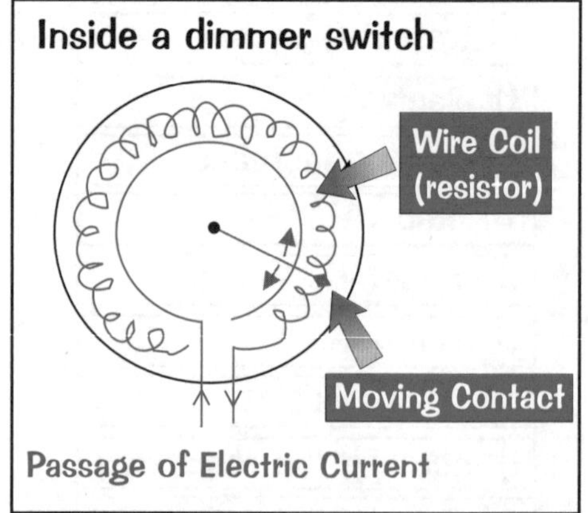

a) Draw the path followed by the current if the lights are *dim*; *medium brightness*; and *bright*.

Below are three readings of current and resistance taken from the switch at different settings.

b) Complete the table using the same descriptions for brightness used in part a).

c) What happens to the size of the current when the resistance is increased?

d) What happens to the size of the current when the resistance is decreased?

Brightness of Lights	Current(A)	Resistance(Ω)
	1.0	6.0
	2.0	3.0
	3.0	2.0

More Devices

Designing Circuits

1) Draw a *circuit diagram* of a battery-operated torch, with 2 cells, a switch and a filament bulb.
2) Draw a circuit diagram of a *loudspeaker*, with a power supply and a switch.
3) Draw a circuit diagram of an *electric heater*, power supply and switch.
4) Draw a circuit diagram of an *intruder alarm*, with an on/off switch, a hidden switch which is triggered when trodden on, and a *loudspeaker* to sound the alarm.
   — Now draw the circuit for a similar alarm which is triggered by light.

Variable Resistors

5) *Use the data* in the table opposite to plot a graph of resistance R, against light intensity. *Draw* the best fit curve.

Resistance / Ω	Light Intensity / units
100,000	0.5
55,000	2.0
40,000	3.0
20,000	5.0
1000	7.5
100	10.0

a) How does the resistance change as the light gets brighter?
b) How does the resistance change as the light gets dimmer?
c) Looking at the *slope* of the graph, describe how *quickly* the resistance changes in bright light compared to dim light, as the light gets brighter.
d) Give *two uses* for LDRs and *explain* how one of them works (drawing the circuit diagram may help).

6) *The graph below shows how the resistance of a thermistor changes with temperature.*
a) Write a sentence to *describe* what happens to the resistance of the themistor as the temperature changes.
b) What is the resistance at 25°C (approximately)?
c) Give an example of where a thermistor is used as a *temperature sensor*.
d) What *change in temperature* increases the resistance from 90Ω to 130Ω?

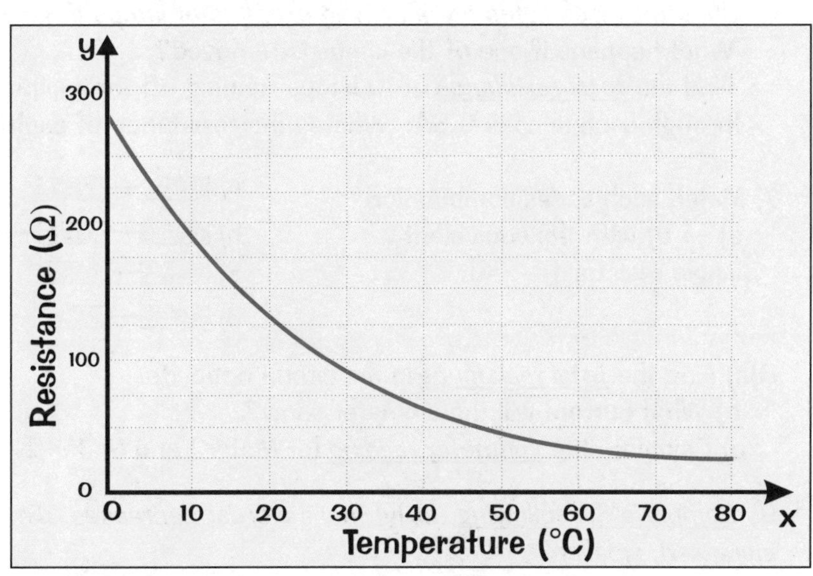

Top Tips

All these components to learn and so little time... Don't worry, the table in question 1 has all the basic details you will need to know. The name tells you what it does, and there is usually a clue in the symbol, too — a motor has a capital M, a diode has a little arrow telling you which way the current can go. Look out for the five "special" components — variable resistor, semiconductor diode, light emitting diode (LED), light dependent resistor (LDR) and thermistor.

Series Circuits

Electrical devices can have dramatically different effects if they are arranged in series or parallel, as you know. The next four pages test if you know the rules for both types of circuits.

Use a pencil and ruler when drawing circuit diagrams so that they're clear, or else you'll only get half marks!!

Drawing Circuits

1) *Draw* a circuit diagram of a 6V battery, a switch and two lamps in series.
2) *Draw* a circuit diagram of a 12V power supply with a fuse and a heater in series.
3) The circuit below shows two lamps. Initially these lamps are of *normal brightness*.
   Work out the brightness of the lamp(s) when the following modifications a) to f) are carried out.
   — Choose from: *off*, *dimmer*, *normal* or *brighter*.
   a) One lamp is unscrewed.
   b) One cell is turned around.
   c) Another cell is added the same way around as the others.
   d) Another cell is added the other way around to the others.
   e) Another bulb is added.
   f) Both cells are turned around.

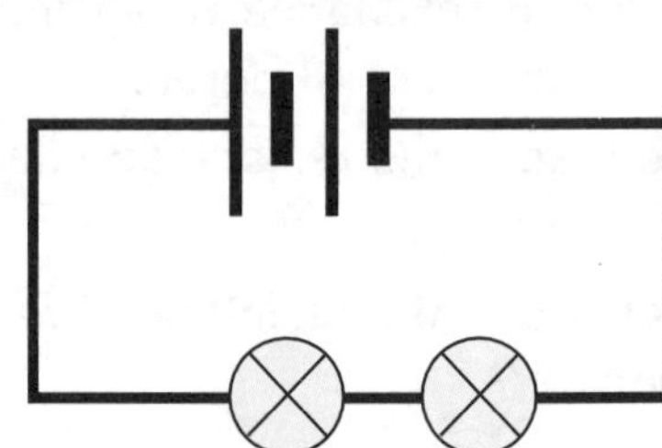

Adding Resistances

4) Draw a circuit with a 2Ω and 4Ω resistor in series with a 6V battery.
   a) What is the total resistance?
   b) Calculate the current flowing in the circuit.

5) The resistances of the resistors in this circuit are equal.
   What are they if the ammeter reads 1A?

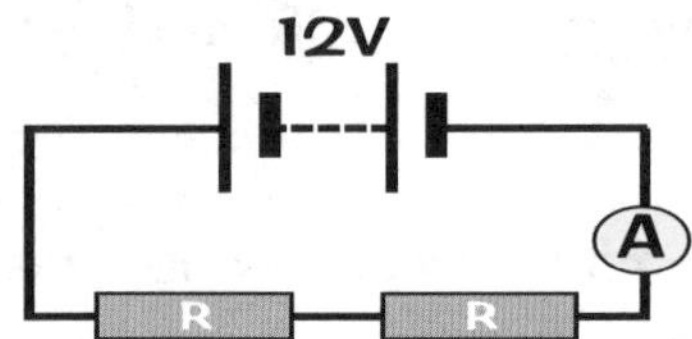

6) *Christmas tree lights are a shining example of lamps in series.*
   What happens if one of the lamps is removed?
   Find the *total resistance* of 10 lamps running off the mains (240V), if the current through each lamp is 0.5A. What is the resistance of each lamp?

7) Match each series combination a) → d) with the equivalent single resistor 1) → 4).

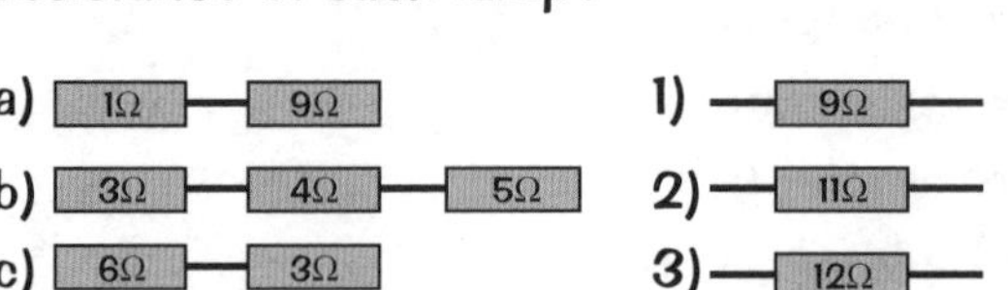

8) a) Find the *total resistance* in the circuit opposite.
   b) What current will the ammeter show?
   c) Calculate the *voltmeter reading* for Meter 1 and Meter 2.

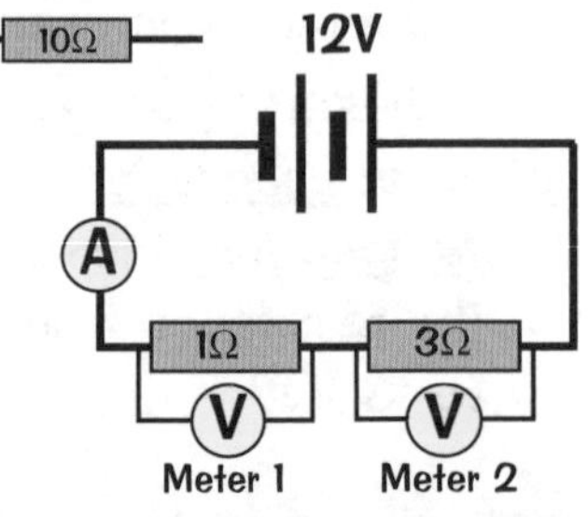

9) *Complete the following, using these words: decreases, dimmer, up, increased, smaller*

If lamps are connected in *series* the current goes through all the lamps in turn. The more lamps you add, the ____________ they get. The ammeter reading ____________ because the current is ____________.
This means the resistance in the circuit has ____________. When we add more resistors to a series circuit, the total resistance goes ____________.

Series Circuits

Current and Voltage

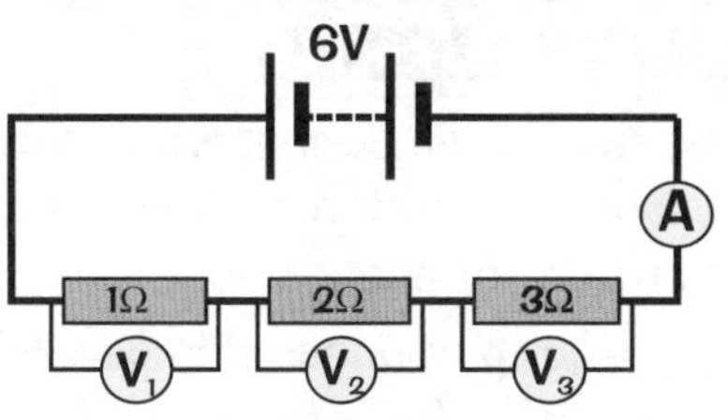

10) Study the circuit on the right.
   a) Calculate the total resistance in the circuit.
   b) What current does the ammeter read?
   c) Work out the voltmeter reading for meters 1, 2 and 3.

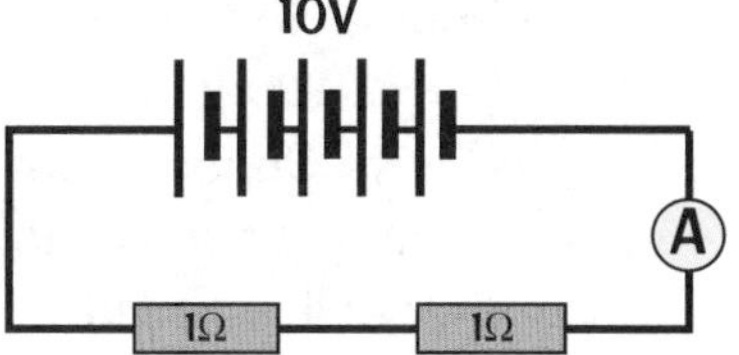

11) *Look at the circuit opposite.*
   a) Find the *total* resistance.
   b) The ammeter reading is 5A. If you wanted to reduce the current to 2A (using the same power supply and ammeter), how many *extra* 1Ω resistors would you have to connect in series?

12) *Draw a circuit diagram* of a power supply, an ammeter and two resistors in series. *Voltmeters are connected in parallel with these resistors.* If the voltmeters read 4V and 20V and the current is 0.5A:
   a) find the resistance of each resistor.
   b) find the voltage supplied by the power supply.

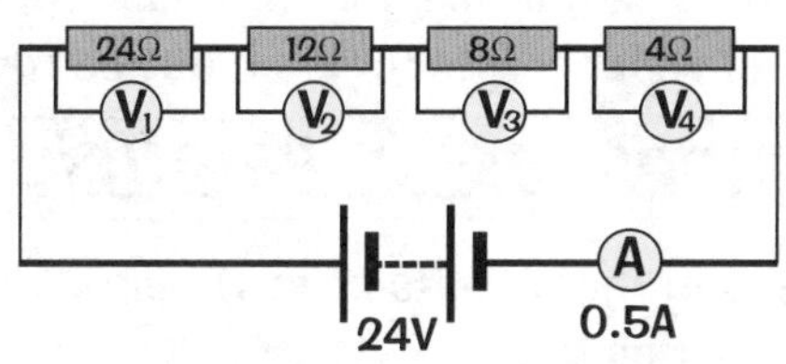

13) Look at the circuit opposite.

   Calculate what each voltmeter, V_1, V_2, V_3 and V_4 will read.

14) Match the "Heads and Tails" to complete the statements about series circuits:

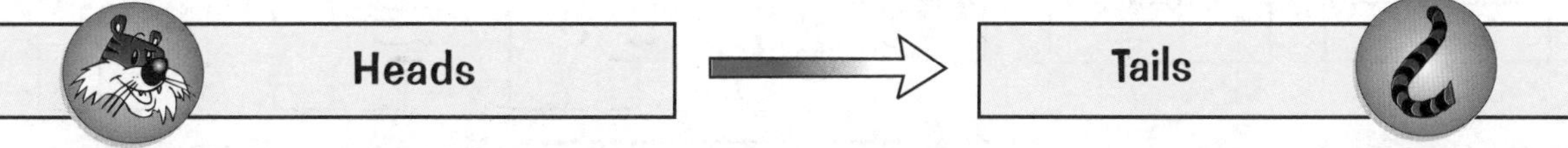

Heads	Tails
a) The bigger the resistance of a component	the source voltage (power supply/cell/battery)
b) The size of the current is determined by	the sum of all the resistances
c) The same current flows	the bigger its share of the total p.d.
d) The voltage in a series circuit always adds up to	through all parts of a series circuit
e) The total resistance is	the total p.d. of the cells and the total resistance of the circuit

15) *Complete the missing values* in this circuit diagram.
   a) What is the potential difference across the 1.5Ω resistor and the 2.5Ω resistor (i.e., across X and Y)?

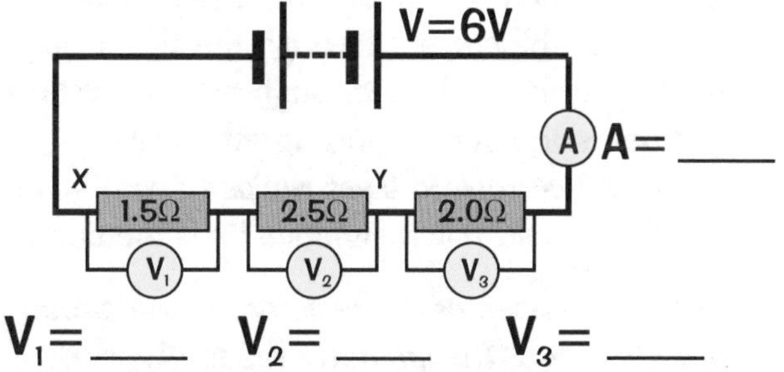

V_1= ____ V_2= ____ V_3= ____

Top Tips

Series circuits are really quite simple to understand. The components are connected one after the other between the +ve and –ve of the power supply (except the voltmeters, which are always connected in parallel). The *same current* goes through everything in the circuit. Don't forget that the down side (and yes, there does have to be one) is that series circuits aren't very common in real life, because if *one component* in the circuit is taken out, then the *whole circuit* is broken and it all stops working.

Parallel Circuits

Drawing Circuits

1) *Draw* two lamps connected in parallel with a 6V battery and...
   a) a switch to switch both lamps off at once.
   b) a switch for each lamp.
2) *Draw* a lamp connected in parallel with an electric motor. Both the lamp and the motor have their own switch. The power supply is 24V.
3) The circuit below shows two lamps connected in parallel. Initially these lamps are of *normal brightness*. Work out the brightness of the lamp(s) when the following modifications a) to d) are carried out. Choose from *off*; *dimmer*; *normal*; *brighter*.
   a) One lamp is unscrewed.
   b) Another cell is added.
   c) The cells are arranged in parallel.
   d) Another bulb is added in parallel with the first bulbs.

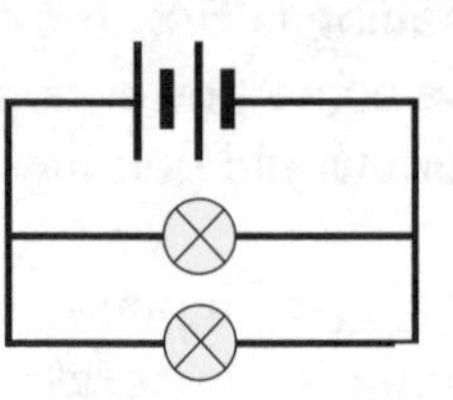

4) *Everything electrical in a car is connected up in parallel.*
   Draw a circuit diagram of a 12V power supply with a fan (motor), light and wiper (motor). Each device needs a separate switch.

Components in Parallel

5) Study the circuits a) to f) below. There are only three different designs. Sort them into pairs of similar circuits.

a) 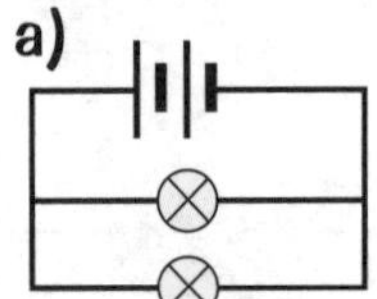
b) 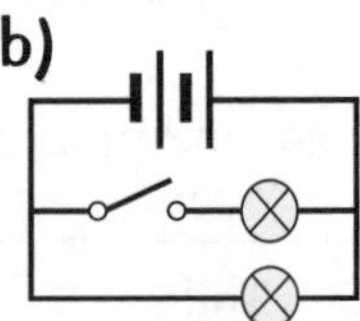
c) 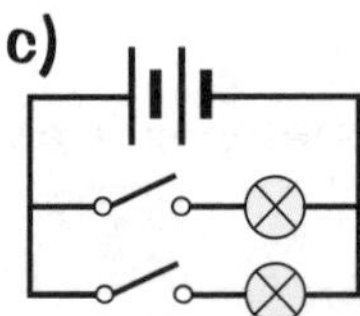
d) 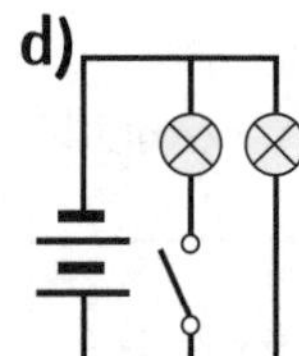
e) 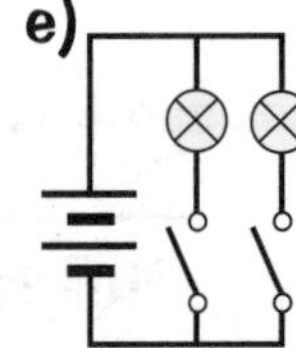
f) 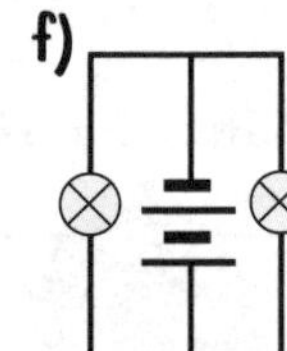

6) Study the circuit diagram opposite. Which lamp(s) (1 → 5) are operated by switches A, B and C?

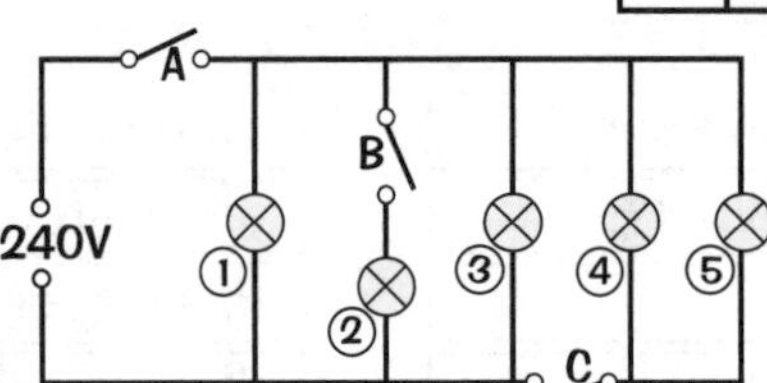

Taking all switches to be closed to start with.
Switch A operates: ________
Switch B operates: ________
Switch C operates: ________

Resistors in Parallel

7) *Draw* a circuit with a 2Ω and a 4Ω resistor in parallel, running off a 6V battery.
   a) What is the current through the 2Ω resistor?
   b) What is the current through the 4Ω resistor?
   c) What is the current through the cell?
   d) *These two resistors are replaced with a single resistor, connected in series with the cell.* What would this resistance be if the current through the cell stayed the same?
8) *The resistances of the resistors in the circuit opposite are identical. The ammeter reads 1A.*
   What is the resistance of these resistors?

12V
A

9) Draw a circuit diagram of a 12V power supply and two resistors, 6Ω and 3Ω, connected in parallel. Find the current in through the power supply and through each resistor. Mark the currents on your circuit diagram.
10) Draw these three resistors in parallel with a 24V power supply. 4Ω 3Ω 2Ω
   Write on the diagram the current through the cell and the current through each of the resistors.

Parallel Circuits

Resistors in Parallel

11) *Match* the statements a) → e) about parallel circuits:

Heads

Tails

Heads	Tails
a) The voltage is the same	across each branch in parallel.
b) The total current flowing is	less than the smallest resistance of any branch.
c) The current through each component	depends on its resistance.
d) The total resistance is	the bigger the current.
e) The lower the resistance	equal to the sum of all currents in separate branches.

12) a) Look at the diagram opposite and *complete the following*:
Use these words: less, branch, parallel, A_2 and A_3, more, A_1

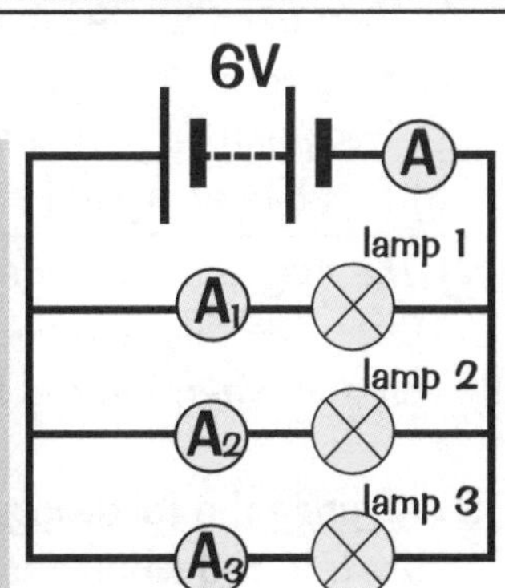

If lamps are connected in ____________, the current in the main part of the circuit splits up and goes through each ____________.
The brightness of the lamps stays the same the ________ lamps you add in ____________.
The ammeter reading at ________ is lower than at (A) but is the same as those at ______ .
The total resistance of lamps in parallel is ________ than the resistance of any of the individual lamps.

b) Look at the diagram again. Work out the *total resistance* of the lamps if each lamp has a resistance of 3Ω. Find the *current* flowing through A, A_1, A_2 and A_3.

13) Look at the two circuits opposite.
a) *Find the current* in each of the parallel branches of circuit (b).
b) *Find the current* flowing in the main branch of both circuits.

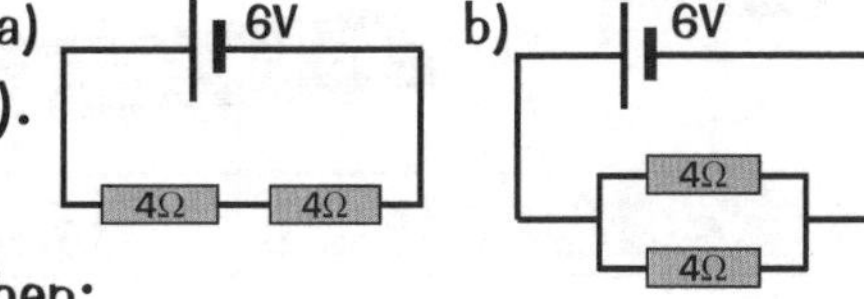

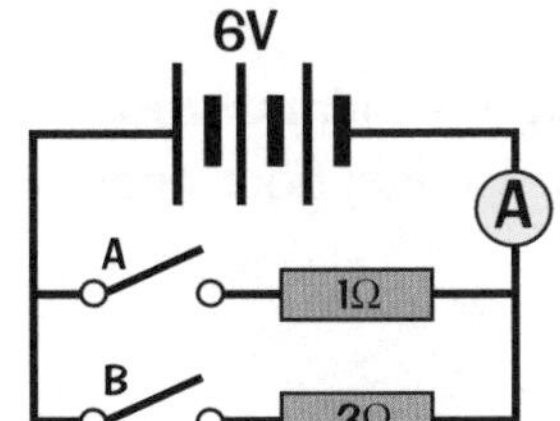

14) *Find the current* in the circuit (left) when:

a) switch A only is closed.
b) switch B only is closed.
c) Find the current through the 2 branches (through the 1Ω resistor and the 3Ω resistor). Then find the current in the circuit when both switches are closed.

15) Study the circuit diagram below and *complete the table*.

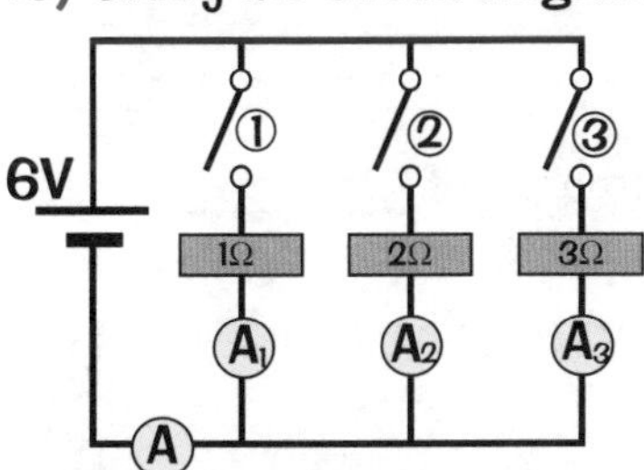

Switch closed	Reading of current on ammeter			
	A	A_1	A_2	A_3
1 and 2				
1 and 3				
1, 2, and 3				

Top Tips

Parallel circuits look a bit more complicated than series circuits, but they're actually a lot more sensible. You can switch everything on and off separately in a parallel circuit, which is obviously what you want in everyday life. Remember that the *voltage* across *each component* is the same as the *source voltage*, and the *current* depends on its *resistance*. The *total resistance* is always *less* than the *smallest resistance* in the circuit. It might sound confusing, but get to grips with the questions, and it'll soon start to make sense.

Static Electricity

Electric Charges

1) *Complete the sentences below:*

a) Positive (+) and negative (–) charges — is caused by friction.
b) Static electricity — repel each other.
c) Negative charges (–) — by connecting it to Earth.
d) Voltage — the greater the voltage.
e) Induced charge — repel each other.
f) The greater the charge — are attracted to each other.
g) Discharge a conductor — builds up if charge builds up.
h) Two negative (–) charges — is lost if the charged rod is moved away.
i) Electrons — move, never the positive charges.
j) Two positive (+) charges — are left on a rod if electrons are rubbed off.
k) Positive charges (+) — are found on a rod if electrons are rubbed on.

2) *The diagram opposite shows a duster and a polythene rod.* Copy the diagram and use arrows to show the movement of charge when the rod is rubbed with a duster.

Polythene rod

3) *Arrange* the following statements in the correct order to explain how static is transferred to an acetate rod when it is rubbed by a cloth duster.

...the rod to the cloth.

...and the rod becomes

...positively charged.

...electrons are transferred from...

...negatively charged

So the cloth becomes...

If you rub an acetate rod with a cloth...

Attraction and Repulsion

4) These two rods, ++++++ ====== attract each other with a force F_0. Study the pairs of rods below and write down if they attract with a force more than or less than F_0. Explain your answers.

a) ++++++ ======

b) ++++++ (vertical rod: ======)

c) ++++++ ======

d) + + + + + + - - - - - -

5) a) Copy the writing about the rod opposite, and *fill in the blanks:*
Use these words: charge, negative, equal, like charges repel, no, positive

+ – + – + – + – + –
– + – + – + – + – +

This rod carries ________ overall charge. It has ________ numbers of ________ and ________ charges. The + and – signs represent the distribution of positive and negative ________. Instead of forming areas of positive charge and areas of negative charge they spread out because ________________________ .

A positively charged object is held near to this copper rod.

b) *Draw* the new arrangement of positive (+) and negative (–) charges in the metal rod. *Explain* the pattern.

c) One end of the metal rod is attracted to the positively charged object and the other end is repelled. The force of attraction is greater than the force of repulsion. *Explain why this is.*

copper rod

Static Electricity

Applications of Static Electricity

6) ***Static electricity can be used to spray paint a car door.***
Complete the following:
Use these words: repel, spread out, positively, attracted, positive, earth, a negative terminal
The spray paint nozzle is connected to a __________ terminal. This makes the spray drops __________ charged. This makes them __________ each other and so they __________ ______. The door is connected to the __________ or __________ so that the droplets are ___________ to it.

7) ***Factories and power stations use static electricity to clean up the effluent gases from chimneys.***
Join up these bits of sentences to explain dust removal in the chimneys.

...in a chimney...
...a set of charged plates.
Every now and then...
...will be attracted to them.
...into a bag and disposed of.
Electrostatic smoke precipitators are...
...the electricity is turned off and...
Charged particles of smoke or dust...
...the dust is shaken...

8) *Draw a simple diagram* to show how static electricity is made use of in a photocopier to position the black toner where it is needed.

Discharging Electricity

9) a) Explain how a moving car can become positively charged.
b) What do you feel if you touch the door of a charged car? Explain why this happens.

10) Why do you sometimes get a shock from your jumper when you take it off? Use the following terms in your answer: "static charges", "movement of electrons", "sparks/shocks" and "negatively charged".

11) *Draw a diagram* to show how lightning occurs. Include on your diagram: the cloud, raindrops, Earth, and positive and negative charges.

12) ***Static electricity can be lethal...***
a) *List* 3 working situations where static can lead to dangerous sparks in the workplace.
b) Choose one situation you listed in a). Draw a diagram to show how the static builds up. *Label* the (+) and (–) charges.
c) For your example in (b), *explain* carefully the solution to the problem.

13) Lightning conductors...
a) Why do tall buildings have lightning conductors?
b) What are lightning conductors made of?
c) Explain how a lightning conductor works.

14) *Describe* how you could make 2 pieces of clingfilm : a) attract each other. b) repel each other.

Top Tips Shocking stuff, this static electricity. It's all about charges that aren't free to move, but discharge with a spark when they do finally move. Build up of static is caused by *friction*. Don't forget that *only electrons move*; if they are rubbed *on*, an object gets a *negative* charge; if they are rubbed *off*, an object gets a positive charge. Charging by induction is a bit more tricky, but question 5 takes you through it. One last point — they will ask you for detailed examples of static electricity in the Exam, so you do need to learn them.

Energy in Circuits

Energy Transfer

1) Use these words to *fill in* the following paragraph about this circuit:

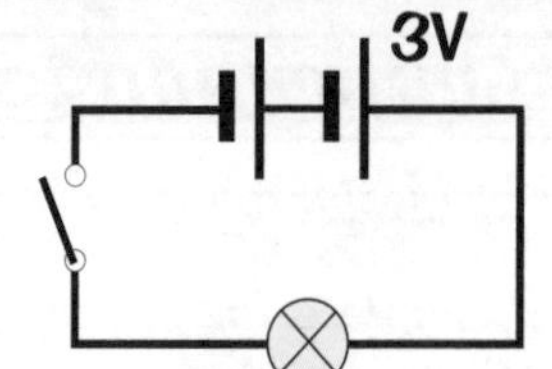

energy, light, heat, electrical, transferred, cells, current, two, light, voltage, flow, brighter, electric circuit, broken

When the switch is closed, a __________ flows around the circuit and the lamp lights up. The 3V battery is made up of _______ 1.5V ________. The energy is ___________ by the __________ __________ to the lamp. The lamp converts _________ energy to _________ and ________ energy; the _______ energy being the useful output.

If the switch is open, the circuit is __________ and there is no current _________ and no transfer of __________. When the battery ___________ is increased to 6V, the lamp glows _______________ and more electrical energy is transformed than with the 3V battery.

2) *Electrical energy can be converted to other useful forms of energy.*

In the 4 examples opposite, *name* the form(s) that electrical energy is transformed into.

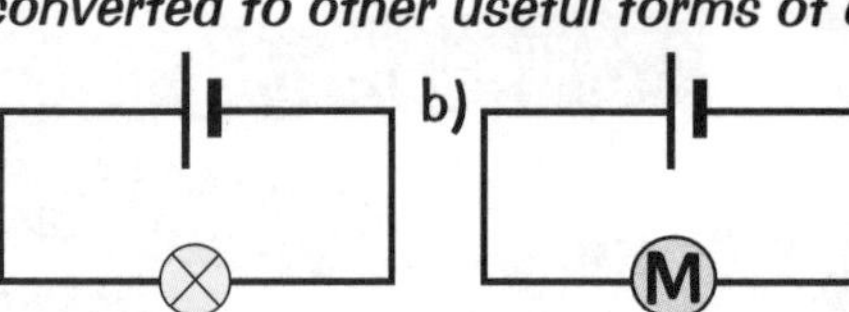

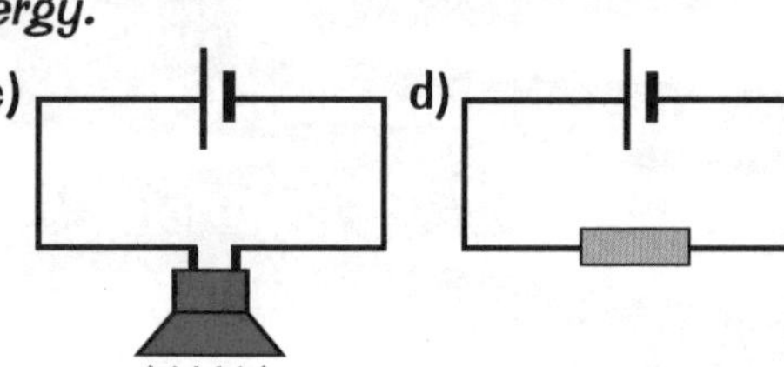

Heating Coils

3) Look at the diagram opposite which shows a water heating experiment.

The experiment is run for a certain time and the water temperature is measured. How will the temperature compare if we:

a) increase the voltage to 24V?

b) replace the heating coil with one of half the resistance?

c) replace the coil with a shorter one of the same total resistance?

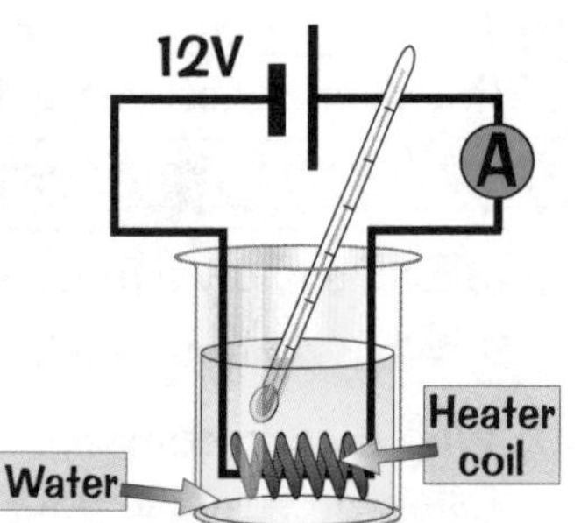

4) Data taken from a heating experiment is shown in the table opposite.

a) Plot the graph of temperature (°C) against time (min).

b) *Explain* the shape of the curve. Why does the temperature stop rising after 7 minutes.

c) What was the temperature of the water after 2½ minutes and 5½ minutes?

d) If a wire of higher resistance replaces the wire in the heater coil, will it take more time or less time to boil the water? *Explain* your answer.

e) What *safety precautions* might you take during this experiment?

f) *How* could you make your readings *more* accurate?

Temperature (°C)	Time (minutes)
20	0
40	1
58	2
71	3
82	4
87	5
94	6
100	7
100	8

Power and Resistance

5) Answer the following questions.

a) *What happens* to some of the electrical energy when current flows through a resistor?

b) What is the effect of increasing the *current* on the amount of heat energy produced?

c) What is the effect of increasing the *voltage* on the amount of heat energy produced?

d) What is the effect of increasing the circuit's *resistance* on the amount of heat energy produced?

e) What measuring instrument would you use to find the quantity of heat produced?

Energy in Circuits

Charge and Energy

6) *Match* the quantities a) → e) with their correct description on the right:

a) One volt	— is the energy transferred per unit of charge passed.
b) Energy	— is current x time.
c) One ampere	— is one coulomb every second.
d) Voltage	— is one joule per coulomb.
e) Charge	— is charge x voltage.

7) *Complete* the two tables below.

What it is?	Letter	Unit	Symbol
Voltage	V	volts	V
Current	I		
		ohms	Ω
	E	joules	
Electrical Charge	Q		
	t	seconds	
Power		watts	

If a current of:	flows for:	-then the charge passing is
1 ampere	1 second	1 coulomb
2 amperes	1 second	
2 amperes	2 seconds	
4 amperes	3 seconds	
5 amperes		15 coulombs
6 amperes	5 seconds	
10 amperes	6 seconds	

8) *Find the energy* supplied by a torch battery, voltage 6V, if 1500C of charge flows.

9) *Find* the missing values of energy, charges and voltage in the table below.

Energy (J)	Charge (C)	Voltage (V)
500	50	
	15	3
4800		240
10 000		20
	75	12

10) Join up these "cuttings". Begin with: "If a voltage in a circuit is changed from..."

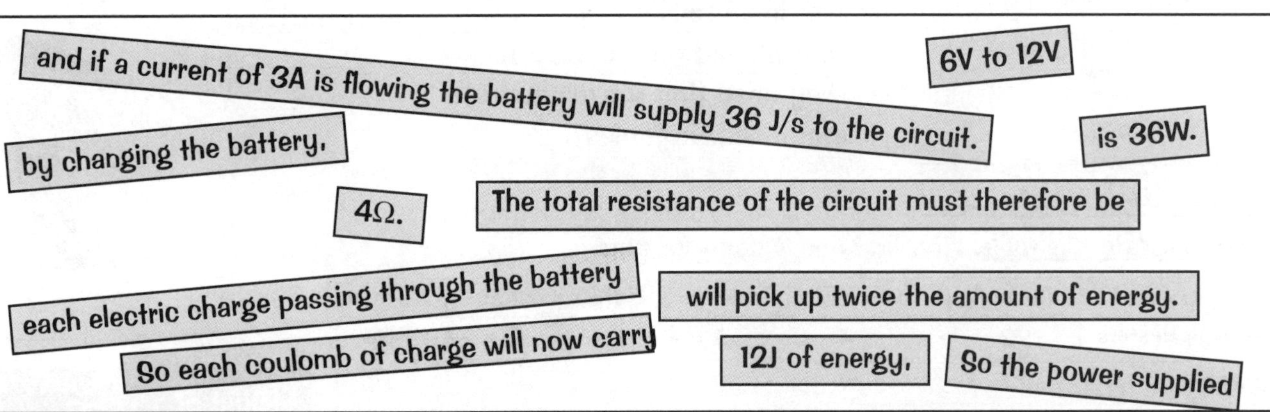

Top Tips This is all just another way of looking at electrical circuits. You can think of voltage pushing the current round and resistance opposing the flow — or you can think of each component converting electrical energy into other forms of energy, which is marginally more exciting. The idea is that when a *charge* passes through a *change in voltage*, *energy* is *transferred*. OK, but I did only say it was *marginally* more exciting. The formula is Energy E = QV, so you can say that *one volt is one joule per coulomb*. Remember that the charge passing is current x the time it flows for.

The Cost of Domestic Electricity

Metering and the Kilowatt Hour

...interesting questions for when you pay the bill!

1) Look at these two electricity bills from Rippov Electricity:

a) Complete the missing figures in these bills.

b) What is the scientific name for the term "units"?

c) If you were estimating the meter reading for a further quarter, what might it be?

Previous meter reading:	47041
Present meter reading:	47525
Number of units used:	---------
Cost per unit (pence):	7.35
Cost of electricity used:	---------
Fixed quarterly charge:	£9.49
Total bill:	---------
VAT on Total bill at 8.0%:	---------
Final total:	£48.67

Previous meter reading:	26935
Present meter reading:	27601
Number of units used:	---------
Cost per unit (pence):	7.35
Cost of electricity used:	---------
Fixed quarterly charge:	£9.49
Total bill:	---------
VAT on Total bill at 8.0%:	---------
Final total:	£63.12

d) If the bills were for the Summer quarter (May, June and July) what difference might you expect in a bill for the Winter quarter (November, December and January)? Explain your answer.

2) *Here are some electrical appliances used at home:*

microwave | toaster | lamp | vacuum cleaner | kettle | electric heater | hairdryer | TV | cooker

Which four appliances are the most expensive to run (for a given length of time)? What do they have in common?

3) Fill in the gaps below.

a) These are units of energy:

----

b) These are units of power:

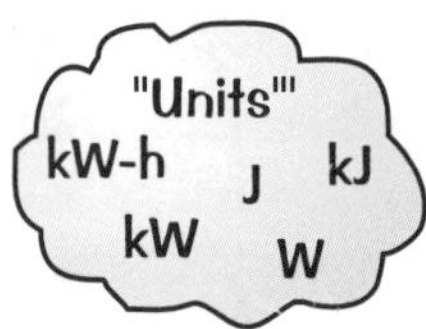

c) "deci" means:

----

d) "kilo" means:

----

100 1000 10 10,000 $\frac{1}{10}$ 100,000

4) Fill in the table opposite to help you work out how many joules a hairdryer uses in one hour...

Power (kilowatts):	1 kW
Time switched on (in hours):	1 h
Power in watts:	------------
Time switched on (seconds):	------------
Energy used (in kilowatt hours):	------------
Energy used (in joules):	------------

Calculating Cost

5) Complete this table. The first one is done for you.

Appliance	Rating(kW)	Time(h)	Energy (kWh)	Cost at 10p per unit
Storage Heaters	2	4	$2 \times 4 = 8$	$8 \times 10 = 80$p
Cooker	7	2		
1-bar Electric Fire	1	1.5		
Kettle	2	0.1		
Iron	1	1.2		
Refridgerator	0.12	24.0		
Lamp	0.06	6.0		
Radio Cassette	0.012	2.0		

[Cost of electricity = power (kW) x time (h) x cost of 1kWh.]

The Cost of Domestic Electricity

Calculating Cost

6) *Complete* the following summary using words from this list:

joules energy energy twice voltage previous take

To find the number of units used on an electricity bill, ______ the ______ from the present meter reading. You pay for the ______ you have used, not the ______ or current supplied. If a label on an appliance says "1kW" it means it will use ______ at the rate of 1000 ______ per second. A "2kW" appliance uses energy ______ as quickly as a "1kW" appliance.

7) Calculate the energy consumed by the following (in kWh):

a) 100W lamp for 10 hours
b) 10W mains radio for 5 hours
c) 500W microwave for 1/2 hour
d) 100W electric blanket for 1 hour

8) *Find the cost* (at 10p/unit) of using:

a) An electric drill, power 300W for 2 hours.
b) A 20W hairstyling brush for 1/2 hour.
c) Two 100W electric lights on for 9 hours a day for a week.
d) A 900W toaster for 15 minutes every day for a month (30 days — it's September!).
e) Four 60W electric lights on 12 hours a day for an old-fashioned working week (5 days).

9) *The picture shows a manual for a 60W stereo radio that runs off the mains.*

a) Calculate how long the radio takes to consume 1kWh.
b) What assumption are you using in your answer to part a)?

10) *It takes an hour to heat up water for a bath. The immersion heater has a power rating of 2.1 kW.*

a) Find the cost of electricity used to heat the bath water (at 10p per unit).
b) Find the cost of electricity used in a shower if the water takes 10 minutes to heat up (2.1 kW heater).

11) In the following questions, work out which of the two appliances consumes the most energy.

a) A 2kW heater for 4 hours *or* a 3kW fire for 3 hours.
b) A 900W toaster for 15 minutes *or* a 800W vacuum cleaner for 20 minutes.
c) A 300W drill for $^1/_2$ hour *or* a 100W light bulb for 1 $^1/_2$ hours.
d) A 1kW iron for 1 hour *or* a 2kW kettle for 20 minutes.
e) A 2.1kW immersion heater for 1 hour *or* a 1.5kW fire for $^1/_2$ hour.

12) *The following table summarises the initial and running costs of filament lamps and CFL (compact fluorescent) lamps.*

Type of Lamp	Lifetime of lamp (h)	Power (kW)	Cost of 1kWh of electricity (£)	Cost of electricity for lamp's lifetime (£)	Cost of 1 lamp (£)	Total running cost for 12000 hr. (£)
CFL	12000	0.02	0.1		10.00	
Filament	1000	0.1	0.1		0.50	

a) Copy and complete the table.
b) Give *two benefits* of CFL lamps over filament lamps. *(A 20W CFL lamp gives the same amount of light as a 100W filament lamp.)*

Top Tips Working out the electricity bill is fairly straightforward — it's just a lot of simple arithmetic. Be careful not to make any simple mistakes, though. In real life the bill is worked out for you, but it won't be in the Exam. The *units* that electricity meters measure are *kilowatt-hours* (kWh), and that means the amount of electrical *energy* used by a *1kW* appliance left on for *1 hour*. Don't be confused by the name, it isn't a measurement of power.

Plugs and Fuses

Electrical Hazards in the Home

1) State the electrical *hazard* in each diagram below, and say what you would do to make each one safe:

a) 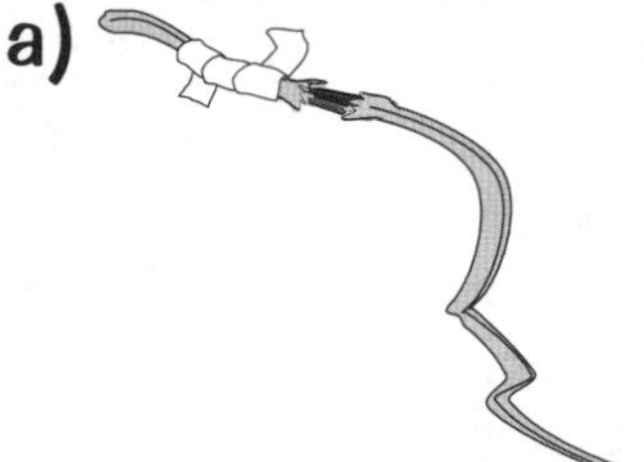

b) 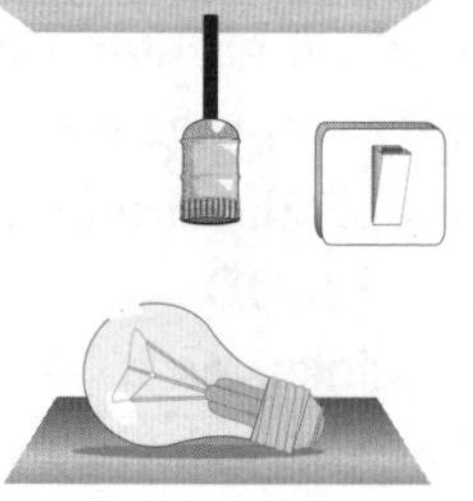 

c)

2) Write down as many other electrical hazards in the home that you can think of. You should be able to write down at least six others.

3) *These are the hazard signs on a hairdryer leaflet.*

Explain what they mean and why they need to be marked on the hairdryer.

Domestic Plugs

4) *Plugging into the mains:*
Label the plug on the right with: *green and yellow*; *blue*; *brown*; *live*; *earth*; *neutral*.

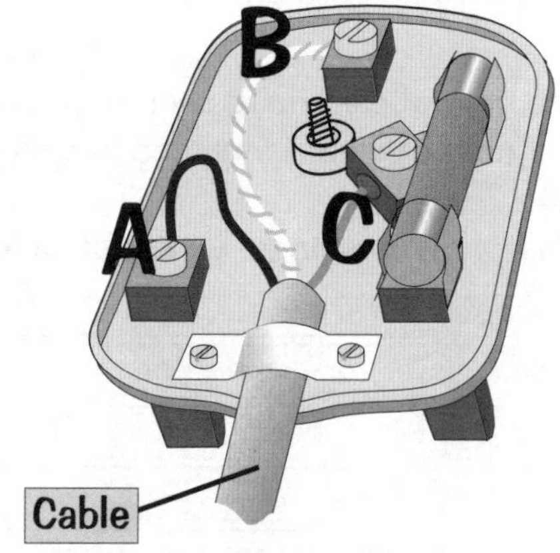

5) *Which parts* of the plug are made out of the following materials, and why?

a) *brass* or *copper*
b) *plastic*

6) Write a *check list* of five things you would check to make sure a newly wired plug is completely safe.

7) *Radios, TVs and lamps do not usually have an earth wire.*
a) What is the *function* of the earth wire?
b) Why are appliances like TVs safe to use *without an earth wire*?

8) *Complete the following paragraph*:
Use these words: safety, alternating, neutral, live, 230, earth, voltage

The ____________ of a live wire is an _____________ voltage of ________V.
Electricity normally flows along the _____________ and _______________ wires only.
The _______ wire is just for _______________.

9) *Find out* about and describe the extra *safety features* used for electric lawnmowers, hedge trimmers and drills.

Plugs and Fuses

Using Fuses

10) *The table opposite shows 7 appliances and the current that passes through them.*

For each appliance, decide if it needs a 3A, 5A or a 13A fuse.

(the first one is done for you)

Appliance	Current taken (A)	Fuse value (A)
Food Mixer	2	3
Cassette Player	3	
Hairdryer	4	
Electric Heater	12	
Toaster	4	
Kettle	9	
Vacuum Cleaner	3.5	

11) *Answer the following questions on fuses.*

a) Why do we use fuses?
b) What is *inside* a fuse?
c) *Explain carefully* what happens when a 6A current supplies an appliance fitted with a 3A fuse?
d) Why should you not use a 1A fuse in a hairdryer plug?
e) *Explain* what would happen if the live wire in a toaster touched the metal case. Say how the *earth wire* and the *fuse* work together to make the appliance safe.

12) *This diagram shows a kettle circuit that has been drawn incorrectly.*

a) Find the 4 mistakes.
b) Redraw the circuit correctly.

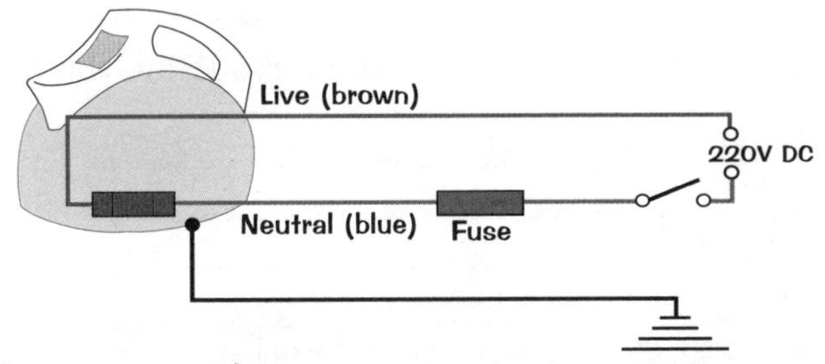

Fuses — Safe Practices

13) *Fill in the gaps* in the box below, using the given words.

cover blown expert wired fuse earth replace

Appliance:	Must be correctly __________ to a plug fitted with the correct __________ and with an __________ wire connected to any touchable metal part.
Blown Fuses:	You must find out why a fuse has __________. If this is not obvious, consult an __________. Do not __________ the fuse with one of a higher rating.
Fire Risk:	Never __________ an appliance, particularly with something that can burn.

14) Study the diagram opposite of a domestic electricity supply. What happens to the lights in the kitchen, lounge and dining room if:

a) fuse 1 blows?
b) fuse 2 blows? c) fuse 3 blows?

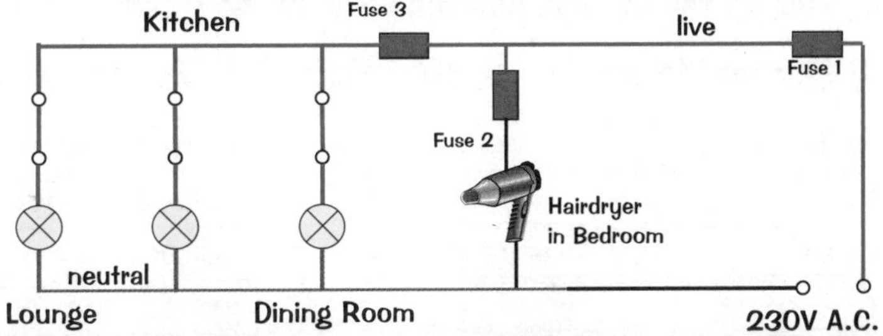

Top Tips

Now, you already know that electricity is dangerous and it can kill you. What you have to do here is to be able to name all the possible *electrical hazards* in the home and say how to *eliminate* them. This is actually just common sense. Don't forget that you need to know how to wire a plug, and what all the parts of a plug are for. The only tricky part is learning how the *earth wire* and the *fuse* work together to protect the appliance and anyone who may be touching it .

The National Grid and Mains Electricity

Mains Electricity

1) *The diagram below shows how electricity is made in power stations, and sent to homes and industry.*

a) Complete the labels on the diagram.

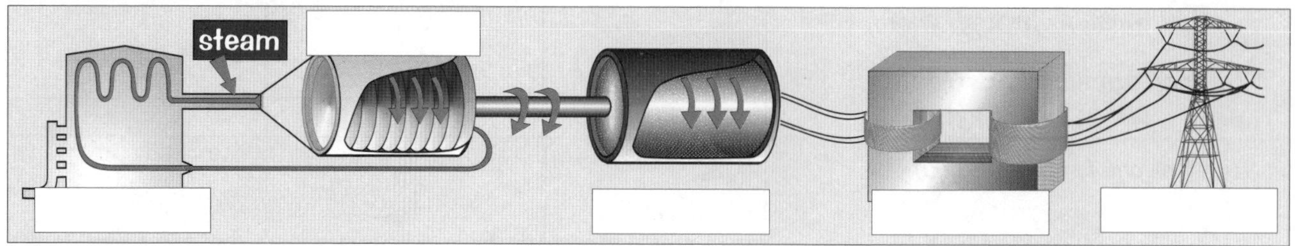

b) Complete the following using these words:

induction, oil, uranium fuel, steam, gas, coal, turbine, generator, magnetic

Heat energy in a power station is produced by burning fossil fuels such as ____________, ____________ or ____________ . ____________ is used in nuclear power stations. The boiler makes ____________ which drives a ____________ , which turns a ____________ . The generator produces electricity using the principle of ____________. This happens when a metal coil is rotated in a strong ____________ field .

2) Match these pairs of statements about the National Grid and Mains Electricity.

a) Cables are high voltage	• due to resistance of the cables
b) Power supplied	• requires transformers as well as big pylons with huge insulators
c) To transmit a lot of power	• equals $I^2 \times R$
d) A high current means a loss of heat	• for efficient transmission
e) Power loss due to resistance in the cables	• best calculated using $V \times I$
f) It's cheaper to boost the voltage up to 400,000V	• to keep the current low
g) Boosting the voltage up to 400,000V	• you need a high voltage or a high current
h) Transformers step-up voltage	• and keep the current very low
i) Transformers step-down voltage to our homes	• to bring it back to safe, useable levels
j) Voltage has to be AC on the National Grid	• because transformers don't work on D.C..

3) *Letter Check! Are you getting confused by all these letters?* Write down what each one stands for.

a) Symbols for quantities: i) V ii) I iii) P iv) R

b) Letters for units: i) Ω ii) A iii) W iv) V

4) Pair up the units in question 3 with the quantities they represent.

5) Pair up the words..  ..and meanings below:

a) Transmit	• rotary motor driven by steam
b) AC	• place for generating and distributing electrical power
c) DC	• direct current
d) Turbine	• send from one place to another
e) Power station	• changes the voltage of an alternating current supply
f) Transformer	• alternating current

6) *Mains voltage is 230V. Find the power of:*

a) a toaster which takes a current of 3A.

b) a drill which takes a current of 2A.

c) a television which takes a current of 0.5A.

The National Grid and Mains Electricity

Current, Power, Voltage and Mains Circuits

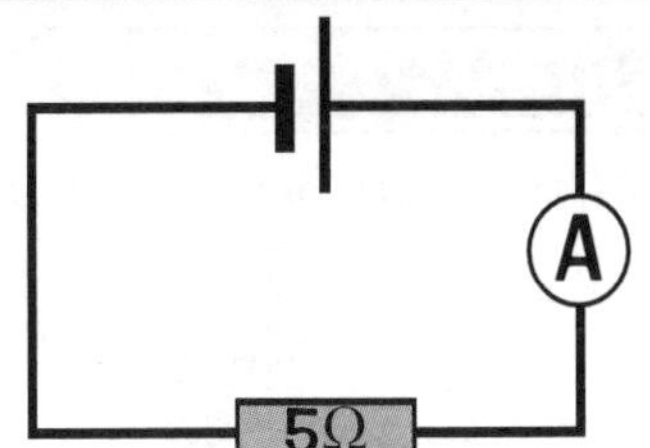

7) *A current flows through a 5Ω resistor.*
Find the power if the current is: a) 2A b) 4A.
How much bigger is your answer to b) than a)? Explain why.

8) Shown below is a circuit with 12V battery and 4Ω resistor.

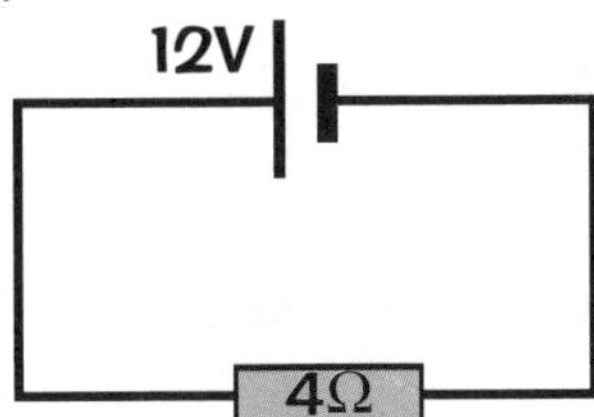

a) Find the power supplied by the battery to the resistor.
b) Find the power if the voltage is doubled to 24V.
c) Find the power if the resistor is replaced with one of 2Ω.

9) Complete the table below. *(Take mains voltage as 230V)*

Appliance	Power in Watts (W)	Power in kilowatts (kW)	Current in Amps (A)	Fuse: 3A or 13A?
Iron	920			
TV	115			
Kettle	2300			
Video Recorder	46			
Fan Heater	1200			

10) *A 1.5kW heater and a 2W clock work off a 230V mains electricity supply.* Work out:
a) The current taken by each.
b) The fuse needed in the plug of the heater and the clock. Why are they different?

11) *The p.d. across 120, 3W fairy lights is 240V. The lights are in series.*
a) Find the voltage drop across each lamp. b) Find the current going through each lamp.
c) Find the current in the whole circuit.

12) *A cable can take a maximum current of 2A when supplied with a mains voltage of 230V.*
a) Find the maximum power that can be carried by the cable.
b) How many 60W bulbs in parallel can you run off the cable?

13) Arrange these phrases into sentences:

A high current gives more power

to spend their energy every second.

because each electron carries more energy.

A high voltage gives more power

because there are more electrons

14) What quantities do the following units represent: C/s, J/s, J/C?

Top Tips These two pages deal with what you need to know about where our electricity comes from, how it's supplied to us and how to calculate the power or current in an appliance running off the mains. All power stations are more or less the same — they have a boiler that makes steam which turns a turbine which drives a generator, producing electricity (the diagram in question 1 will help you to remember all of that). The trickiest bit here is explaining why pylon cables are at such a high voltage to keep the current low. It's all there, in question 2.

Magnetic Fields

Bar Magnets

1) State whether these materials are magnetic or not;

iron copper aluminium brass steel silver gold nickel

2) *This question concerns sprinkling iron filings onto a piece of paper, with a magnet underneath.*

a) Where do most of the iron filings collect and why do they collect there?

b) *Draw* the pattern of the magnet field around a single bar magnet. Put arrows on the field lines that point towards magnetic south.

3) On the diagrams below, label the North and South poles of the magnets a, b, c and d. State whether each pair of magnets are attracting or repelling each other.

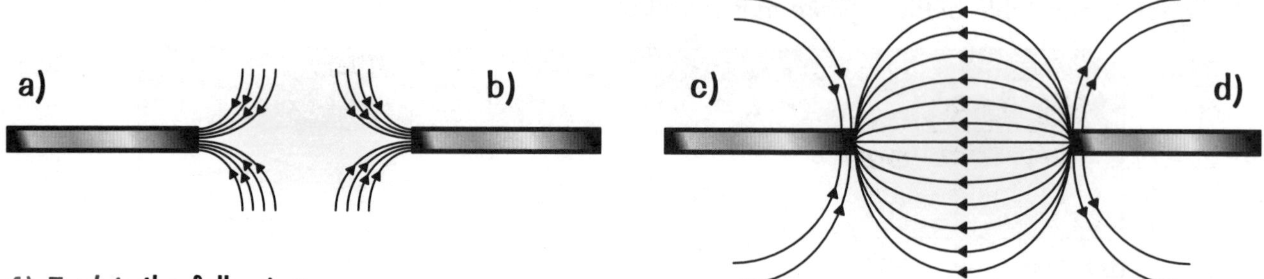

4) *Explain* the following:

a) Magnets are often fitted to the doors of cupboards.

b) Flour is usually passed near a magnet before it is packed.

c) If a magnet is broken in half, each half is a magnet.

d) If an iron bar or a steel bar are near a magnet, they become magnetised.

e) If the bars in d) are taken away from the magnet, the steel bar keeps its magnetism, but the iron bar does not.

5) *Suppose you were given a small bar magnet with nothing on it to tell you which was "S" and which was "N".*

a) *Explain* how you could find which end is "S" and which is "N".

b) *Explain* how you could do this *without* using another magnet with the poles already labelled "N" and "S".

The Earth's Magnetic Field

6) a) Use the following words to complete the sentences below (you will need to use one of the words more than once).

suspended south opposite poles plotting freely

Magnetic __________ are __________ to geographic poles: that is, the __________ magnetic pole is at the north pole. The black end of the black and white double arrow compass needle is the __________ pole. Any magnet __________ so that it can turn __________ will come to rest pointing north–south. A compass can also be used for __________ magnetic fields around bar magnets.

7) a) What navigational problem might mountaineers have if they come across magnetic rocks?

b) In what direction does a freely hanging magnet point at the magnetic North Pole?

c) In what direction does a compass needle point at the magnetic North Pole?

d) Towards which country would a compass needle point at the geographic North Pole?

Magnetic Fields

Magnetic Fields around Wires

8) Put these phrases together to make a sentence describing magnetic fields.

like iron and steel	is a region where	and also wires carrying currents
A magnetic field	magnetic materials	experience a force
	acting on them	

9) *This question is about the magnetic field around a current-carrying wire:*

a) *Compasses are put on card around a wire through which a high current flows up through it.* Draw in the direction the compass needles are pointing in figure a).

b) *The experiment was repeated with the current flowing DOWN through the card.* Draw in the direction the compass needles are now pointing in figure b).

c) Describe a simple rule to work out the direction of the magnetic field around a wire through which an electric current flows.

d) Choose the correct words:
The magnetic field is stronger closer to / further from the wire. Increasing / Decreasing the current makes the magnetic field stronger. The field lines run from north / south to north / south.

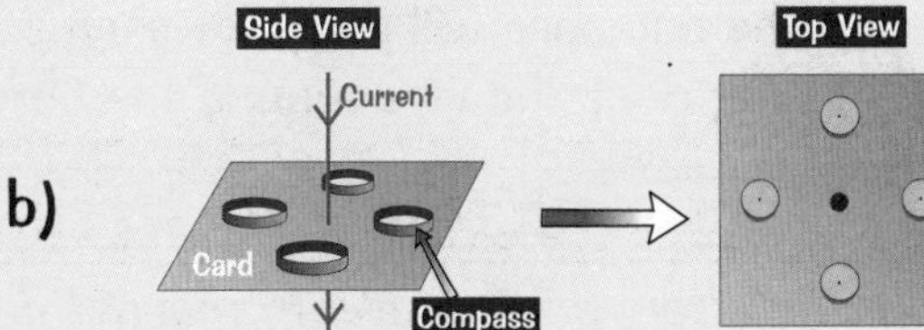

Solenoids

10) A magnetic field is produced when a current flows through a solenoid.

a) Copy the diagram opposite and draw in the magnetic field pattern surrounding the coil.

b) Describe the magnetic field inside the solenoid.

c) Describe two ways of increasing the strength of the magnetic field.

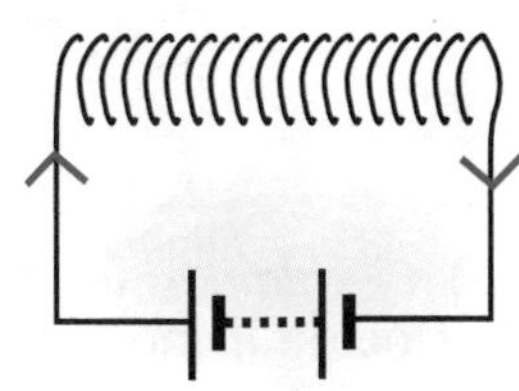

11) *Four students set up different coils, all with the same current running through the wires.*

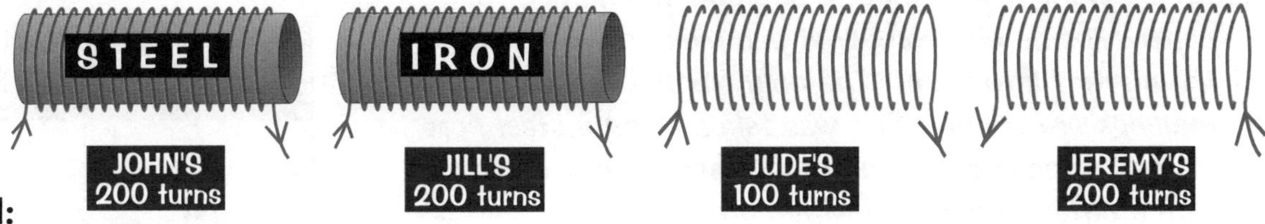

Whose coil:

a) gives the weakest magnetic field?

b) has a South pole at the left-hand end?

c) will still possess a magnetic field when the current is switched off?

d) Is the wire in the coil insulated, and why?

Top Tips Magnetism, there's an attractive subject for you. You won't go far wrong if you learn this definition: A magnetic field is a region where magnetic materials (like iron and steel) and also wires carrying currents experience a force acting on them. The diagrams of a field around a magnet and a solenoid come up in the Exam, so learn the diagrams on questions 2,3 and 10a. Don't forget it's the RIGHT hand rule for a field around a current carrying wire

Electromagnets and Electromagnetic Devices

The Parts of an Electromagnet

1) *Look at the diagram of this electromagnet.*

A

B

D

E

C

   a) Label the diagram with these words:

   iron core | solenoid | current in | current out | magnetic field pattern

   b) Explain what an electromagnet is.

   c) What is the purpose of the iron core?

   d) Why is the core made of iron, and not say, copper?

   e) Why is the core not made of steel?

   f) Which end of the electromagnet is the north pole?

   g) How could you make the north and south poles of the electromagnet swap around?

   h) A plotting compass is placed at A, B, C, D and E. Draw which way the north end of the compass will point for each position.

   i) Why does the wire around the core have to be insulated?

Factors affecting the Strength of an Electromagnet

2) *The strength of an electromagnet depends on three factors.* Unjumble these words to reveal what these are...

   the the the what of of core current
   is size number the turns of of the coil made

3) Look at the two solenoids below.

A

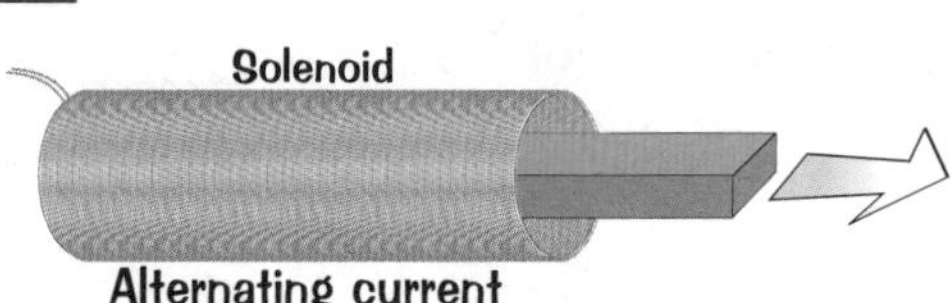

B

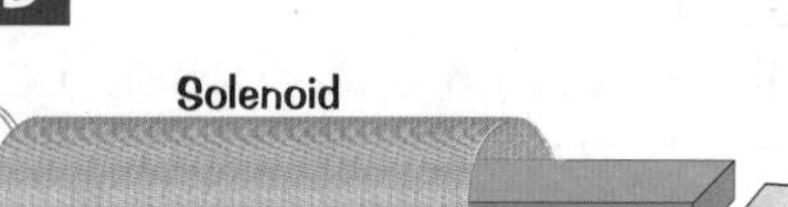

   a) Decide if the solenoids in A and B are magnetising or demagnetising the steel bar. Explain the process in both cases.

4) *An experiment was done to see how the number of paper clips an electromagnet can pick up varies with the current through it. The only trouble is, two of the readings are wrong. One was taken using a steel core instead of an iron one, and the other reading taken with a different solenoid with more coils.*

   First of all, say why this is an example of bad science.

   a) Redraw the table with the figures in order, and identify the 2 odd readings. (Label "more coils" and "steel core".)

   b) Plot a graph of number of paperclips (vertical axis) against current, leaving out the two odd readings. Draw a "best fit" line.

   c) Make a labelled drawing of the apparatus you would need to carry out this experiment.

Number of paperclips	Current (A)
13	3.0
4	1.0
8	2.0
3	1.5
1	0.5
2	1.0
14	3.5
5	1.5
11	2.5

Electromagnets and Electromagnetic Devices

Electromagnets in Action

5) a) *Which* circuits (x or y) match with the electromagnets in 'a' and 'b'.

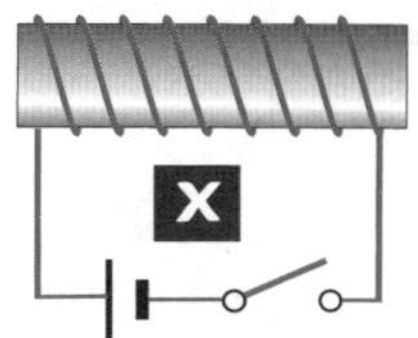

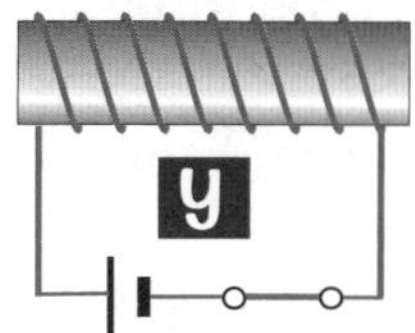

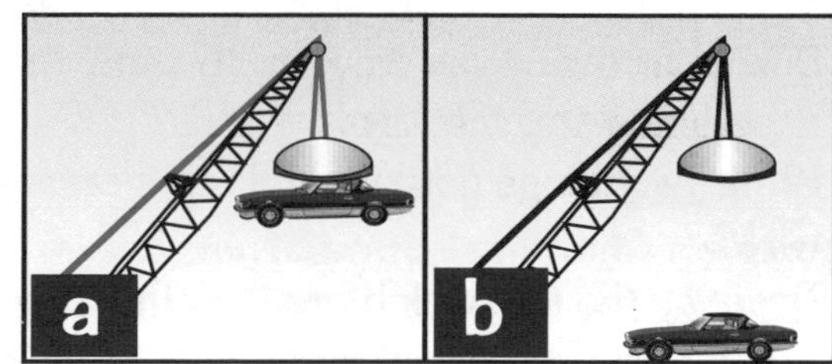

b) *Explain* briefly how the scrap yard electromagnet works. *What* are its main components?

6) The diagram opposite shows a circuit breaker with the labels missing.

a) *Label* the diagram correctly using these words:

Pivot | Spring | Iron Core | Iron Rocker | Brass Contacts

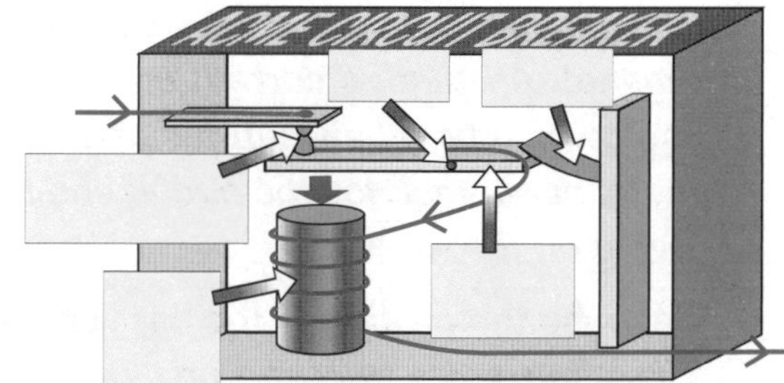

b) *Put the following sentences about circuit breakers in order.*

It can be reset manually. This trips the switch. The circuit breaker is placed on the incoming live wire. It will flick itself off again if the current is too high. If the current gets too high, the magnetic field in the coil pulls the iron rocker. This breaks the circuit.

The Starter Motor Relay

7) *The diagram opposite shows a starter motor relay.*

a) *Draw* in the missing right-hand part of the diagram, and label it.

b) *What part* of the car electrics uses a relay, and what is the relay's function?

c) *Describe* what happens in the relay when the switch is closed.

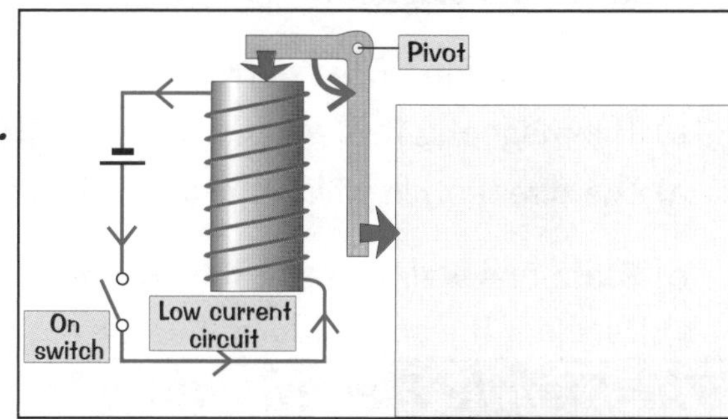

The Electric Bell

8) *Someone closes the switch of this electric bell.*

a) What happens to the fixed iron cores?

b) *Explain* why the hammer moves and hits the gong.

c) *This movement breaks the circuit. Explain why.*

d) What happens to the iron bar after the hammer has hit the gong?

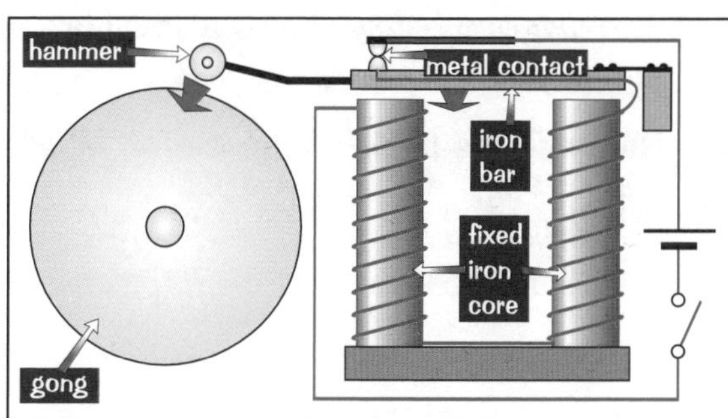

9) Which of the following are magnetic materials?

iron *copper* *zinc* *steel* *nickel* *brass*

Top Tips Electromagnets — like magnets, only even more attractive. An electromagnet is a solenoid with an iron core. Remember this essential definition: The strength of an electromagnet depends on *three* factors: the *size* of the *current*, the *number* of *turns* the coil has and *what* the core is *made of*. You also need to know the difference between iron and steel, and how to demagnetise a piece of steel. Lastly, learn the examples on this page, they come up in the Exam.

The Motor Effect

Magnets and Electric Currents

1) *The diagram opposite shows a current-carrying wire at right-angles to a magnetic field.*

a) Use an arrow on the diagram to show the direction of the force experienced by the wire.

b) State *two* things you could do to increase the size of the force on the wire?

c) *Describe* the rule which predicts the direction of the force on the wire.

d) If the wire was turned through 90° so that it ran along the magnetic field, would there still be a force? *Explain* your answer.

2) *The diagram opposite shows a horseshoe magnet. An electric current can be made to flow in a wire between the poles. A metal bar completes the circuit and rests freely on the wires.*

Describe the *motion* of the bar when a *direct current* is switched on.
Describe the motion of the bar when an *alternating current* is switched on.

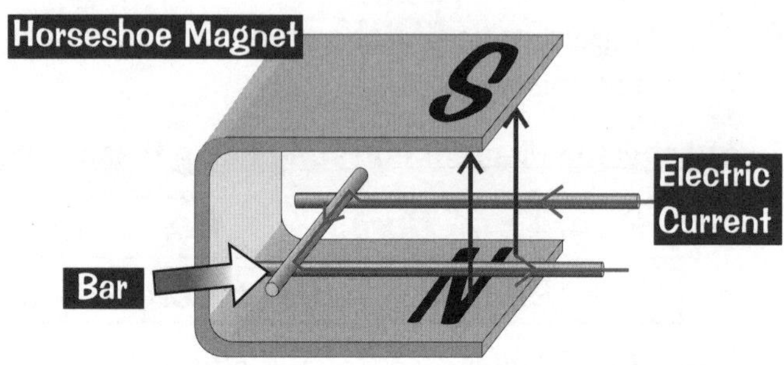

3) *Copy* the diagram below showing two magnets with a current-carrying wire between them.

Draw on the diagram:

a) The direction of the current.

b) The magnetic field and its direction (N to S).

c) The direction in which the wire will move.

d) State one way to make the wire move in the opposite direction.

The Simple Electric Motor

4) *The diagram below shows a small laboratory version of a simple electric motor.*

a) Name all the parts of the motor, labelled A to J.

b) Which of the parts from A to J are made from insulating materials?

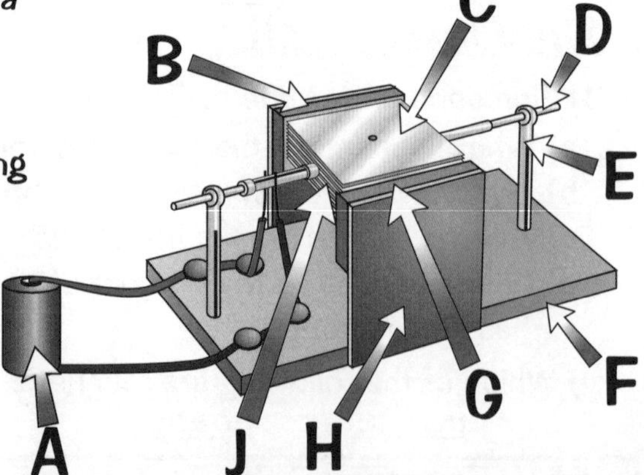

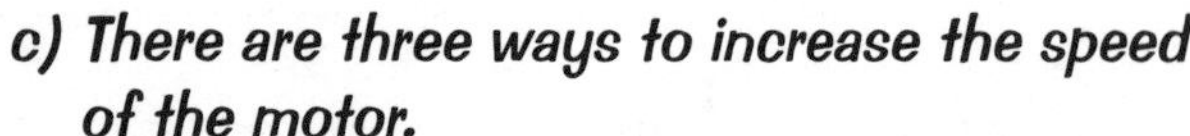

c) *There are three ways to increase the speed of the motor.*

Fill in the gaps in the sentences opposite describing how to speed up the motor.

Use these words: Turns, core, increase, iron

1. Put more ________________ on the coil.
2. ________________ the magnetic field.
3. Put a ____________ ____________ in the coil.

The Motor Effect

The Simple Electric Motor

5) *The diagram shows how a simple motor works. The coil is free to rotate between the poles of the magnet. The split ring commutator is fixed to the coil and turns with it.*

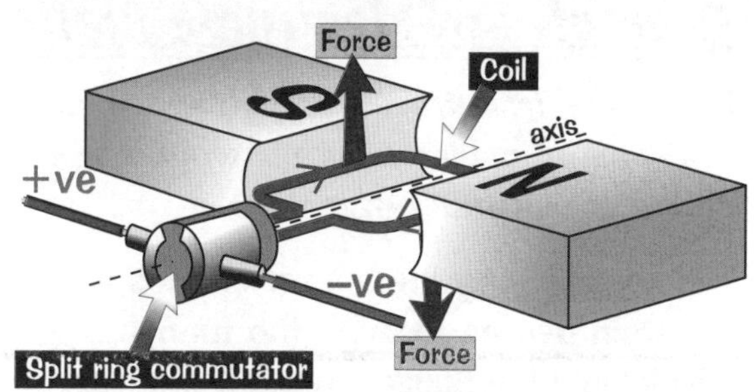

Fill in the gaps below using the *following words:*

Current *up* *torque* *coil* *forces* *turn* *down* *right*

When a current flows through the ___________ , the left side is pushed ___________ and the ___________ side ___________. When the coil is vertical, the forces can not ___________ it any further because there is no ___________. As the coil shoots past the vertical, the split ring commutator changes the direction of the___________. Now the ___________ point the other way around and the coil is pushed around and around and around...

6) *Redraw* the circuit with an ammeter and a voltmeter correctly placed to measure the current through and voltage across the motor M.

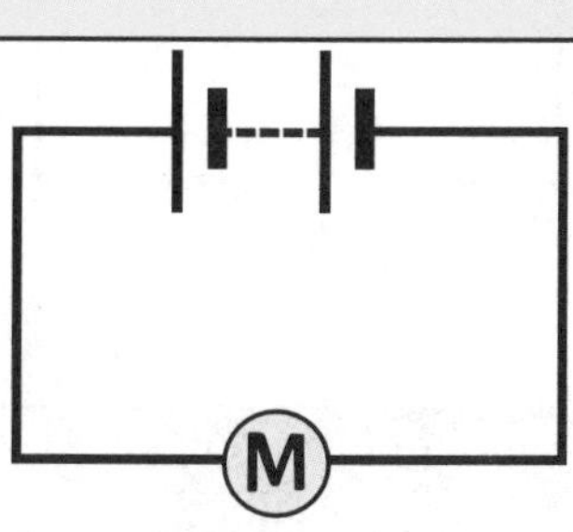

7) *Name 5 appliances* at home that contain an electric motor.

The Loudspeaker

8) *Put these statements* about how a loudspeaker works into the *correct order:*

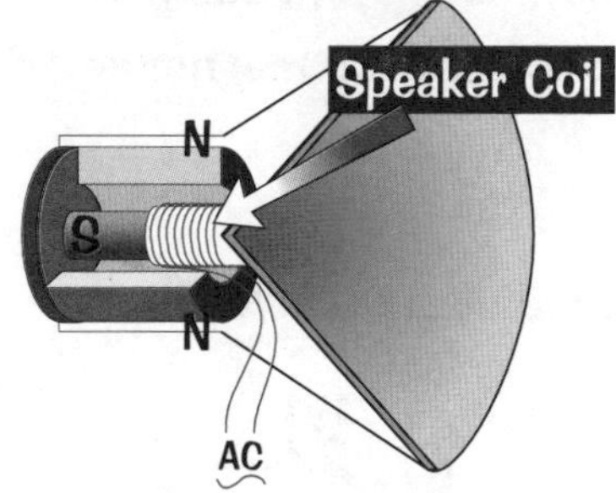

- This creates sounds.
- These make the coil move back and forth
- over the North pole of the magnet.
- are fed into the speaker coil.
- the cardboard case vibrate.
- These movements make
- AC signals from the amplifier

Word Revision

9) *Link up* each description a) to f) with the correct word from the right-hand column.

a) Swaps the contacts every half turn in an electric motor	• vibrates
b) Converts electrical energy into sound energy	• coil (armature)
c) Converts electrical energy into kinetic energy	• polarity
d) Turns around on an axis	• electric motor
e) Move quickly forwards and backwards but not changing position	• loud speaker
f) Positive and negative	• split ring commutator

Top Tips

The point here is that a *current carrying wire* in a magnetic field experiences a *force*, which gets bigger if the current or the magnetic field is made bigger. Learn the diagrams in questions 1 and 2. You need to know how the motor and the loudspeaker work. The best thing about the motor effect is looking at your left hand to answer the question (Believe me, in the Exam doing this will seem like entertainment). Remember thumb = motion, first finger = field and second finger = current. And it's Fleming's LEFT hand rule, important, so learn it.

Electromagnetic Induction

Examples of Electromagnetic Induction

1) *A model train travels at high speed into a tunnel. A bar magnet is fixed to the top of the train. A coil of insulated wire is wound around the tunnel and underneath the track (connected in the circuit to a buzzer).*

a) Explain why the buzzer sounds when the train passes through the tunnel.
b) Would the buzzer sound if the train stopped in the tunnel? Explain your answer.
c) Suggest two ways to make the buzzer sound louder (without dismantling the tunnel).

buzzer

2) *A magnet is being pushed towards a coil of insulated wire.*

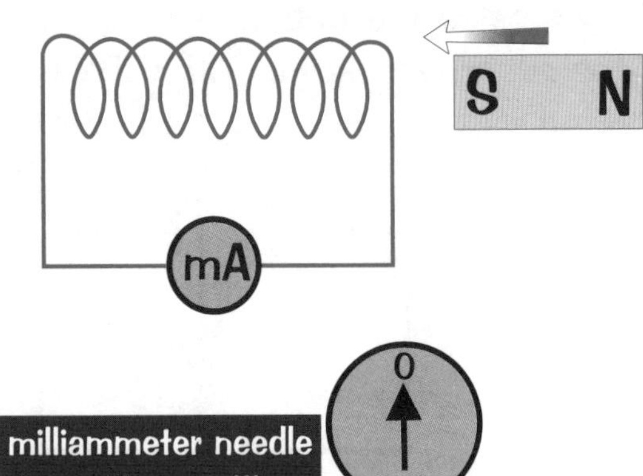

Magnet pushed in	Needle moved to the right
Magnet in the coil - not moving	
Magnet pulled out	
Magnet pulled out faster	

a) The table above summarises four experiments with the magnet. Copy and complete.
b) Which type of pole (N or S) is produced at the ends of the coil when the magnet is pushed in? Explain your answer.
c) Suggest two ways to reverse the poles produced in the coil.

3) *A wire is moved upwards through a magnetic field, as shown in the diagram below.*

a) What is the direction of the induced current?
Is it: X to Y or Y to X?
b) What would be the effect of:
i) using a stronger magnet.
ii) moving the wire faster.
iii) moving the wire downwards.
iv) moving the wire towards one of the poles.

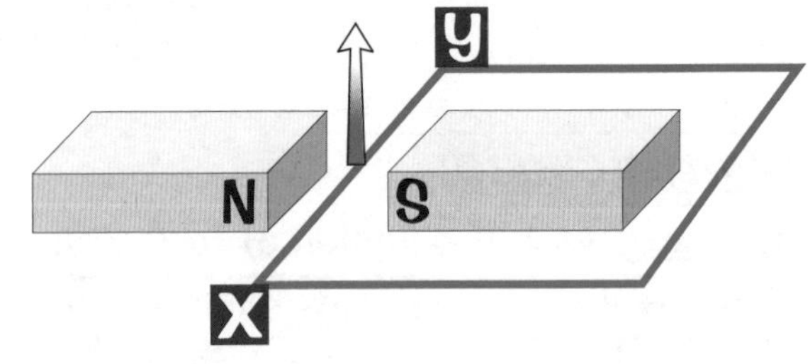

Factors affecting the Size of the Induced Voltage

4) The *size* of the induced voltage depends on...
a) Unjumble these words to reveal the four factors.

The the The the The The the the speed coil area turns
strength of of of of on number magnet coil movement

b) Unjumble the following sentence about cutting magnetic flux lines.
The size of the of cutting is proportional to the voltage induced rate of the flux.

Electromagnetic Induction

5) *Word check!* Match up the following words and phrases a) to f):

a) North pole	• Measures small amounts of current
b) South pole	• Type of current produced by an alternator
c) Milliammeter	• A generator needs more of these for more current
d) Coils	• Field lines point away from this pole
e) Dynamos	• When turned, they produce currents
f) Alternating current	• Field lines point towards this pole

Generators and Dynamos

6) Fill in the missing words about generators.

Swap slip motor voltage rotate higher more voltage faster magnetic

Generators __________ a coil in a __________ field. Their construction is quite like a __________, except there are __________ rings instead of a split ring commutator, so the contacts don't __________ every half turn. This means they produce AC __________ as shown on the CRO displays. __________ revolutions produce not only __________ peaks, but __________ overall __________ too.

7) *Below is a CRO display for a generator.* Fill in the trace to show how the current from a generator changes as the coil rotates, and also the blanks in the following sentences.

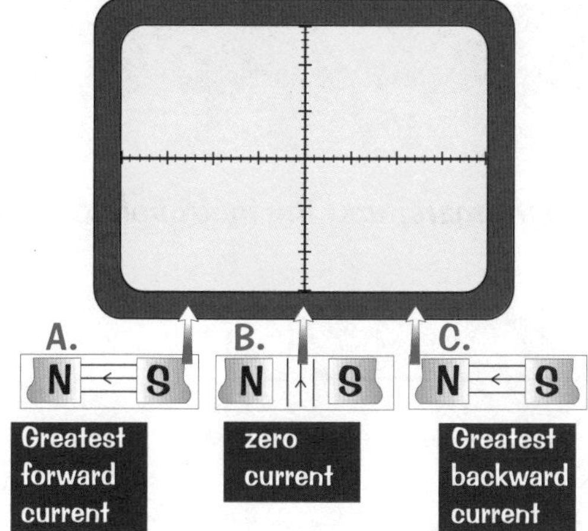

A. The current is __________ when the coil is __________. The coil __________ magnetic field lines most __________ in this position.

B. The current is __________ when the coil is __________. The coil does not cut __________ lines in this position.

C. Once again, the current is greatest when the coil is horizontal.

Use these words: field, cuts, horizontal, vertical, zero, greatest, rapidly

8) Give three ways an generator could be altered to produce more current.

9) *Below is data about a small lab generator, a generator in a power station, and a dynamo.*

a) Uses a spinning electromagnet instead of a permanent magnet.
b) Uses a permanent magnet which rotates.
c) Generates a current of 20,000A at a voltage of 25,000V.
d) Generates a current less than 1A.
e) Uses a stationary permanent magnet .
f) Produces alternating current, AC.
g) Producing direct current, DC.
h) Has a magnet spinning at 50 times a second.
i) Has a magnet spinning at variable speeds.

Draw a table with the columns: *"lab generator", "power station generator" and "dynamo".* Write out the data in the correct column. *You can use the data once, more than once or not at all.*

Top Tips Electromagnetic induction *is* really weird, but it isn't that difficult to learn the definition: The creation of a *voltage* (and current) in a wire placed in a *changing magnetic field*. *Four* factors affect the size of the induced voltage, and yep, you need to learn them. You can explain all four in terms of rate of change of flux, but quite honestly it is a bit hard to grasp.

Transformers

Basic Features of Transformers

1) *A model train is connected to the mains supply via a transformer. The following information is on the back of the transformer...*

Input:	230V	50Hz	12W
Output:	12V	1A	12W

a) What is the *function* of this transformer?
b) Is this a *step-up* or a *step-down* transformer? Explain your answer.
c) What is the frequency of the *mains* supply?
d) *State* what the symbols V, Hz, A and W stand for. Also, state what they are the *units* for.

Input and Output Voltage

2) *There are 2 step-up and 2 step-down transformers here. Which is which? (The primary column is on the left and the secondary on the right).*

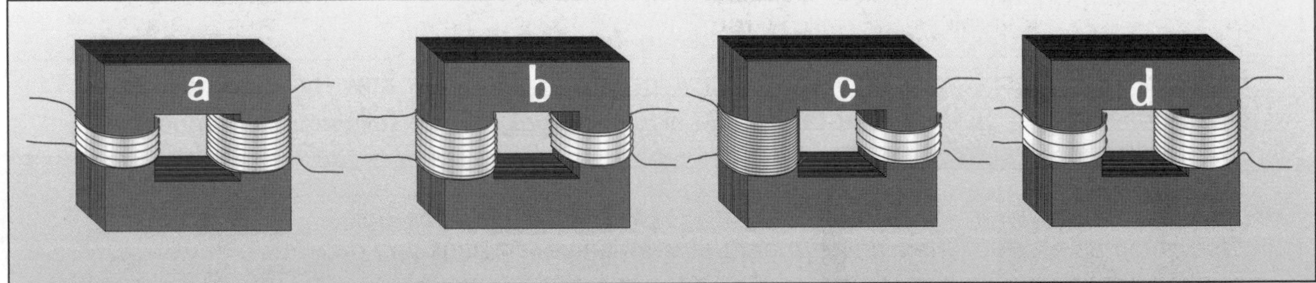

3) *This table shows the number of turns on the above transformers, and the input voltage.* Find the *output voltage* in each case.

Transformer	a	b	c	d
Input turns	5	8	16	3
Output turns	10	4	4	9
Input voltage	230	230	24	24
Output voltage				

4) *This table shows the input and output voltages and the number of turns on the input coil.*

Transformer	t	u	x	y
Input voltage	180	230	12	20
Output voltage	9	23	180	50
Input turns	400	100	9	16
Output turns				

a) Complete the table above.
b) Which of the transformers; t, u, x and y are *step-up* transformers?
c) Which of the transformers has a ratio of turns 10:1?
d) Which of the transformers has the *greatest number* of output turns?

Transformers

Running a 9V radio off the Mains...

5) *A 9V radio takes a current of 2A. The supply to the radio is from a transformer connected to a 230V mains.*
   a) What is the ratio of turns on the input and output coils of this transformer?
   b) What is the power used by: i) the radio ii) the mains?
   c) What current is taken by the mains?

6) *This is the diagram of part of a burglar system.*

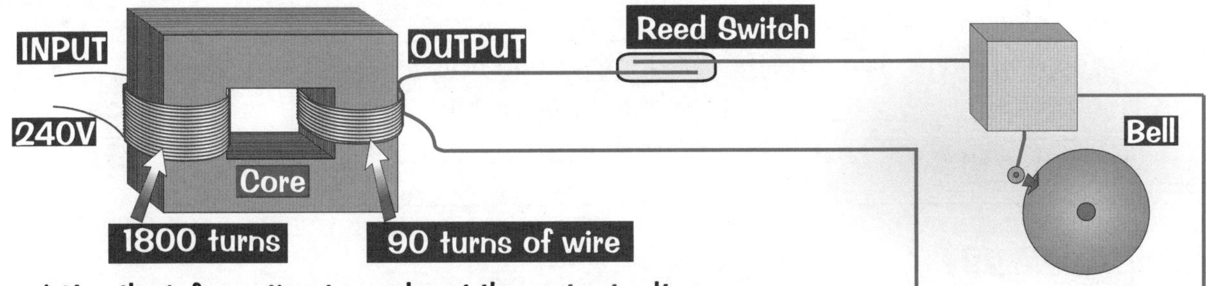

   a) Use the information to work out the output voltage.
   b) Explain carefully how a voltage is produced in the secondary coil.

Transmitting Electricity from Power Stations to Homes

7) *Step-up transformers are used to transmit electricity at high voltage over long distances.* Explain how this reduces the energy losses.

8) *This question is about the transformers between power stations and peoples' homes.*

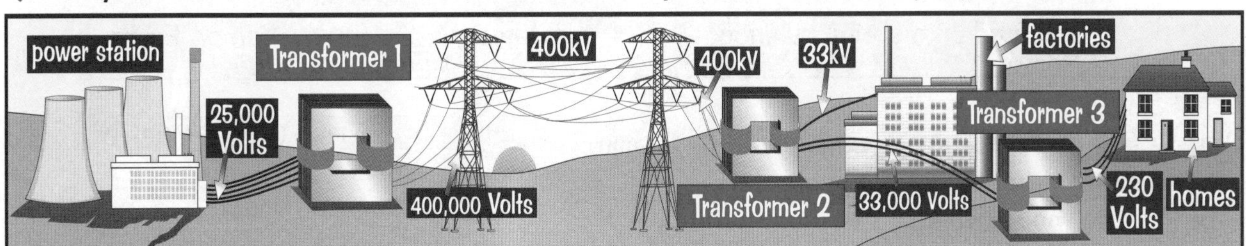

Work out the ratio of input : output voltage for each transformer 1-3. Write down if a step-up or step-down transformer is needed.

9) a) Complete the table opposite for the transformers e, f, g and h.

   b) Find the power output for each of the transformers e, f, g and h.

Transformer	e	f	g	h
Voltage (Primary)	24	230	12	
Current (Primary)	1	2	3	0.5
Voltage (Secondary)	6		6	6
Current (Secondary)		1		1.5

10) Explain the following terms:
   a) Laminated iron core b) Eddy currents c) Magnetic flux d) Electromagnetic induction
   e) Primary coil f) Secondary coil g) Ratio h) Reversing

11) Explain why we can not get transformers to work with DC (direct current).

Top Tips Transformers work by Electromagnetic Induction, so they only work on AC. Remember that no current flows around the iron core, only magnetic flux. If current did flow, it'd be a waste of energy. This is the formula you need to learn — it goes either way up.

$$\frac{\text{Primary voltage}}{\text{Secondary voltage}} = \frac{\text{Number of turns on Primary}}{\text{Number of turns on Secondary}}$$

Mass, Weight and Gravity

The Force of Gravity

1) Fill in the *gaps*:
Use these words: bodies, large, attraction, weak, strong, field, centre, newtons, weight

Gravity is the force of ____________ between __________. It is a ____________ force, but if the mass is very very __________ as with a planet or a star, the gravity can be very ____________. The region where a gravitational force can be felt is often referred to as a gravitational ______________. The Earth's gravitational field attracts every object on Earth. This gives an object a ____________. Weight is measured in ____________, and always acts towards the __________ of the Earth.

Mass and Weight

2) *"Mass and weight" are used in everyday language almost as if they were the same thing.* Draw a table with 2 columns, one headed "*mass*" and the other "*weight*". Decide which information belongs to which column, and write them in:

- amount of matter
- measured in newtons
- measured by a balance
- not a force
- measured by a spring balance
- is a force
- caused by the pull of gravity
- same anywhere in the universe
- measured in kilograms
- is lower on the moon than on Earth

3) a) *"A bag of flour weighs one kilogram".* Explain why this statement is not accurate.
b) Rewrite the above statement so that it is accurate.
c) *Complete* the table opposite for a range of masses on Earth (g = 10 N/kg).

Mass (g)	Mass (kg)	Weight (N)
5		
10		
100		
200		
500		
1000		
5000		

Weight on the Moon and the Planets

4) *The strength of gravity on Earth is g=10 N/kg.* Find the *weight* of rocks with the following masses:
a) 5kg b) 10kg c) 2.5kg

Find the *mass* of rocks with the following weights on Earth:
d) 30N e) 150N f) 450N

5) *The strength of gravity on the Moon is g=1.6 N/kg.* Find the *weight* of moon rocks with the following masses:
a) 5kg b) 10kg c) 2.5kg

Find the *mass* of rocks with the following weights on the Moon:
d) 16N e) 80N f) 960N

Mass, Weight and Gravity

Orbital motion and weightlessness

6) *Match the words* a) to j) with the correct descriptions from the list on the right.

a) Accelerate	• moving
b) Gravity	• forces in equilibrium
c) Motion	• curved path of a planet or satellite
d) Balanced	• to undergo a change in velocity
e) Weight	• amount of matter
f) Mass	• orbits around a star
g) Orbit	• downwards force
h) Planet	• orbits around a planet
i) Satellite	• attraction between two masses

7) An astronaut is in a spacecraft far away from any star or planet. His mass is 70kg.

a) What is his weight?

b) The astronaut enters orbit around the strange planet Vulcan, a replica of planet Earth. What is the force that keeps him in orbit?

c) Explain, very carefully, why the astronaut experiences 'weightlessness' when orbiting Vulcan, even though he has a mass and is in a gravitational field? (Think about the motion of the astronaut, the spacecraft and the force pulling them downwards).

8) *Use the data in the table below to answer the following questions (the strengths of gravity given are at the planet's or star's surface):*

Planet	Radius (m)	Mass (kg)	Strength of Gravity, g (N/kg)
Earth	6.378×10^6	5.978×10^{24}	9.8
Mars	3.375×10^6	6.420×10^{23}	3.8
Sun	6.96×10^8	1.989×10^{30}	274

a) Suppose an astronaut of mass 95kg (including spacesuit) visits the surface of Mars. What would his weight be in newtons?

b) When on Earth he can lift a maximum of 120kg above his head. What is the largest mass is he able to lift on Mars?

The gravitational force, F between two masses, m_1 and m_2 can be calculated using the formula:

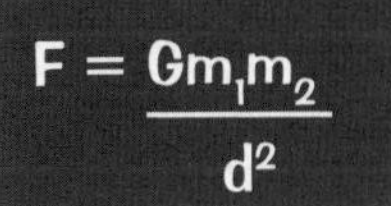

$$F = \frac{Gm_1m_2}{d^2}$$

where d is the distance between the masses and G is Newton's gravitational constant: $G = 6.67 \times 10^{-11}$ Nm²/kg².

c) Calculate the average force between the Earth and the Sun if their mean distance apart is 1.50×10^{11}m.

d) Occasionally, the Sun, Earth and Mars form a straight line in space, at which time the distance between Mars and Earth is 7.8×10^{10}m, approximately. Calculate the gravitational force between Mars and the Earth when this happens.

e) What do your answers to c) and d) tell you about the influence of Mars upon the Earth's orbit?

Top Tips Lots of practice on mass, weight and gravity here. Remember, *mass* and *weight* are *not* the same. Mass is the *amount of matter* (in kg) — weight is the *force of gravity* pulling on something (in N). Don't forget the formula W = m x g that ties them all together.

Moments: Turning Forces

Seesaws and pivots

1) For each of the seesaws a) to d), write down if it is balanced or unbalanced.

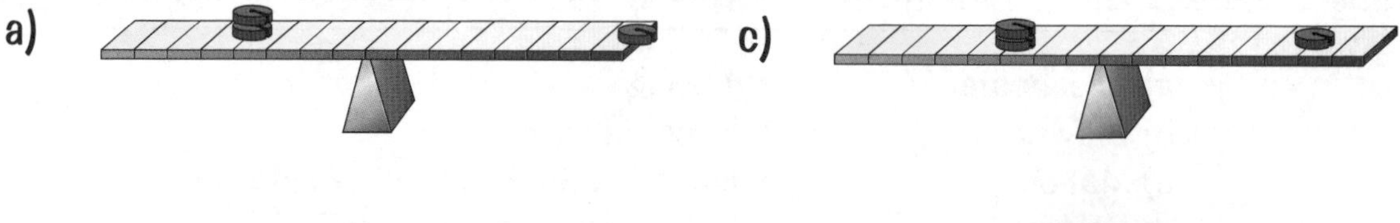

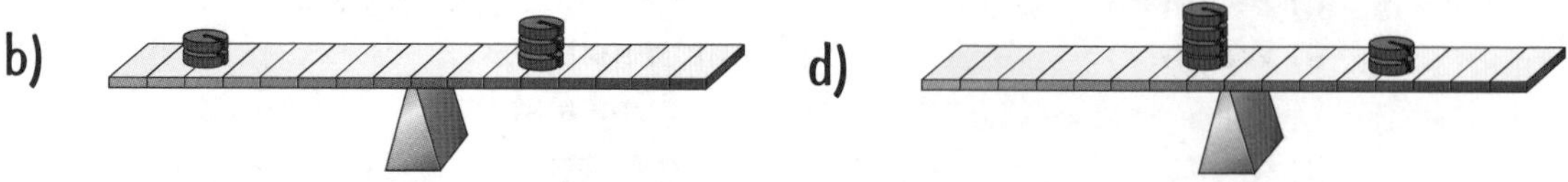

2) For each of the seesaws A to D, calculate the clockwise and the anti-clockwise moment, and state whether the seesaw is balanced or unbalanced.

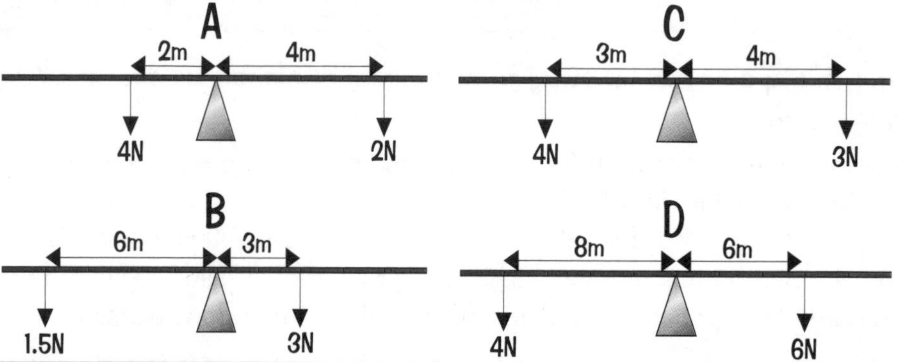

Which Way will they Tip?

3) The diagrams i) to iv) show four thin rods pivoted at X with forces applied at various distances from X

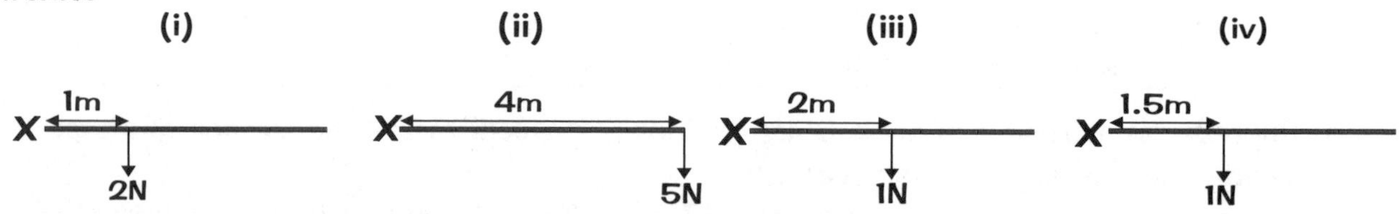

a) Which rod has the largest moment about the pivot X ?
b) Which rod has the smallest moment about the pivot X ?
c) Which 2 rods have an equal moment about the pivot X ?

4) For the seesaws below, work out the total *clockwise* moment and total *anticlockwise* moment. *Which way* will the seesaws tip — to the left or to the right?

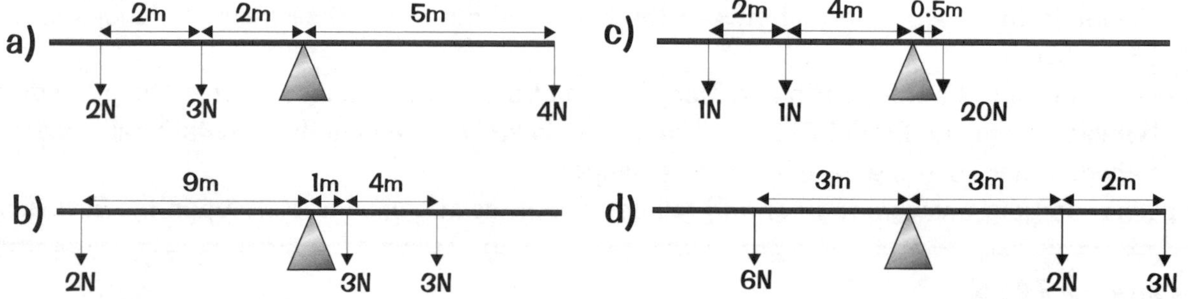

5) A load of 100N is placed on a thin, light rod 4m from the pivot. *What force* do you need to apply 2m from the pivot on the opposite side to *counterbalance* the load ?

More Moments

6) a) *What* is the weight of the paving stone if its mass is 50 kg? *(taking the pull of the Earth to be 10 N/kg)*

b) If the total length of the metal bar is 2.0m, what is the *minimum force* you need to apply at the other end of the metal bar to lift the paving stone?

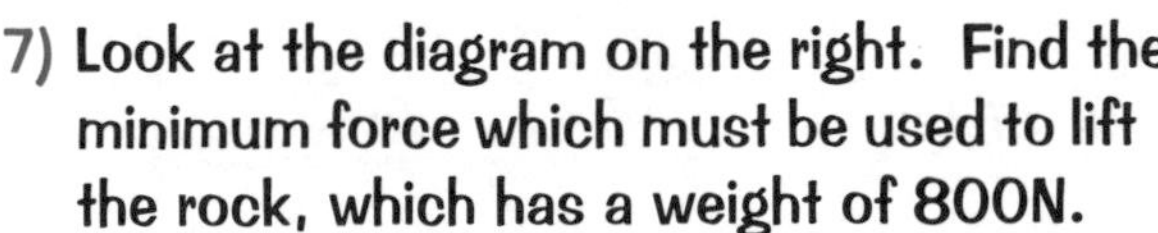

7) Look at the diagram on the right. Find the minimum force which must be used to lift the rock, which has a weight of 800N.

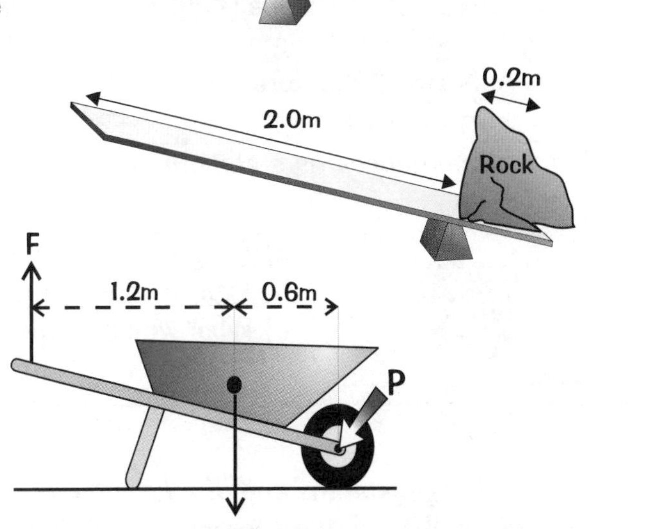

8) *Point P marks the pivot point on the wheelbarrow.* Take moments about P to find the *vertical* force, F, that needs to be applied to the handles of the wheelbarrow to just lift it off the ground.

Balancing the Books

9) Sally is handing over an overdue book to a librarian. The book has a mass of 2kg.

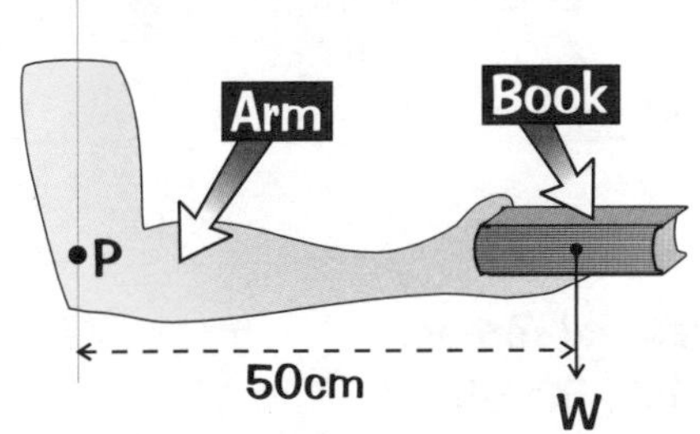

a) Find the weight, W, of the book.

b) Copy the diagram and draw an arrow for the vertical force, T, needed to support the book in this position (think carefully about where this force will be acting).

c) Calculate the moment of the book's weight about the pivot, P.

10) a) Look at the diagram on the right. What's the reading on the two spring balances if the two readings are *equal*?

b) If four spring balances were used with the same 1 Kg block, what reading on each balance would you get if the values are again equal?

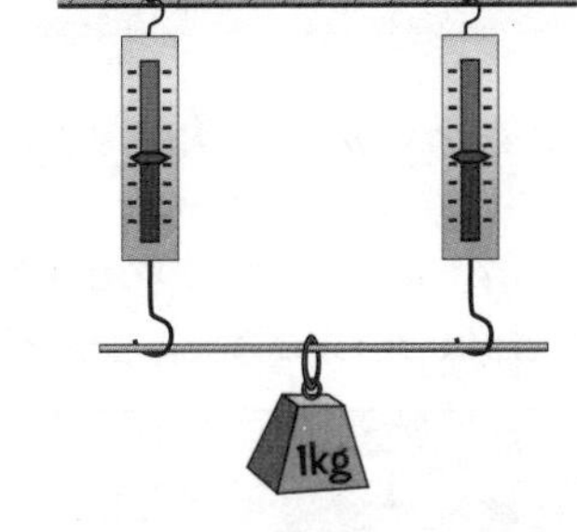

Forces on Planks

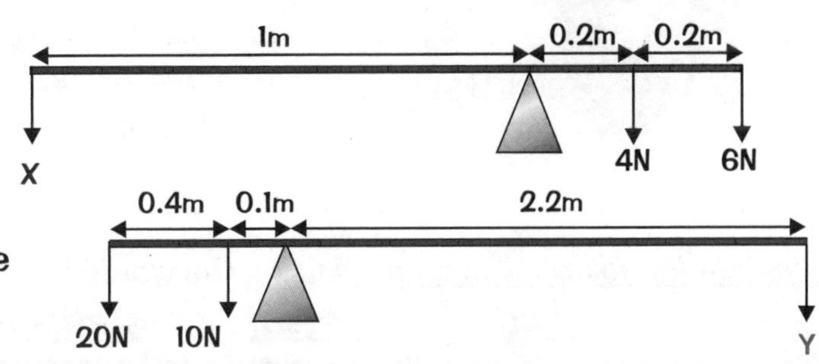

11) *Find* the force X to be applied on the left side of the plank to balance it.

12) *Find* the force Y to be applied on the right side of the plank to balance it.

Top Tips Lots of tedious seesaw questions, I know, but you need plenty of practice with these. When a *force* acts on something which has a *pivot*, then you have a *moment*, which is a *turning force* making the thing *rotate* about its pivot. The equation you need to learn is *Moment = Force × perpendicular distance*, which makes sense if you think about pushing an open door near the hinge or near the handle.

Force Diagrams

1) *Identify* these different forces:

a) Acts straight downwards.	TENSION
b) Slows things down.	GRAVITY or WEIGHT
c) In a rope or cable.	LIFT
d) Due to an aeroplane wing.	THRUST or PUSH or PULL
e) Speeds something up.	REACTION FORCE
f) Acts straight upwards on a horizontal plane.	DRAG or AIR RESISTANCE or FRICTION

2) *This question concerns a stationary object — a mug of tea.*

a) *Copy* the diagram and *draw in* the 2 vertical forces. *Label them*.
b) *Explain* how you know that this pair of forces is equal.
c) *What* would happen if there was only one *vertical* force?

3) *A fish is hanging on the end of a fishing line.* *Copy* the diagram and *draw in* the 2 vertical forces. *Label them*.

4) *A car is moving forward with a steady horizontal velocity.*

a) *Copy* the diagram and *draw in* the *two* vertical forces. *Label them*.

b) *Draw* in the *two* horizontal forces. Is one force bigger than the other?

5) *Rifle shooting and rocket engines provide forward motion.*
a) *Draw* diagrams to show the forces occurring during the firing of each (don't worry about drawing the rifle and rocket).
b) Why does a rifle "kick back" when it is fired?

6) *After jumping out of an aeroplane, a skydiver accelerates until he reaches a steady vertical velocity, known as the terminal velocity.* *Draw* in the *two* vertical forces for when the diver is at terminal velocity, and *label them*.

7) *Complete the following sentences* using the words below:

drag *constant* *stationary* *downwards*
equilibrium *weight* *gravity*

If all forces acting on an object are in ___________ , the object is either ___________ or moving with a ___________ velocity. The force of ___________ acting upon an object (giving it a ___________) points ___________. If the object is falling through the air, another force called ___________ acts in the opposite direction.

Force Diagrams

8) Study these diagrams of a submarine which is horizontal. The forces acting on the submarine are represented by arrows such that the length of the arrow is proportional to the size of the force. If the submarine starts from a constant velocity, state for each case if it will accelerate up/down/forwards/backwards or remain at that velocity. One example is done for you.

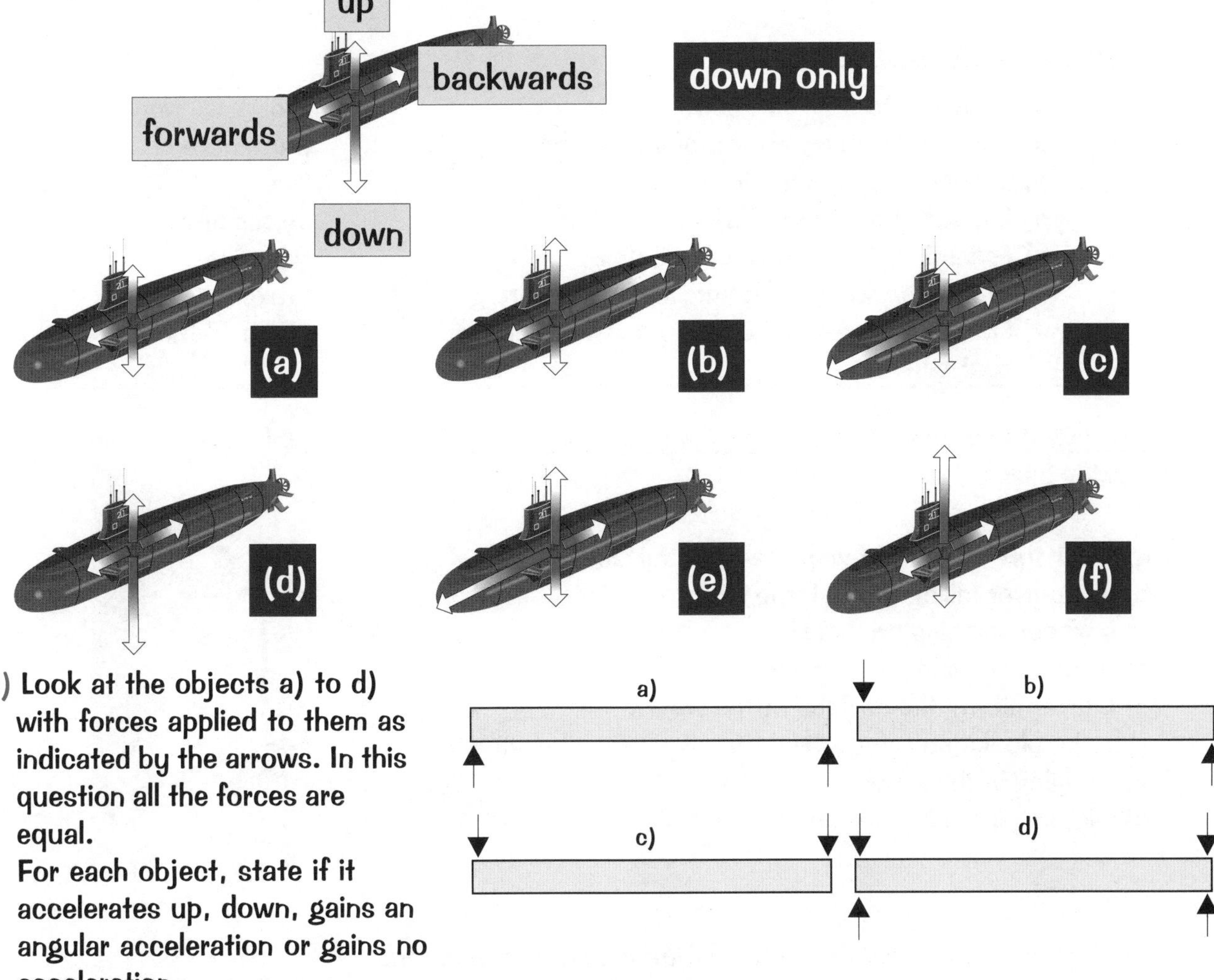

9) Look at the objects a) to d) with forces applied to them as indicated by the arrows. In this question all the forces are equal.
For each object, state if it accelerates up, down, gains an angular acceleration or gains no acceleration.

a) b) c) d)

10) *Complete* the following sentences with the words below:

unbalanced *faster* *greater* *greater* *thrust* *upwards*
downwards *weight* *reaction* *drag* *drag* *force* *smaller*

Acceleration means getting ____________. You only get acceleration with an overall resultant (____________) force. The ____________ the unbalanced ____________ the ____________ the acceleration. The ____________ the unbalanced force, the smaller the acceleration. A car which is accelerating forward has a larger ____________ than ____________ force, but the vertical forces (____________ and ____________) are the same. A skydiver accelerating ____________ has a weight force downwards, but less ____________ ____________.

Top Tips

More force questions for you to enjoy, this time with pictures, wow. Seriously, though, you *really do* need to be able to draw a diagram showing *all* the forces acting on an object. Don't forget to include *pairs* of forces that are in *equilibrium*. Remember all the forces in Question 1 — these are the only six you need to know about.

Friction

1) a) If an object is stationary and has no forces acting on it, *what happens*?
   b) If an object is moving at a steady speed over a rough surface and has no forces propelling it along, *what happens*?
   c) To continue travelling at a steady speed across a rough surface, *what* does an object need and *why*?

2) *Match the words and the meanings*:

a) On a car, to grip the road.	sliding friction
b) Change direction after braking too hard.	parachute
c) Shaped to overcome friction.	tyres
d) Increases drag in the air.	streamlined
e) Essential if a car is to stop safely.	skid
f) Friction between solid surfaces which are gripping.	brakes
g) Friction between solid surfaces which are sliding past each other.	static friction

3) *State whether* friction should be *as low as possible* or *as high as possible* in each of the following cases:

a) a car tyre in contact with the road surface.
b) a skydiver falling through the air.
c) a wheel spinning on its axle.
d) a skater moving over the ice.
e) a diver hitting the surface of the water.
f) brake blocks pressing against the rim of a bike wheel.
g) sledging in the snow.
h) climbing a mountain using a rope.

4) *This diagram shows how the force of friction can be measured.*

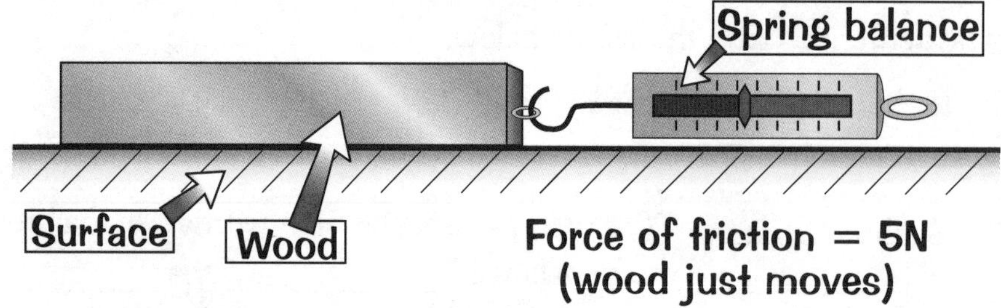

a) Give two ways you can *increase* the force of friction.
b) Give two ways of *decreasing* the friction.

5) *Why* do:

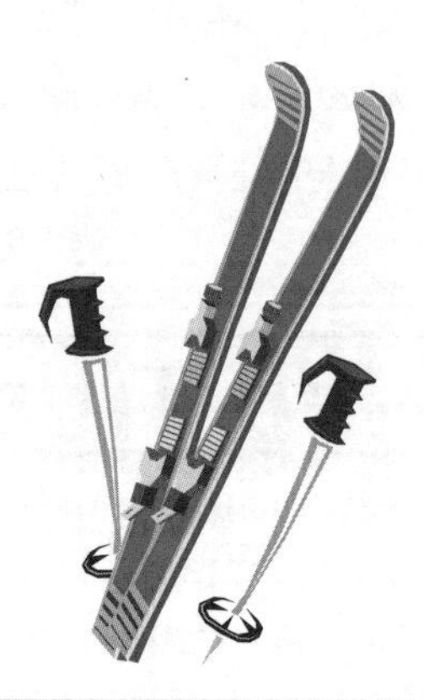

a) Skiers wax their skis?
b) Machines have to be lubricated by oil?
c) Climbers wear rubber-soled shoes?
d) Ballroom dancers wear leather-soled shoes and dance on a highly polished floor?

Friction

6) *Riding a bicycle gives us plenty of examples of friction being useful and a nuisance.* Divide these up into *"useful"* and *"nuisance"* and *explain* your decision each time.

air resistance	saddle	handlebar grips	
pedals	wheel bearings	tyres	brakes

7) *Put these sentences into their correct sequence*:

- compared to 30 mph
- A car has much more friction
- than it would going just as far at 30 mph
- It therefore uses more petrol
- just to maintain a steady speed
- as the speed increases
- to work against when travelling at 70 mph
- So at 70 mph the engine has to work much harder
- Air resistance always increases

8) *Friction causes wear and heating.* Answer these questions about these *two* effects of friction.

a) *Give three examples* where friction acts between surfaces that are *sliding* over each other.
b) Friction produces *heat* energy. Give two examples where this is *useful*.
c) What can be used to keep friction in *machinery* as *low* as possible?
d) *Explain* what will happen to an engine running without oil?
e) *Explain* why brakes might need to be replaced more often for a racing car than for a car that is only used around town (30 mph speed limit).

9) *Suppose someone invented a frictionless material.* Which of the following would be *impossible* to do with it, and *why*:

a) Run across a thin sheet of it.
b) Slide across a sheet of it.
c) Stop sliding across a sheet of it.

Which of the following would be *useful* if made out of it:

d) Nuts and bolts.
e) Tables.
f) Tyres.
g) Car bodies.
h) Roofs.

Top Tips Don't let it rub you up the wrong way, now. Friction is always there to slow things down — you can't afford to ignore it, so learn all the stuff on these pages. Remember the *three* ways that friction occurs. Don't forget that friction can be *helpful* as well as a *nuisance*. Lastly, because friction causes wear and heating, machinery needs *oil* to *lubricate* it and stop it from wearing down — or *even worse*, welding itself together from the extreme heat.

The Three Laws of Motion

Newton's First Law

1) *Newton's First Law of Motion states that balanced forces means no change in velocity.*
   a) Explain clearly the underlined terms (balanced forces and velocity).
   b) Draw a diagram of something (a car, bus, stick man) moving at a constant velocity. Draw in the horizontal forces.
   c) Describe what is meant by the term "resultant" force.
   d) For your diagram in b) what is the resultant force?

2) a) Draw a diagram of a submarine with the forces acting on it, if it's resting on the ocean bed.
   b) What is the velocity of the submarine?

Newton's Second Law

3) Newton's Second Law of Motion states that a non-zero resultant force means acceleration. Complete the following sentences about this law, using the words below.

force unequal slowing down speeding up stopping
accelerate decelerate direction starting

If there is an unbalanced ___________ , then an object will ___________ or ___________ in that ___________ . This change in motion can take five different forms: ___________ , ___________ , ___________ ___________ , ___________ ___________ and changing direction. On a force diagram, the arrows will be ___________ .

4) Answer TRUE or FALSE. Explain your answer.
   a) "If something is moving, there must be an overall force on it".
   b) "You get steady speed from balanced forces".
   c) "You get acceleration/deceleration if there is an overall force acting on an object".
   d) "The bigger the force, the smaller the acceleration".
   e) "The bigger the mass, the smaller the acceleration".
   f) "To get a small mass to accelerate as much as a big mass, it needs a bigger force".

5)
   a) In the equation F = ma, explain what F, m and a stand for.
   b) What are the units of F, m and a?
   c) Rearrange the equation as "a = ".
   d) Rearrange the equation as "m = ".

6) Fill in the gaps:
   Use the following words: force, acceleration, mass, one newton, mass, double

To give a ___________ of 1 kilogram an ___________ of 1 metre per second squared, a force of ______ ________ is needed. Twice the ___________ pushing on the same ___________ would produce ___________ the acceleration.

7) Find the force acting on these objects:
   a) mass 10kg, acceleration 5 m/s^2.
   b) mass 50kg, acceleration 2.5 m/s^2.
   c) mass 400kg, acceleration 8 m/s^2.

The Three Laws of Motion

8) *Find* the acceleration of these objects:

a) Resultant Force 100N, mass 10kg.
b) Resultant Force 500N, mass 25kg.
c) Resultant Force 75N, mass 2.5kg.
d) *One of the above objects is falling towards Earth.* *Which one* is it?

9)

a) Which masses have the same accelerations?
b) Which has the biggest acceleration?
c) Which has the smallest acceleration?

10) *An astronaut, who weighs 900N on Earth, climbs into his space craft and takes off. Once in orbit, he engages his super thrust booster engines which, according to 'Which Interstellar Spaceship?' magazine, has a maximum output force of 60 million newtons. He accelerates from 0 to 60 (that's 60 km/sec) in 10 seconds. Checking his copy of 'Which Interstellar Spaceship?', he finds that the figure for the mass of his craft is smudged.* Can you *work out* what it is?

11) *When Sarah is sitting in her go-cart, the total mass is 50kg. Starting from rest at the top of a hill, she experiences a force of 100N down the hill, and a constant resistance of 10N in the opposite direction. She sets off with a tiny push, and travels for ten seconds before the hill levels off.* *What* is her *velocity* when she reaches the bottom?

Newton's Third Law

12) *This question is about Newton's Third Law of Motion.*

a) *State* the law. *Start off with* "If object A exerts a force on object B then .....".
b) *Explain* what happens when you push on a wall, in terms of Newton's Third Law. *Draw a diagram* to explain your answer. Include the forces.
c) If an object is on a horizontal surface, *what force* will there be pushing upwards?
d) *What* other force acting on the object is this force equal to?
e) *Draw a diagram* which illustrates your answers to both c) and d).

13) *A circus cannon is fired, sending Coco the Clown flying out accelerating at 5 m/s^2. He weighs 90kg.*

a) What force propelled Coco?
b) What force is exerted on the cannon?
c) If the cannon has a mass of 450kg, how fast will it accelerate, and in what direction?

Top Tips

Newtons Laws of Motion might sound a bit obscure, but you really *absolutely* do need to *learn* them. The three laws are the basic facts you need to understand forces and motion. If you learn them and understand them — and they're pretty *simple*, then you'll *never* get caught out saying something *totally stupid*, like "if something's moving there must be an overall force acting on it". That's wrong, really really wrong.

Speed and Velocity

1) *Getting going!* *How fast is*:

a) An athlete who runs 100m (metres) in 10s (seconds)?
b) A racing car zooming 240m in 12s?
c) A student, walking 600m in 240s?
d) A tortoise with a twisted ankle, shuffling 10m in 100s?

2) *Keeping going....*

a) *Sir misses a paper aeroplane thrown from the middle of the classroom, which is 5m away. It takes 1.5 seconds to reach him.* *What* is its speed? *How long* would it have taken to reach him if it had been thrown from the back row of desks, 10m away?
b) *A snail creeps 1m in 500s.* *What* is its speed?
c) *Find* the speed of a rocket zooming 280,000m in 20s. What is this speed in km/s?

3) *How long?!*

a) *Your flashy neighbour reckons his new racing bike can reach 18 m/s.* He finished 10 laps of 120m track in 70s. *Work out* his speed. *Could* he be telling porky pie *lies*?
b) *A sprinter crosses the 100m race finish line.* His speed throughout the race was 10 m/s so *how long* did it take him?
c) *The greyhound racetrack is 750m long.* If Droopy's speed is 25 m/s, *what* is his time?

4) *How far?*

a) *How far* around the track would a racing car get, going at 90 m/s for 30s ?
b) *Concorde's travelling across the sky at 650 m/s.* *How far* can it go in 25s, travelling at this speed?
c) *Find* how far a cheetah could get if its speed is 30 m/s (70 mph) and it runs for 500s.
d) *How far* would a roadrunner go travelling at a speed of 25 m/s (56 mph) in 700s.

5) *Speed and velocity! Remember that speed is how fast you're going, and velocity has direction. If you change direction, you change velocity, even if the speed stays the same.*

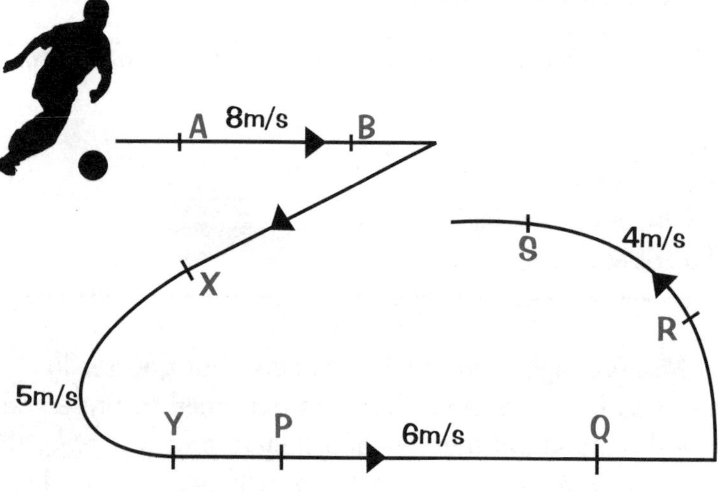

Between points *A and B*, *x and y*, *P and Q*, *S and R* *Ronaldo moves with the constant* *speeds* *shown. Between which of these points has he also constant* *velocity*?

Speed and Velocity

6) *Complete the sentences*:

Use these words: fast, direction, how, direction

> Speed is ___________ ___________ you're going with no regard to ___________ .
> Velocity, however, must also have the ___________ specified.

7) *Divide* these into *3 columns* — "Units of speed", "Units of velocity" and "Other units":

m/s *m/s WEST* *m* *s* *m/s NORTH* *mph*

Speed Questions

8) *A cat skulks 50m in 90s. Find*:
  a) its speed.
  b) how long it takes to go 120m.

9) *A car travels 600m in 30s.*
  a) Find its average *speed*.
  b) *The car's* average speed is usually different from its speed at any particular instant in time? *Explain* the reason for this.
  c) *How far* would the car travel at the same speed in 1500s?

10) *Find* the speed of:
  a) a train going 1200km in 8 hours.
  b) a walker who travels 12km in 2½ hours.

11) How far does:
  a) a cyclist travel in 3 hours at an average speed of 12 km/h?
  b) a ship travel in 5 hours at an average speed of 25 km/h?

12) *How long* does it take:
  a) a car to cover 560km at an average speed of 70 km/h?
  b) light to travel from the Sun to the Earth (150,000,000 km) at a speed of 300,000 km/s? (answer in minutes and seconds).

Velocity Questions

13) Find the velocity of a car travelling 2000m due North in 100s.

14) Find the velocity of a walker travelling a distance of 1000m East in 500s.

15) Find the velocity of a bird flying 450m South-East in 5s.

16) *A walker starts in Barchester at 10am. He walks 5km North-East to Histon, getting there at 11am. He takes a half-hour break, then walks back to Barchester in 50 minutes.*
  a) What is his velocity when walking to Histon?
  b) What is his velocity when walking back to Barchester?
  c) What is his average speed for the whole trip?

Top Tips

Speed and *velocity*, they're not quite the same. Speed and velocity are both how *fast* you're going measured in m/s (or km/h or mph), but velocity also has to specify the *direction* e.g. 30m/s north. Remember Speed = Distance/Time. Don't forget, if you write it as a *formula triangle* it makes things a whole lot easier.

Acceleration

1) a) In the equation $a = \frac{\Delta V}{\Delta t}$ state *what* a, ΔV and Δt *stand for*.

   b) State the usual *units* of a, ΔV and Δt.

   c) *Explain* how acceleration is different from speed and velocity.

2) *Complete these sentences*:

   Use these words: acceleration, second, 3 m/s, second, acceleration, 4 m/s, velocity, velocity

   a) A motorbike has a steady __________ of 3 m/s^2. This means that every __________ its __________ changes by __________.

   b) A car has a steady __________ of 4 m/s^2. This means that every __________ its __________ changes by __________.

3) Complete the charts showing steady acceleration and deceleration.

Time (s)	1	2	3	4	5	6
Speed x (m/s)	2.0	4.0	6.0		10.0	
Speed y (m/s)	17.5	15.0	12.5		7.5	

   What is the *acceleration* of X?

   What is the *deceleration* of Y? *How* can you tell that it is decelerating?

4) *Find* the acceleration of:

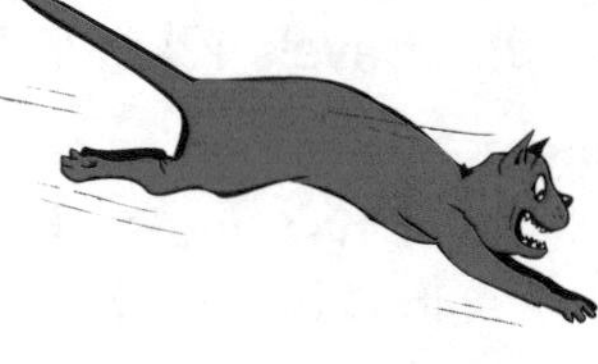

   a) A cat, pouncing from 0 m/s to 5 m/s in 4s.

   b) A car, speeding from 10 m/s to 30 m/s in 5s.

   c) A runner, going from 3 m/s to 8 m/s in 3s.

5) *A car has a steady acceleration of 2 m/s^2.* If it starts from rest, *what's its velocity* after 10s?

6) What is the deceleration of a car that takes 8s for its speed to drop from 20 m/s to 0 m/s?

7) How long does a motorbike take to stop if it's travelling at a speed of 16 m/s and then *decelerates* at a rate of 2 m/s^2?

8) *PC Bacon is cruising along in his car at 15 m/s.*

   a) *He keeps on going for an hour.* *How far* does he go, in kilometres?

   b) *A car shoots past at 80 mph. One mile is about 1.6 kilometres.* How fast is the car going in kilometres per hour, and in metres per second?

   c) *PC Bacon gives chase, and accelerates steadily at 1 m/s^2 up to 40 m/s.* *How long* does this take?

   d) *After travelling along for 3 minutes, he catches up with the speeding car.* *How far* has he travelled since reaching 40 m/s?

   e) *The speeding car is now travelling at 28 m/s. PC Bacon flags it down, and it pulls over into a layby.* If it takes 15s to halt, *what* is its deceleration?

Acceleration

1) *This question is about a car whose motion is described by a velocity/time graph.*

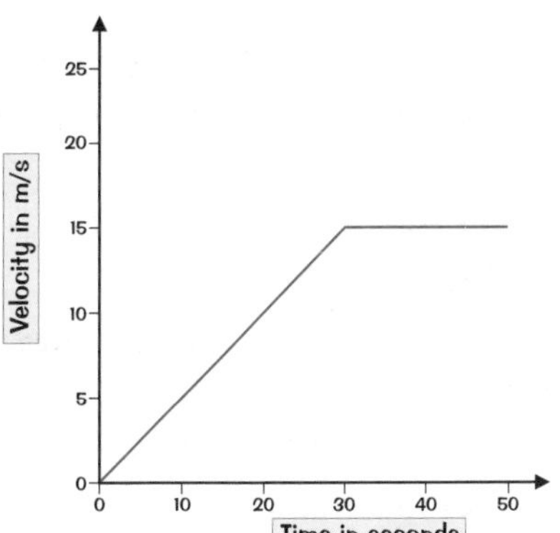

a) How far does the car travel in the first 30 seconds?
b) Describe the motion of the car in the next 20 seconds.
c) Copy the graph with the time axis extended to 100 seconds and complete the graph using the following information:
(i) between the times of 50 and 60 seconds, the car undergoes a steady acceleration to 20 m/s.
(ii) for the next 20 seconds the car's speed is steady at 20 m/s.
(iii) during the next 20 seconds, the car slows to a stop at a steady rate.

d) Calculate the acceleration occurring in c) (i).
e) Calculate the deceleration occurring in c) (iii).
f) Work out the distance travelled during the last 40 seconds of this short trip.

2) *This question is about the motion of a motorbike described by a a distance/time graph.*

a) What is the maximum speed of the motor bike?
b) What distance does the motor bike travel in the first 20 seconds?
c) Calculate the motor bike's speed between 20 and 40 seconds.
d) Describe carefully how the motor bike moves during the 60 seconds (use words like accelerates, decelerates, steady speed).

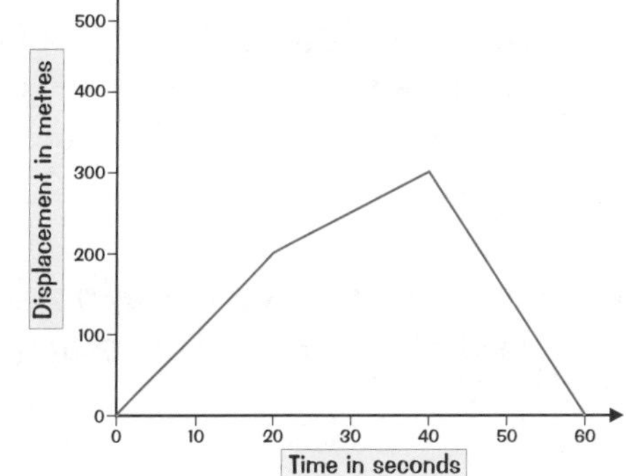

3) *Here's another question about a car moving.*

Velocity (m/s)	Time (s)
0	0
2	1
9	2
18	3
27	4
36	5
45	6
54	7
54	8
54	9
54	10

a) Plot the graph of velocity in m/s (vertical axis) against time in seconds (horizontal axis) but extend the time axis to 50 seconds.
b) What is the acceleration of the car during the first 6 seconds?
c) Describe the motion of the car between 0 and 10 seconds.
d) What steady deceleration is required by the car between 10 and 15 seconds to bring it to a halt at 15 seconds?
e) Find the total distance travelled by the car.

Top Tips

Acceleration isn't the same as velocity or speed. Acceleration is how fast the velocity is changing — it's a bit more subtle. The equation you need to remember here is Acceleration = Change in Velocity/Time taken (use a formula triangle, it'll help). The units of acceleration are m/s^2, which you can think of as metres per second per second. Lastly, watch out for the differences between distance/time graphs and velocity/time graphs.

Distance/Time and Velocity/Time Graphs

1) *This question is about a distance/time graph describing the motion of a car.*

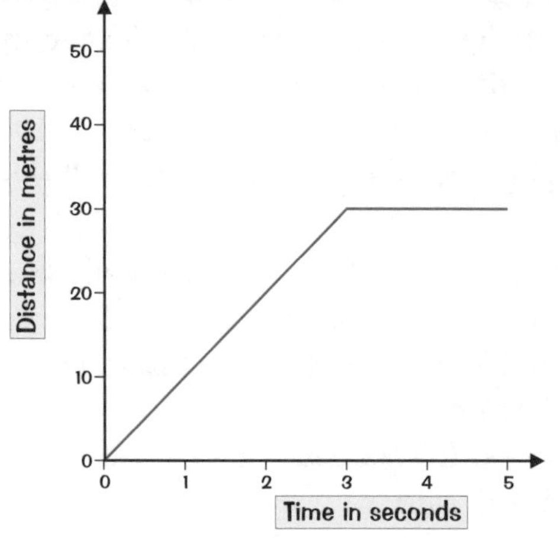

a) How far does the car go in 3 seconds?
b) Find the speed of the car during the first 3 seconds.
c) Describe what happens between 3 seconds and 5 seconds.
d) Copy the graph and draw a line showing the motion of a different car that, during the first 3 seconds, travels at half the speed of the original car.

2) *This question is about a cyclist riding a bike.*

a) How far does the cyclist travel during the first 20 seconds of his journey?
b) Between the times of 20 and 40 seconds, what is the deceleration of the cyclist?
c) How far does the cyclist travel during the period of deceleration described in (b)?
c) What happens over the next 20 seconds of the journey?
d) What is the total distance travelled by the cyclist for the whole 60 seconds?

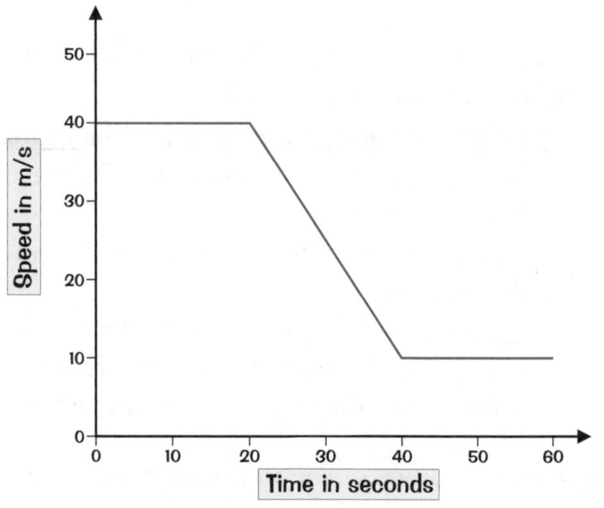

3) *A car passes a crossing. Its distance from the crossing is measured every second.*

Distance (m)	Time (s)
0	0
2	1
9	2
18	3
27	4
36	5
45	6
54	7
54	8
54	9
54	10

a) Plot a graph of distance in metres (vertical axis) against time in seconds (horizontal axis).
b) Mark on the graph where the car (i) is accelerating, (ii) is travelling at a steady speed, (iii) is stopped.
c) What is the average speed of the car in the first 7 seconds?
d) What distance has the car travelled after 5.5 seconds?
e) How long did the car take to travel 23 metres?

Distance/Time and Velocity/Time Graphs

1) *Complete* the table by stating the significance of features sometimes observed on Distance/Time and Velocity/Time graphs.

Feature on Graph	Distance/Time	Velocity/Time
Gradient equals		
Flat sections show		
Curves show		
Downhill section shows		
Area under the curve shows	NOT APPLICABLE	

2) *Draw* the velocity/time graph using these measurements taken during a car journey.

a) *Describe* the motion of the car (*write on the graph*).
b) *Calculate* the acceleration of the car in the first 12 seconds.
c) If the car had a mass of 1000 kilograms, *what force* was needed to produce the acceleration in (b)?
d) *Calculate* the deceleration of the car in the last 4 seconds.

Velocity (m/s)	Time (s)
0	0
4	2
8	4
12	6
16	8
20	10
24	12
24	14
24	16
12	18
0	20

3) *Draw* a distance/time graph using these measurements taken during a bike journey.

Distance (m)	Time (s)
0	0
20	5
40	10
60	15
80	20
100	25
100	30
50	35
0	40

a) *Describe* the motion of the bike for the whole journey (write on the graph).
b) *Calculate* the speed of the bike between the times of 20 and 25 seconds.
c) *For how long* is the bike stationary?
d) *Calculate* the speed of the bike between the times of 30 and 40 seconds.
e) What is the *total distance* covered by the cyclist?

Top Tips

These graphs *look* similar, and it would be *tempting* to try and avoid learning all the differences between them. *Be warned*, if you *don't* know what all the details mean and you *can't* distinguish between the two types of graph, then you will get all these questions *wrong*. If it all seems a bit tricky, then the best way to go is simply to *learn* all the facts in Question 1 on this page and remember them. You need to know how to calculate speed, acceleration and distance travelled from a velocity/time graph. The thing that isn't immediately obvious is that *distance* travelled is the *area* under the graph — remember your formula triangle.

Resultant Force and Terminal Velocity

1) *Complete the following sentences* using these words:

adding *subtracting* *resultant* *forces* *direction* *overall* *motion* *same* *accelerate* *decelerate* *steady*

In most real situations, there are at least two __________ acting on an object along any ____________ . The __________ effect of these forces will decide the __________ of the object — whether it will __________ , ____________ or stay at a ____________ speed. The overall effect is found by ____________ or ____________ the forces which point along the _____________ direction. The overall force you get is a ____________ .

2) *A car of mass 2,000kg has a faulty engine which provides a driving force of 5,500N at all times. At 70 mph the drag force acting on the car is 5,400N.*

a) *Draw a diagram* for both cases (rest and at 70 mph) showing the forces acting on the car. *There is no need to show vertical forces.*
b) *Find* the car's acceleration when first setting off from rest. (The drag can be neglected).
c) *Find* the car's acceleration at 70 mph.

3) *A smaller car of mass 1,500kg has an engine which provides a maximum driving force of 4,500N. At 70 mph the drag force acting on the car is 4,450N.*

a) *Draw a diagram* for both cases (starting from rest and travelling at 70 mph) showing the forces acting on the car. *There is no need to show vertical forces.*
b) *Find* the car's acceleration at 70 mph if the driver's foot is to the floor.
c) *What* force is needed to accelerate the car steadily to a speed of 4 m/s in 2 seconds, if it is starting from rest? Assume the drag to be negligible.

4) *This information about cars and free-fallers reaching a terminal velocity is in the wrong order.* Put the following statements in the correct order.

- the forces due to resistance.
- until eventually the resistance forces balance the accelerating forces,
- When cars and free-falling objects first set off
- at which point the cars or objects are unable to accelerate any more.
- the forces accelerating them are greater than
- As the body's velocity increases the resistance forces rise

5) Consider the parachutist on the right:

a) *Copy* the diagram and *label* the two vertical forces acting on her.
b) Sketch a *velocity/time graph* showing the change in velocity of the parachutist as she falls (include the period of free fall and the period when the parachute is open). Explain the graph in terms of the forces acting on the parachutist.

6) *What is another name* given to each of the following?

a) The downward force acting on falling bodies.
b) Air resistance.
c) The maximum velocity reached by a falling object.
d) A useful piece of equipment to increase air resistance.
e) A shape which will decrease air resistance.

Resultant Force and Terminal Velocity

7) *Answer true or false*.

a) A feather and a hamster will not land at the same time if dropped from the same height above the Moon.
b) Acceleration equals force times mass.
c) The drag force depends on shape and area.
d) The forces of air resistance and weight are equal when a falling object is travelling at its maximum speed (terminal velocity).
e) The speed at which weight equals air resistance is the same whether a falling sky diver has a parachute open or not.

8) *Fill in the gaps*

same *weight* *drag* *resistance* *falling*

The downward force acting on all ____________ objects is gravity, which would make them fall at the ____________ rate if it wasn't for air ____________ . The terminal velocity of any object is determined by its ____________ in comparison to the ____________ of it.

9) *Plot the graph* of velocity (in m/s) [vertical axis] against time (in s) [horizontal axis] showing the motion of a human skydiver after jumping out of an aeroplane.
Then answer these questions:

a) *Find* the terminal velocity of the skydiver. (Be sure to give the units)
b) *Estimate* the velocity of the skydiver after:
i) 5s ii) 12.5s.
c) At what time does the skydiver reach terminal velocity?
d) The skydiver opens her parachute 20 seconds after jumping out of the aeroplane. Describe the extra force acting on her and its effect upon her speed.
e) Will the skydiver reach a new terminal velocity? *Explain* your answer.

Velocity (m/s)	Time (s)
0	0
4.5	2
16.5	4
23.0	6
29.0	8
36.0	10
43.5	12
50.0	14
56.0	16
60.0	18
60.0	20

10) *Draw* the diagrams below showing the resultant forces. If the body is accelerating, write down the direction (up, down, right or left) in which it is accelerating.

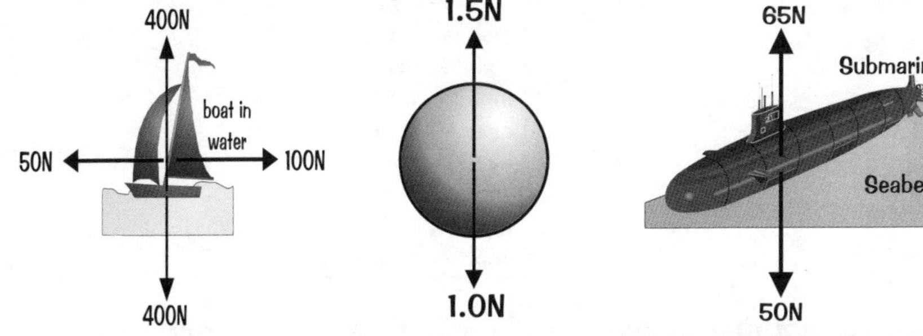

A boat in the water | A ball in the air | A model submarine on the sea bed | A shuttlecock in the air

Top Tips The idea of *Resultant Force* is really important. The resultant force is just the *overall force* acting on an object. You get it by adding or subtracting forces that act in the same direction. Obviously, it's the overall resultant force that decides if the object *accelerates*, *decelerates* or stays at a *steady speed*. Free-fallers reach a terminal velocity when the force of drag is equal to the force of gravity — remember drag depends on *shape* and *area*.

Stopping Distances

1) *The distance it takes to stop a car is divided into the thinking distance and the braking distance.*

a) *Explain carefully* the term *"thinking distance"*. Include the words "distance", "hazard" and "brakes".

b) *Explain carefully* the term *"braking distance"*. Include the words "distance", "deceleration" and "brakes".

Thinking Distance

2) *State* and *explain* carefully *three* different factors which affect the "thinking" distance.

Braking Distance

3) *This question is about the braking distance of a car.* State which of the following takes the *longer* to stop. *Explain* your answer.

a) The same car travelling at 50 mph or at 70 mph.

b) A car with four people and holiday luggage or the same car with just the driver.

c) A car before it had new brakes or the same car after they were renewed.

d) A car with worn front tyres or the same car after the tyres have been replaced with new ones.

e) A car driving on roads on a dry day or the same car driving on a wet day.

4) *Plot a graph* of braking distance in metres (vertical axis) against the velocity of the car in metres per second (horizontal axis) using the data in the table.

a) What is the braking distance at 30 mph, approximately?

b) What is the braking distance at 50 mph, approximately?

c) Estimate the braking distance at 70 mph.

Braking Distance (m)	Velocity of car (mph)
6	20
24	40
55	60

5) *Explain carefully* using the words "grip", "slippy", "brake", "tread", "friction", "water" and "skid" why it's illegal to drive a car with a tyre tread of less than 1.6mm deep.

6) *Match* these "thinking", "braking", and "total stopping distances" to the speed a car is travelling. *It's well worth learning these because you will be tested on them in your driving theory exam as well as for your GCSE.*

Speed of car/type of distance
a) 70 mph — total
b) 30 mph — braking
c) 50 mph — thinking
d) 30 mph — total
e) 30 mph — thinking
f) 70 mph — thinking
g) 50 mph — braking
h) 70 mph — braking
i) 50 mph — total

Distances (m)
14
9
75
15
23
53
21
38
96

7) *Copy the table* in Qu. (4) but *add another column* for the kinetic energy, $\frac{1}{2}mv^2$, where v is the velocity of the car, and m, is the car's mass, which equals 2000kg.

Plot a graph of:

a) Braking distance in metres (vertical axis) against $\frac{1}{2}mv^2$ (horizontal axis).

b) *Explain* what the graph shows you.

c) *Complete this*: if you double the speed, you ____________ the value of v but the v^2 means that the Kinetic Energy is then increased by a factor of ____________, so the breaking distance must ___________ by a factor of __________ to stop the car.

Stopping Distances

8) *Here are the speed limits in mph for different vehicles on different types of roads in the UK.*

TYPE OF VEHICLE	BUILT-UP AREAS	SINGLE CARRIAGEWAY	DUAL CARRIAGEWAY	MOTORWAYS
CARS	30	60	70	70
GOODS VEHICLES (not exceeding 7.5 tonnes maximum laden weight)	30	50	60	70*
GOODS VEHICLES (exceeding 7.5 tonnes maximum laden weight)	30	40	50	60

*60 if articulated or towing a trailer

a) *Suggest* why the speed limit for all vehicles is 30mph in built up areas.
b) *Give reasons* for the different speed limits imposed upon the 3 types of vehicle on single carriageway roads.
c) *Suggest* a reason why goods vehicles not exceeding 7.5 tonnes, have a 60mph speed limit imposed upon them if they are articulated (having joints) or towing a trailer.

9) *The table shows the stopping distance for cars at different speeds.*

Speed		Thinking distance (m)	Braking distance (m)	Stopping distance (m)
m/s	mph			
15	34	9	19	
20	45	12	30	
25	56	15	48	
30	67	18	70	

a) *Copy* the table and *complete* the column 'stopping distance (m)'.
b) *Explain* why the driver's thinking distance increases with increasing car speed even though the reaction time (approximately 0.6s) stays the same.
c) *Alcohol slows people's reactions significantly.* If a drunk driver has a reaction time of 2 seconds:
i) find his *thinking distance* at 56mph (25m/s).
ii) find his *stopping distance* at 56mph (25m/s).

10) *Find* the kinetic energy transferred from a vehicle when braking to a standstill, if it has:
a) Mass 7,500kg travelling at 20m/s.
b) Mass 10,000kg travelling at 30m/s.
c) Weight 400,000N travelling at 15m/s (take g = 10 N/kg).

11) *Find* the maximum braking force of a vehicle, mass 520kg travelling at 20m/s (braking distance 30m). Give your answer *correct* to 3 significant figures.

12) A van of mass 7,500kg, decelerates steadily from 20m/s to 5m/s in 5 seconds, over a distance of 20m.
a) Calculate the *work done* by the brakes.
b) What is the *power* dissipated by the brakes in this case?
c) Name two types of energy that the car's kinetic energy is converted to as it slows down.

Top Tips This topic does keep coming up in the Exam, so make sure you know it. The important things to remember are the definitions of *thinking distance* and *braking distance*. You also need to know the *factors* that affect each of these. The tricky thing here is understanding why the braking distance increases so much with extra speed. Remember that the *work done* by the brakes has to *balance* the *kinetic energy* that the car's got by moving. It's the v^2 in the kinetic energy that means that if you double the speed, the braking distance increases by a factor of four.

Hooke's Law

1) Use these words to complete the following paragraph:

extension total length proportional original
force increase stretch new

Hooke's law states that extension is ____________ to the load applied. That means, if you ____________ something with a steadily increasing ____________ , then the ____________ will ____________ steadily too. The important thing in a Hooke's law experiment is to measure the __________ which is the _________ length subtracted from the __________ length.

Hooke's Law Experiment

2) a) Draw the apparatus you would use to carry out a Hooke's law investigation using a steel coil spring. Label the apparatus carefully.

b) *Here are results obtained by measuring the extension of a steel spring produced by increasing the load applied to it.*

Extension (cm)	Load (N)
0	0
8	1
16	2
24	3
32	4
36	5
38	6

(i) Plot a graph of extension in cm (vertical axis) against load in N (horizontal axis).
(ii) Mark the elastic limit on your graph. What happens to the spring beyond the elastic limit?
(iii) Why should the smaller loads be applied first?
(iv) Why should each new load be gently applied?

c) What load would produce an extension of 28cm?
d) What load is needed to make the spring stretch to 35cm if it was 15cm long to start with (before a load was hung from it)?
e) What extension would you expect if a load of 4.5N was applied to the spring?
f) What extension would you expect if you hung a 0.3kg mass on the unloaded spring? (take g = 10 N/kg)

3) *A physics teacher sets up an experiment to investigate Hooke's Law for a small spring.*

a) *When a mass of 100g is hung from the spring, its total extended length is 12cm long. When a 300g mass is hung from it, its total extended length is 16cm long.* How long will it be when a 200g mass is hung from it?
b) What is the unstretched length of the spring?
c) *The elastic limit is reached when a force of 5N is hung from the spring.* How long will the spring be when it reaches its elastic limit?
d) *If a weight of 10N is hung from the spring, it will exceed its elastic limit.* What will happen to the spring once the weight is removed?
e) *If a weight of 1000N is hung from the spring, it will exceed its elastic limit and behave in a more dramatic way.* Describe *briefly the dramatic behaviour of the spring?*

4) Explain what the following words mean: a) elastic b) brittle c) flexible d) plastic.

Hooke's Law

5) The graph shows results obtained from a Hooke's law experiment for a spring.

a) *What* is the point O on the graph referred to as? What is its significance?
b) If a force less than 100N was applied to the un-extended spring, and then taken off, *what would happen* to the spring?
c) If a force of 150N was applied to the un-extended spring and then taken off, *what would happen* to the spring now?
d) *Explain* Hooke's law carefully.

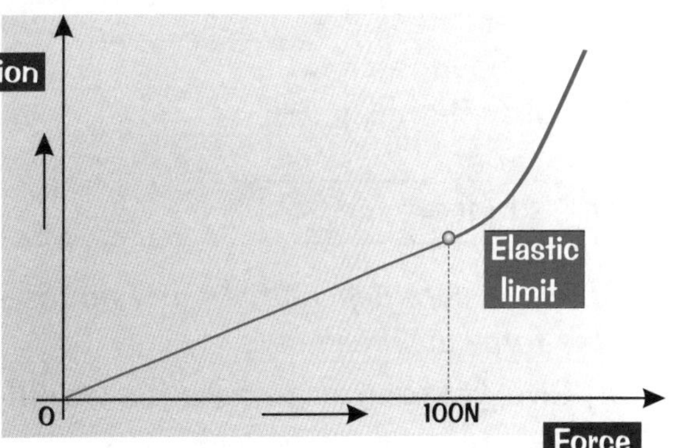

6) *Sketch* the forces in the right places for the solids shown in the box below. *State* where the solid is under *tension* and/or *compression*, if at all.

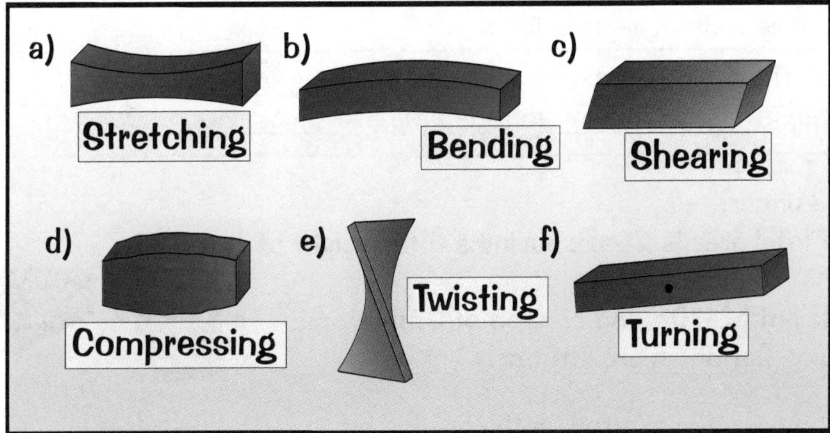

7) *Name* and *sketch* the forces in:

a) The guy line of a tent.
b) A seesaw in balance.
c) A pole, as a pole vaulter puts it in the ground.
d) The bumpers of two cars colliding.
e) The cables of a lift.
f) A jelly wobbling side-to-side on a plate.
g) A footballer kicking a ball

Top Tips

Nice springs and elastic bands to think about, and a *very easy* law to remember. Hooke's Law says that for elastic materials, like wires and springs, *extension* is *proportional* to *load*. If you stretch something with a steadily increasing force, the length will increase steadily too until you get to the *elastic limit*. Now it won't go back to its original length. The important thing to remember here is that you measure the *extension*, *not* the *total* length. Don't forget to learn all the weird and wonderful effects that combinations of forces can have on solids, because you can be asked to fill in the labels on a diagram in the Exam.

Pressure on Surfaces and in Liquids

1) *Copy out* the following passage, *filling in* the blank spaces.

Use these words: small, area, doesn't, sink, high, larger, smaller, force

> Pressure is the ____________ acting per unit ________ of a surface. A force concentrated on a ____________ area creates a ___________ pressure which means that the thing will __________ into the surface. But with a ____________ area, you get a ____________ pressure which means the thing ____________ sink into the surface.

2) *The pressure depends not just on the amount of force, but also on the size of the area the force is spread over.*

a) Give *five* examples where the weight of an object is spread over a big area, giving rise to a low pressure and no sinking.

b) Give *five* examples where a force concentrated on a small area produces high pressure and damage. Carefully *explain* how *one* of your examples leads to high pressure.

3) *Complete the following*:

Use these words: pascal, Force/Area, metres^2, newtons, force

> Pressure = ____________. The normal unit of pressure is the __________, if the _____________ is measured in ____________ and the area in ____________.

4) *Find* the pressure exerted under:

a) concrete slabs, whose total area is 20m^2, having a total weight of 160,000N.

b) a suitcase, having a weight of 170N and an area of 0.1m^2.

c) the same suitcase, laying flat on an area of 1m^2.

5) For each example, find the *pressure* exerted on the ground by:

a) a man, whose mass is 90kg, standing in his flat shoes whose soles have a total area of 0.05m^2.

b) the same man, wearing snow shoes whose soles have a total area of 0.18m^2.

6) a) Find the *pressure* on a pair of jeans from an iron whose base area is 0.02m^2 and has a weight of 12N.

b) What *extra downward force* must the person ironing exert to achieve a pressure of 1500 Pa on the jeans?

Hydraulics

7) *Hydraulic systems are an important application of "P = F / A".* *Fill in the blanks* using the following terms:

areas *flexible* *force* *applied* *liquid*
transmitted *pipes* *multiplied* *pistons*

> In a hydraulic system:
> Pressure is ___________ throughout the ___________, so that the ___________ can be easily ___________ wherever it is wanted, using ___________ ___________.
> The force can be ___________ according to the ___________ of the ___________ used.

Pressure on Surfaces and in Liquids

8) *Label* this diagram of the hydraulic system in car brakes:

brake fluid

tyre

slave cylinder

master cylinder

brake disc

brake pedal

a) Which cylinder has the *largest* area?

b) *Which* cylinder has the *smallest* area?

c) If the car master piston has an area of 4cm^2 and a force of 500N is applied to it, calculate the *pressure* created in the brake pipes. If the slave cylinder has an area of 40cm^2, calculate the *force* exerted on the brake disc.

d) *Why* isn't water used in a brake system?

9) *Hydraulic jacks can be used to lift very heavy objects, by acting as force multipliers.*

a) *Explain*, with the aid of a diagram, how a hydraulic jack is used as a force multiplier.

b) If a force of 16N acts on the master piston, whose area is 0.01m^2, what upward force will be produced if the area of the slave piston is 0.1m^2?

10) *Here is a simple hydraulic jack:*

a) Find the pressure at A.

b) Find the pressure at B.

c) What is the force on the load?

d) *Would* the force on the load be *greater* or *smaller* if the area at A was less? (keeping the same force of 20 N)

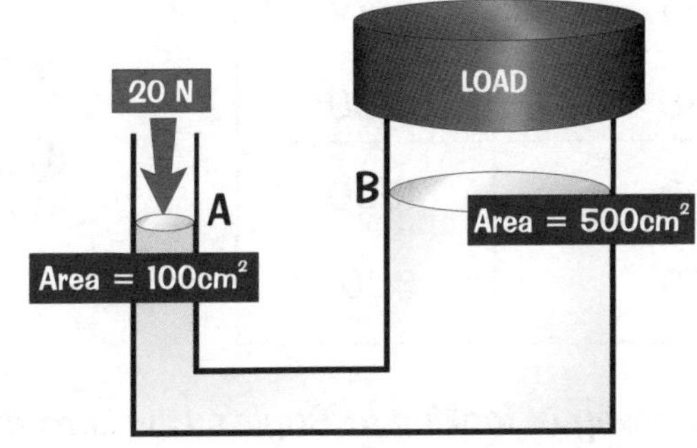

11) *An archaeologist uncovers an ancient idol (mass 7kg) protected by a crude version of a hydraulic jack. To get to the idol, she must step on a master piston. On the slave piston, which is four times the size of the master, is a huge boulder, delicately balanced so that it would roll off and crush anyone standing on the master piston if it experienced a force of more than 3000N. The archaeologist's mass is 73kg.*

Could she safely pick up the idol?

Top Tips

Pressure and *force* are another two things that people get mixed up — they're *not* the same. Learn the definition of pressure, and the equation. Remember, a force spread out over a *big area* gives a *low* pressure and a force concentrated on a *small area* gives *high* pressure. You need to know that in a liquid the pressure's acting outwards in all directions, and it increases the deeper you go — which is why dams are thicker at the bottom than the top. Also, you have to explain the workings of hydraulic systems in terms of the pressure equation, which is slightly tricky, so do the questions on this page *carefully*.

Boyle's Law

An Experiment to Demonstrate Boyle's Law

1) *Shown in the diagram below is the apparatus used to demonstrate Boyle's Law.*

a) Write down the corresponding names that go with the labels A to H.

oil   volume scale

Bourdon gauge   glass tube

air from pump   tap

trapped air   reservoir

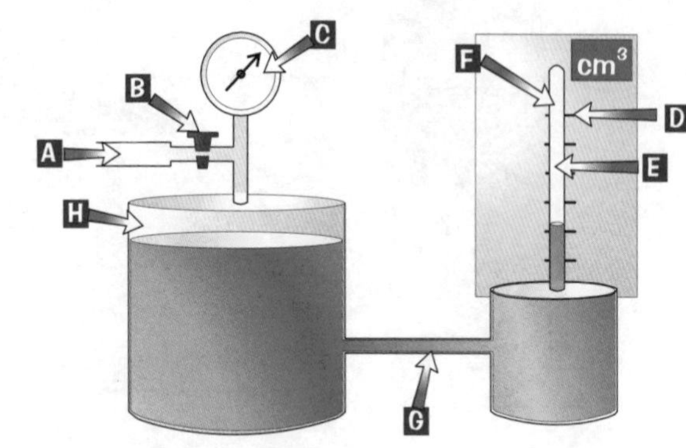

b) What is the purpose of the oil?

c) Why should you be careful to ensure the temperature of the laboratory remains constant throughout the experiment?

2) *Here are some readings obtained using the above apparatus:*

Pressure P in mm of mercury	Volume V in cm^3
10	4000
20	2000
30	1330
40	1000
50	800

a) Plot a graph of pressure, in mm of mercury (vertical axis) against volume V in cm^3 (horizontal axis). Describe its shape.

b) Copy the results chart and add a third column 1/V (V in cm^3). Now plot a graph of P (vertical axis) against 1/V (horizontal axis).

c) Write an equation relating P and 1/V using a constant of proportionality.

d) By considering the equation for a straight line, $y=mx+c$, and comparing this to your equation found in (c), find, using your graph in part (b), the value of the constant of proportionality.

3) *Another way of looking at Boyle's Law is to think about weights on gas syringes.*

Think of what happens to the pressure and volume of the gas when:

a) F is replaced with ½F.

b) F is replaced with 4F.

c) F is replaced by 6F.

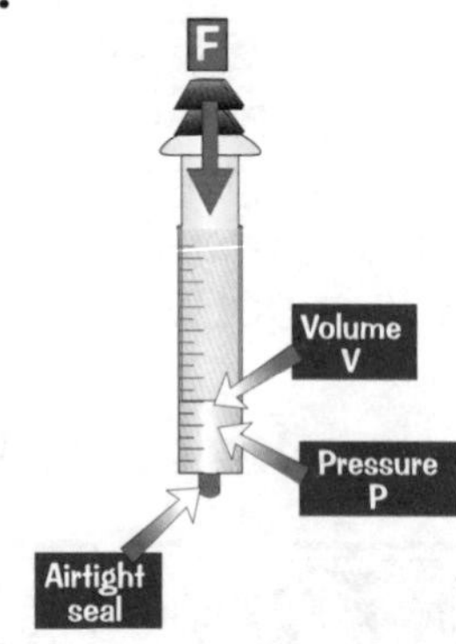

d) Explain Boyle's law and this experiment in the simplest way you can.

e) If the gas in the syringe is then heated will a greater or smaller force than F be required to compress the gas to volume V?

4) Work out the change in pressure of a fixed mass of gas at constant temperature in the following examples:

a) If the gas is compressed from a volume of 250cm³ at a pressure of 3 atmospheres down to a volume of 150cm³.

b) If a gas expands from a volume of 540cm³ at a pressure of 1 atmosphere to a volume of 2160cm³.

Boyle's Law

5) *Work out* the new volume of a fixed mass of gas at constant temperature in the next examples:

a) If a gas of volume 480cm^3 is compressed so that its pressure changes from 2.0 to 2.5 atmospheres.

b) If a gas of volume 60cm^3 expands so that its pressure decreases from 5 to 4 atmospheres.

6) *Complete* the following table of data from a Boyle's Law experiment. *P_1 and V_1 are the pressure and volume of the gas under the first conditions and P_2 and V_2 under the second set of conditions.*

	P_1 / atm.	V_1 / cm^3	P_2 / atm.	V_2 / cm^3
a)	10	100	2.5	
b)	6	12		36
c)	2	250		1500
d)	5	500		200
e)		40	8	100
f)	1	600	2.5	
g)		20	1	80

Kinetic Theory

7) *Sequence* these sentences about "Kinetic Theory".

- It depends on two things,
- The pressure a gas exerts on a container
- bashing into the walls of the container.
- how often they hit the walls
- is caused by particles whizzing about
- how fast they're going
- and
- and

8) *Explain* Boyle's Law in terms of kinetic theory. Use diagrams to help you explain your points more clearly.

9) *The equipment in question 1 is used to measure volume V of a mass of air at different pressures, P. Here are the results obtained.*

Pressure P (atmospheres)	Volume V (cm^3)	P × V
1.0	60	
1.5	40	
2.0	30	
2.5	24	
3.0	20	
4.0	15	

a) *Copy* the table, completing the third column 'P x V'.

b) From these results, what conclusion do you come to about the relationship between pressure and volume?

c) *Estimate* the volume (cm^3) if the gas was compressed to a pressure of 5 atmospheres.

10) *Explain* in terms of kinetic theory:

a) Why a balloon increases in size when air is blown into it.

b) Why you can smell bacon cooking in the kitchen when you're in the lounge.

c) Why a tyre needs to be inflated to a pressure about three times normal air pressure.

d) Why a piston will increase the pressure of a gas inside a cylinder when compressing it.

e) Why most stars are stable against gravitational collapse.

Top Tips

Boyle's Law is one of those things that sound more complicated than it really is. It's actually *common sense*. If you squash something up into half the space, it'll be at twice the pressure it was before. Remember how *kinetic theory* (lots of particles moving about and colliding into the walls of the container) *explains* Boyle's Law.

Basic Principles of Waves

Key Words

1) Copy the following sentences and *fill in the gaps*.

a) There are two different types of wave motion: ______________ and ______________.
b) The number of waves per second passing a fixed point is called the ______________ and is measured in ________.
c) The time taken for two adjacent crests to pass a fixed point is called the__________ and is measured in __________ .
d) The maximum distance of particles from their resting position is called the ___________.
e) The highest point of a wave is called a ____________.
f) The lowest point of a wave is called a ____________.
g) The distance travelled each second by a wave is called its ____________ and is measured in ___________.
h) Waves will change their speed and wavelength when they go into different materials; this is called ______________.
i) Waves will spread out when they pass through a small gap; this is called ____________.

Wave Motion

2) Describe the motion of the particles in an ocean wave.
3) Describe the motion of the particles in a sound wave moving through air.
4) Give a definition of "wavelength". What unit is it measured in?
5) What does a wave transfer?

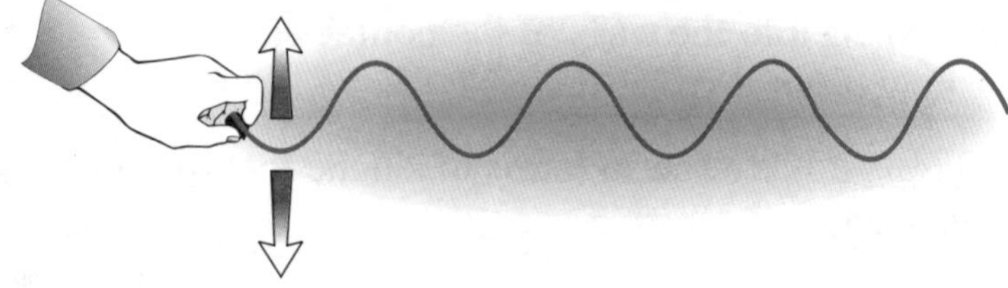

Properties of Waves

6) *You can send a wave along a piece of string by shaking one end up and down (see diagram).*

a) What do we call the up and down movement of the string?
b) How would you increase the frequency of this wave?
c) How would you increase its amplitude?
d) This wave is a transverse wave. Explain why a longitudinal wave of a similar frequency can not be made to travel along the string.

7) *You are floating in the sea, measuring waves (as you do). You time 5 seconds between one crest passing and the next.*

a) What is the period of this wave?
b) What is the frequency of this wave?
c) *By watching the waves move along a breakwater you estimate that the distance between 10 crests is about 30m.* Calculate the average *wavelength* of the waves.
d) *How far* have the waves travelled each time a crest passes you?
e) *How long* does it take the wave to pass you?
f) How far does the wave travel in ONE second?
g) What is the *speed* of the wave?
h) Which way do you move as the wave passes through you?

8) *A sound wave will not travel for ever.*

a) What happens to, a) The wavelength and b) The amplitude, if no energy is supplied to it?
c) What form of energy is the energy transformed into?

Basic Principles of Waves

The Wave Equation

9) There are six equations below; some of which are incorrect.

a) Write down the correct versions, first in words, then using the usual symbols.

$$\text{Frequency} = \text{Speed} \times \text{Wavelength}$$

$$\text{Frequency} = \frac{\text{Wavelength}}{\text{Speed}}$$

$$\text{Wavelength} = \frac{\text{Speed}}{\text{Frequency}}$$

$$\text{Speed} = \frac{\text{Frequency}}{\text{Wavelength}}$$

$$\text{Speed} = \text{Frequency} \times \text{Wavelength}$$

$$\text{Frequency} = \frac{\text{Speed}}{\text{Wavelength}}$$

b) Write an equation relating a wave's period T, with its wavelength and speed.

A Wave Example

10) *The diagram below shows a piece of string with a wave travelling along it. There are beads attached to the string in positions A, B, C, D, E, F, G, H and I.*

a) Draw on the diagram where the stationary string would lie after the wave has died away.

Which bead(s) are:

b) at the crests?
c) at troughs?
d) moving up?
e) moving down?
f) changing direction?
g) stationary?
h) moving with the greatest speed?
i) accelerating?

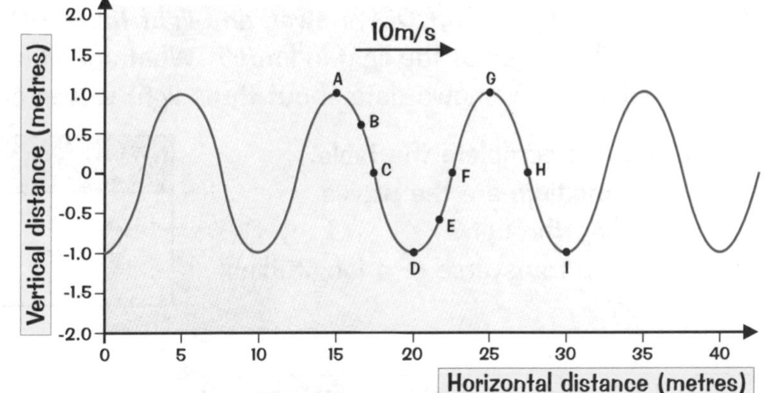

j) Calculate the amplitude, wavelength and frequency of the wave.

Wave Calculations

11) A certain radio programme is broadcast on a wavelength of 2.250km. If the speed of radio waves is 3×10^8 m/s, calculate the frequency of the transmission.

12) *A ruler was flicked on the side of a table and viewed under a rapidly flashing light (stroboscope). The time between the flashes was increased until the tip of the ruler appeared stationary. This happened when the light produced 48 pulses of light per second.*

a) Why did the ruler look like it was stationary under this light?

b) What is the period of oscillation of the ruler?

c) *The stroboscope flash rate is gradually decreased. The ruler appears to move again and then becomes stationary for a second time.*
How many flashes per second is needed for this to happen? Explain your answer.

Top Tip Right, you've all seen waves on the ocean, and you've heard of sound waves and microwaves. Waves are a bit different from what you've seen in Physics so far — they have features which you have to know about. You really need to know *amplitude*, *wavelength*, *frequency* and *period*. Don't forget the difference between *transverse* and *longitudinal* waves. You'll need to be able to give three examples of each type of wave. One more thing, and that's the wave formulae. Don't be afraid of them, they're just formulae like all the others. Remember when you need to use them, and *watch out for the units*.

Light Waves

Shadows and Light

1) *The lamp in the diagram is giving out light, making the doll cast a shadow.*

a) What is the name for something that gives out its *own light* (such as a lamp or the Sun)?

b) The doll does not give out its own light, *so how do we see it?*

c) The fact that the shadow is made demonstrates one fact about the doll and one fact about light. *What are these facts*?

The Speed of Light

2) What does the fact that light waves can travel from the Sun to the Earth tell us about light waves?

3) *The Sun is 150,000,000km away and light takes 500s to reach us.* What is the *speed* of the light in km/s? What speed is this in m/s?

4) The table below shows data about three light waves coming from the Sun.

a) Copy and complete the table.

b) What medium are the waves travelling through?

c) Is light a transverse or a longitudinal wave?

Wavelength (μm)	Frequency (GHz)	Speed (km/s)
40		300 000
60	5000	
50	6000	

The Colours of the Rainbow

5) Describe how *rainbows* are formed and explain what this tells you about the *composition of sunlight.*

6) Give two different methods of splitting white light into its constituent colours in the laboratory.

7) *Copy and complete* the table opposite comparing red and violet light. Use the following words to fill in the gaps.

Long, Low, Same, High, Short

Wave Property	Red Light	Violet Light
Speed		
Frequency		
Wavelength		

8) a) *Copy and complete* the diagram to show the path of the light beam through the prism and the coloured light exiting the opposite face. Label the colours in the right order.

b) What is the name given to this effect?

c) Which colour shows the largest angle of deviation?

d) Mark on your diagram where infra-red and ultra violet light should exit (although they are invisible).

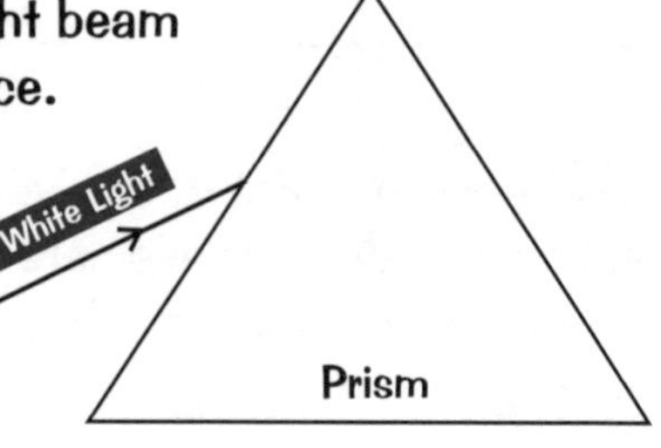

Light Waves

The Visible Spectrum

9) *Getting the green light......*

a) What is the correct order of the colours in the visible spectrum?

b) *Write down* which of these sentences you think are correct.

- *Green has a longer wavelength than yellow light.*
- *Red light has a lower frequency than blue light.*
- *Increasing the frequency of green light could make it blue.*
- *Yellow light travels more slowly than violet light.*
- *Orange light has a higher frequency than red light.*

A particular light source gives out green light. What changes in the light would you see if you increased the...

c) *amplitude* of the light?

d) *frequency* of the light?

e) *wavelength* of the light?

10) The waves A, B and C below represent red, green and violet light waves (not in that order).

Read the sentences below and *write down* the ones which are correct.

- *B is violet.*
- *The red light has the largest amplitude.*
- *C has the highest frequency.*
- *Green has the smallest amplitude.*
- *A has the shortest wavelength.*

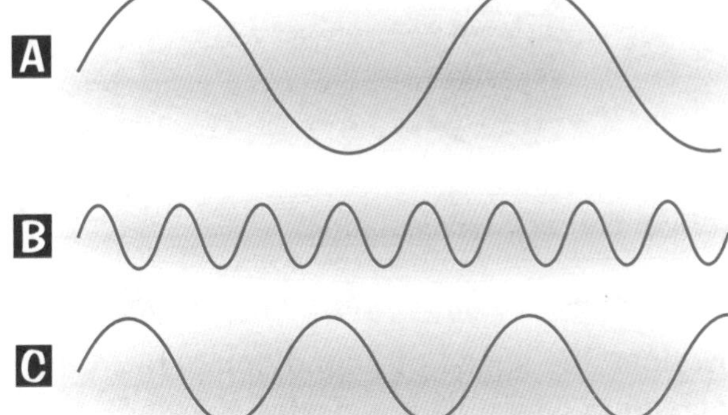

Colour Mixtures and Filters

11) *At the school disco, students are dancing to the latest hit. Coloured lights flash around the hall and light up people's clothes.*

a) A pure *green* light lands on a *red* shirt. What colour does the shirt appear now?

b) A pure *yellow* light lands on a dress with red, green and yellow stripes. What colour do the stripes appear to be?

12) A pop star is driving through the Scottish highlands one night when a *red* deer suddenly leaps out in front of him. The deer is lit up in the pure *white* light of the headlights. What colour does the deer look to him if he is wearing *green*-tinted contact lenses?

Top Tip Bright lights, pretty colours, it's all happening on this page. You need to know that different *colours* of light have different *wavelengths* — and that you can split white light up into the colours of the rainbow. You can work out the frequency of light waves quite easily, because the *speed of light* is always the *same*. Calculations of wavelength, frequency and speed for light use very large and very small numbers because the speed of light is so large. Remember how to write very large or very small numbers using the form $a \times 10^n$.

Sound Waves

Creating Sound

1) What has to happen for a sound wave to be created?

2) What *vibrates* in the above objects to start a sound?

3) How does the vibration travel from the object to your ear?

How Sound Travels

4) *Sketch the diagram* below and complete the labelling.

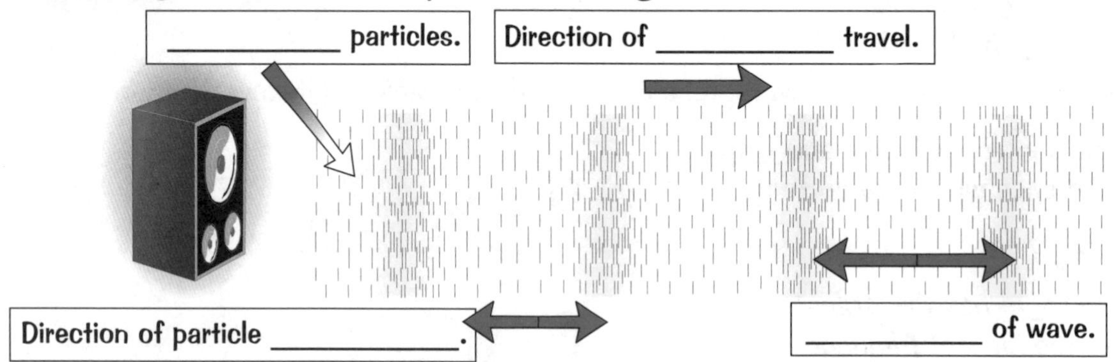

5) Are sound waves *longitudinal* or *transverse*?

6) How does the speed of sound compare to the speed of light? *Describe* an everyday observation which demonstrates this fact.

7) *The diagram below shows a sound wave experiment. The bell is switched on and the pump started.*

a) What happens to the sound coming from the bell once the pump is started?
b) What conclusion can be drawn from this?
c) What is the purpose of the foam block?

Ringing bell
Glass bell jar
Foam
air
To vacuum pump

Audible Frequencies

8) *Six frequencies are listed below.*

2Hz, 20Hz, 200Hz, 2000Hz, 2kHz, 20kHz

a) Which two frequencies are *identical*?
b) Which is closest to the lowest frequency *humans* can hear?
c) For which one could you easily count the vibrations without instruments?
d) Which is closest to the *highest* frequency humans can hear?

9) *Copy and complete* the statement below adding the missing words:-

As people get ___________ the ___________ frequency of sound that they can hear gets ___________. This makes it ___________ to clearly distinguish spoken words. This damage happens faster if people are regularly exposed to ___________ noises.

Sound Waves

Noise Pollution

10) Complete the sentences a) to c) below:

a) Noise is defined as unwanted__________ and is a form of ___________ in the environment.

b) Levels of noise are measured in _____________.

c) Materials which reduce noise are called sound ______________ and include carpets, curtains and ______________ glazing.

11) List *five* sources of noise pollution.

12) List *six* measures that can be taken to *overcome* noise problems.

Include:
- *Two measures that can be taken by national or local government.*
- *Two that can be taken by individuals to prevent making unwanted noise.*
- *Two that can be taken by individuals to protect themselves from excessive noise.*

Movement of Sound Waves

13) *Sound travels through some things, but not through others.*

a) Which of the following can sound travel through? *Mark* with a tick.

☐ SOLIDS ☐ A VACUUM ☐ LIQUIDS ☐ GASES

b) For each of the media you have chosen in a), give *ONE piece of evidence* to show that sound can travel through that medium.

c) *Which* medium in a) does sound generally travel the fastest in?

14) *If sound is a wave it must be able to do three things that all waves do*

a) These are ____________, ____________ and _____________.

b) What is the common name for a sound reflection?

c) *When you are in a room with the door open, you can hear sounds coming from outside the room wherever you are standing in the room.*

Describe how this is possible.

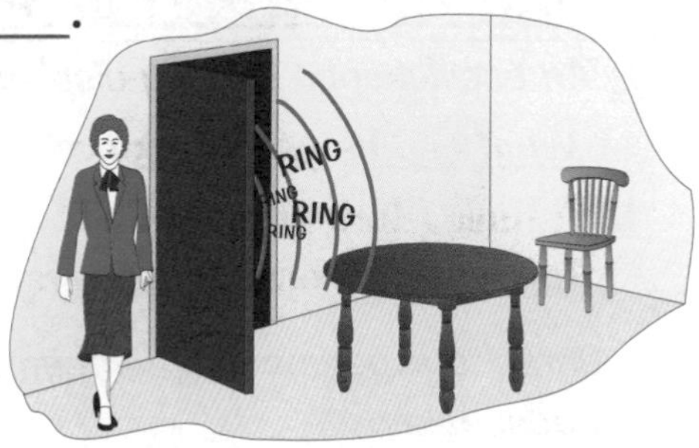

Using the Wave Equation

15) A spectator on a sports field is 200m from the start. She sees the starting gun fire and then hears the sound of the shot 0.6s later.

a) *Calculate the speed* of the sound.

b) What will be the *wavelength*, if the frequency of the sound is 200Hz?

c) Another sound wave has a frequency of 2000Hz. How does its frequency compare to the wave in part b)? What will the ratio of their *wavelengths* be?

16) *In water a sound wave of 200Hz has a wavelength of 7m.*
How fast does it travel?

17) *Calculate the wavelength* of a sound travelling in steel with a frequency of 200Hz, if the speed of sound in steel is 5000m/s.

Top Tip More waves, more calculations, more fun. You have to know what makes sound waves and how they travel — remember that sound won't travel in a vacuum. You won't need to know the range of human hearing by heart, but you will need to have a good idea of what frequencies we can't hear. You do need to know about noise pollution, and be able to name some ways of reducing it — easy marks in the Exam.

Pitch and Loudness

Revision of the Basics

frequency medium vacuum 400 transverse vibration wavelength wave 330 longitudinal amplitude

Copy and complete, choosing words from the box opposite.

1) Sound is a type of _____________ motion.
2) To make a sound wave there must be a _____________ .
3) Sound is a ____________ wave.
4) Sound waves travel at about ____________ m/s in air.
5) The distance between successive peaks of the wave is the __________ .
6) The number of vibrations per second is called the ____________ .
7) The maximum distance of particles from their resting position is called the __________ of the wave.
8) Sound cannot travel through a _____________, but needs a __________ to travel in.

The Tuning Fork

9) *A tuning fork is struck producing a high pitched sound.*

a) Explain *how* the sound is produced.

b) Describe a way of measuring the frequency of the tuning fork.

c) What difference would you hear if a tuning fork with longer prongs is struck?

d) How could you visually display the sound waves without the aid of an oscilloscope?

Oscilloscope Traces of Sound Waves

10) *An oscilloscope visually displays electrical signals.*

a) *What can be used* to convert sound into an electrical signal, needed by the oscilloscope?

b) A tuning fork produces a single pure note. *Sketch* the shape of the wave you would expect to see on an oscilloscope trace.

11) *Sarah is experimenting with an oscilloscope and a signal generator connected to a loudspeaker.*

She draws an oscilloscope trace for a range of frequencies and amplitudes (see opposite) but gets the labels mixed up.

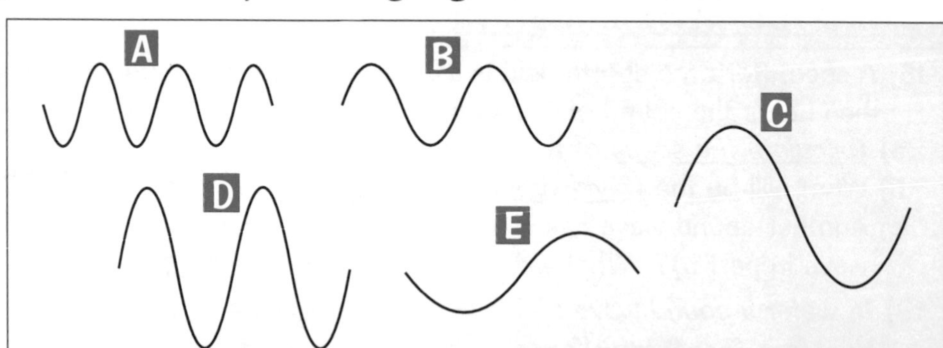

a) Study the traces above and complete the missing data in the table opposite.

b) What is the difference in the sound of the traces B and D.

Oscilloscope Trace	Frequency (Hz)	Amplitude (V)
	100	2
	100	4
	200	2
	200	4
	300	2

Pitch and Loudness

Frequency and Amplitude

12) *Changing the frequency or amplitude of a sound wave affects the type of sound you hear.*

Choose the correct words to complete the paragraph below:-

"Increasing the [frequency / amplitude] of a sound will [raise/lower] the pitch of the sound, producing a [higher / lower] note. Decreasing the [frequency / amplitude] will [raise/lower] the pitch of the sound.
Increasing the amplitude will increase the [pitch / loudness] of the sound and decreasing the amplitude will make the sound [louder / quieter / higher / lower]."

13) *Kerry is using the equipment shown below to investigate high frequency sounds.*

She records:

- *the frequency*
- *the amplitude*
- *what she hears*
- *a drawing of the signal*

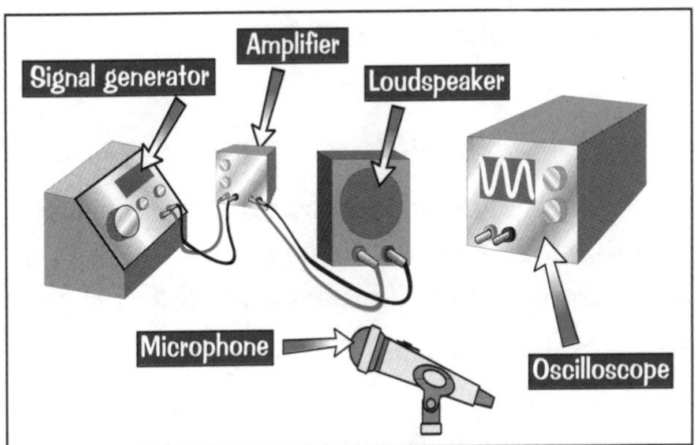

She recorded the results in a table like the one below. The first line of her table is filled in.

Drawing	Frequency (Hz)	Amplitude (V)	Sound heard
	10 000	2V	High and Quiet
	15 000	4V	
	20 000	2V	
	25 000	2V	

a) *Complete* the table with the results you would expect her to find for the other frequencies.
b) *Why is it difficult* to be certain about the last column for 20 000Hz?
c) What animal might hear the highest frequency in the table?

Top Tip Yet more waves, frequencies and amplitudes. They *really* want you to know this stuff, so you need to practise. It's *mega-important* to be able to understand an oscilloscope picture — questions about oscilloscope pictures are *very popular* in exams. Remember that a *taller* trace means a *higher amplitude* which means a *louder sound*. Remember that more ups and downs means a *higher frequency* which means a *higher pitch*.

Ultrasound

Ultrasound is sound with a higher frequency than we can hear.

Signal Generators

1) *A signal generator can be used with a loudspeaker and amplifier to make sounds of a large frequency range (see below). An oscilloscope displays the sounds as traces.*

a) What *kind of signal* is produced by a signal generator?

b) What does the *loudspeaker* do to this signal?

c) What can the oscilloscope be used for in this set up?

d) Why does the oscilloscope need a microphone attached to it?

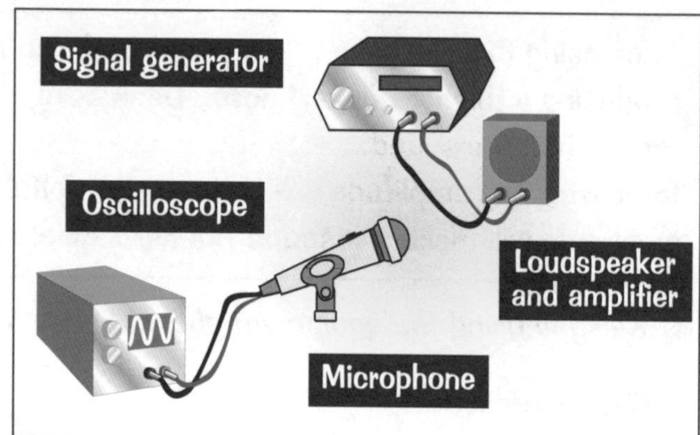

2) *An oscilloscope is set to give a clear signal at 10 kHz.*

a) What change would you see on the oscilloscope if the frequency is changed to *20kHz*.

b) What change would you *hear*?

c) If the frequency is increased to 25kHz what changes would you see and hear?

3) Copy and complete the following:

"Sounds above 20 000Hz have too high a ____________ to be heard by the human ear. Such sounds can be converted from ______________ oscillations using a loudspeaker. Sounds above this frequency are called ______________."

Ultrasonic Frequencies

4) Calculate the wavelengths of the following ultrasound frequencies *(in air)*.
— *Take the speed of sound in air to be 330m/s.*

a) 25kHz	b) 30kHz	c) 50kHz	d) 100kHz

5) Why is it important to state that the sounds are travelling through air?

6) *What frequency* will a sound wave have if its wavelength is 0.5cm?

7) *Bats use ultrasound to catch their prey. A typical victim would be a mosquito or a small moth.*

A bat can not sense anything smaller than the wavelength of sound it uses.

What frequency does the bat need to send out, to help catch a mosquito?

Hint *(you first have to estimate the size of a mosquito...)*

Ultrasound

Uses of Ultrasound

8) *You should be able to describe several applications that humans have found for ultrasound.*

Below is a table summarising six uses of ultrasound. The information is all mixed up.

Application	Category of use	Ultrasound used to	Basic principles
Removal of kidney stones	Industrial	Image the foetus	Use of energy in ultrasound to physically alter material
Quality control	Medical	Shatter stones allowing them to be passed out in urine	Use of energy in ultrasound to physically alter material
Removal of tartar	Military / Scientific	Break up tartar deposits on teeth	Use of energy in ultrasound to physically alter material
Sonar	Medical	Check for cracks in metal castings	Detection of reflected ultrasound to build image
Pre-natal screening	Industrial	Cleaning delicate mechanisms without dismantling them	Detection of reflected ultrasound to build image
Cleaning	Medical	Measure distances to objects or map the sea bed	Detection of reflected ultrasound to build image

Redraw the table with the information in the correct places.

Benefits of using Ultrasound

9) Copy and complete:-

"Ultrasound is useful for imaging because it is partially ____________ at the boundaries of different ____________. The reflection can be processed to form an ____________ of the internal ____________ of the object under study."

10) Why is ultrasound..
   a) better than X-rays for looking at a foetus?
   b) better for cleaning delicate mechanisms than traditional methods?
   c) better for treating kidney stones than open surgery?
   d) the chosen method for checking for flaws in metal castings?
   e) used to remove tartar?

11) There are other commercial uses of ultrasound.
   a) Submarines use it to calculate the distance to objects. How?
   b) What is this process called?
   c) There are less obvious uses for ultrasound such as in autofocus cameras. How do you think it is used in this case?

Top Tip Well, it's pretty obvious what ultrasound is. In the syllabus, they expect you to be able to name four examples of where ultrasound is used, and to say what the benefits are of using ultrasound rather than some other mechanism. There's more practice with the standard wave equation on these pages, too.

The Speed of Sound

Using Reflected Sound to Find The Speed of Sound

1) What is the speed of sound in *air* in metres per second?
2) What is the name for a *reflected* sound?
3) How is the speed of sound different in *water* compared to *air*?

4) *A group of students has been sent outside to estimate the speed of sound. One student bangs two wooden blocks together. Two other students measure the time between the bang and hearing the reflected sound from a large wall. They measure the time interval several times. The distance to the wall is 200m.*

Their ten different recorded times are shown in the table below.

Time Interval (s)				
1.11	1.23	1.29	1.17	1.15
1.19	1.21	1.13	1.27	1.25

a) Calculate the *average* of these times.
b) *How far* did the sound actually travel during this time?
c) What is the *speed of sound* deduced from this experiment?
d) Why is it a good idea to repeat the experiment?
e) If they had calculated the speed of sound using *only one* of their measured times, what is the maximum error that could have occurred in their calculation?

5) *Another group of students try a different way of measuring the speed of sound.*

The students are positioned at 200m intervals across the field. Each has a stopwatch. The student with the starting pistol simultaneously pulls the trigger and drops his arm. The students start their stop watches when they see the arm fall, and stop the watches when they hear the bang.

Their times are summarised in the table below.

Distance (m)	200	400	600	800	1 000
Time (s)	0.9	1.2	1.8	2.4	3.0

a) *Plot a graph* of distance from the pistol against time.
b) Use your graph to calculate the speed of sound.
c) One point does not quite fit the pattern. Why might you expect this point to be the one *least accurately* measured?

The Speed of Sound

Sonar — The Submarine

6) *A small submarine is using sonar to locate objects in murky water. There are several objects in it's projected path. These objects are: a large submarine; a whale; a shipwreck; the seabed. The submarine sends a pulse out in front and receives four echoes. It moves forward 75m and sends another pulse, again receiving four echoes.*

The table below shows the time taken for the first and second echoes to be received from each of the 4 objects.

Object	Time for First Echo (s)	Time for Second Echo (s)
1	0.2	0.1
2	0.1	0.1
3	0.4	0.2
4	1.0	1.1

The speed of sound in water is 1500m/s.

a) What distance away is each object at the time of the first echo?
b) What distance away is each object at the time of the second echo?
c) Remembering that the small submarine has moved between receiving the first and second echoes: *What can you say* about the movement of the other objects?
d) *Identify* the seabed and the shipwreck.
e) Now choose which of the objects left is the whale and which is the submarine? It will be helpful to note that submarines are more inquisitive than whales.

Sound Propagation in a Metal

Sound is a wave and there are two equations for calculating the speed of a wave.

7) *A sophisticated method of measuring sound involves the use of a metal bar and an oscilloscope. A sound with a frequency of 10 kHz takes 0.0004s to travel along a 1m steel bar and return.*

a) How far has the sound wave travelled?
b) What equation would you use to *calculate the wave's speed*?
c) What is its speed? Is this faster or slower than speed in air?
d) What equation would you use to calculate the wavelength?
e) What *is* its wavelength?

Top Tip The loud noises and echoes on this page might give you a headache, but the calculations won't. It's simple — *speed = distance/time*. Questions about measuring distance using reflected sound come up a lot in the Exam, so you need to learn all this stuff carefully. The *really important* thing to remember when doing the *echo questions* is that the sound has to travel *to* the wall *and back*, so it's travelled *double* the distance. Light travels so fast that you can just assume that you see something at the exact moment that it happens. Don't forget that the speed of sound changes depending on what it's travelling through — it's a lot *faster* in *water* than in *air*, which you might not expect.

Reflection

Some Basic Facts

1) *Like sound, light can be reflected off surfaces. Complete the gaps in the sentences below.*

a) Some objects give out their own light. All other objects we see because they ______________ light.

b) Some objects reflect light without disrupting it. This is called a ___________ reflection and objects which do this look ____________.

c) Most objects disrupt the reflected light giving a ___________ reflection. These objects look ____________.

d) The law of reflection states that "the angle of ____________ is ______________ to the angle of ______________."

2) What is the name for a beam of light used to represent a light path?

3) What is the name for the line drawn at right angles to a mirror or lens surface?

The Law of Reflection

4) The diagrams 1, 2 and 3 shows rays arriving at a surface.

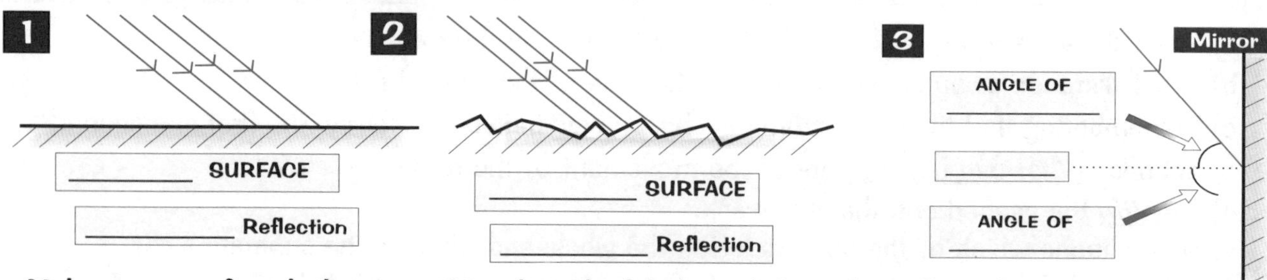

Make a copy of each diagram. Complete the labels and draw the reflected rays.

5) Study this plan view of two people sitting on a park bench.
They can see some statues reflected in the window.
Use the law of reflection to decide *which of the statues*, A, B, C, and D, persons 1 and 2 can see?

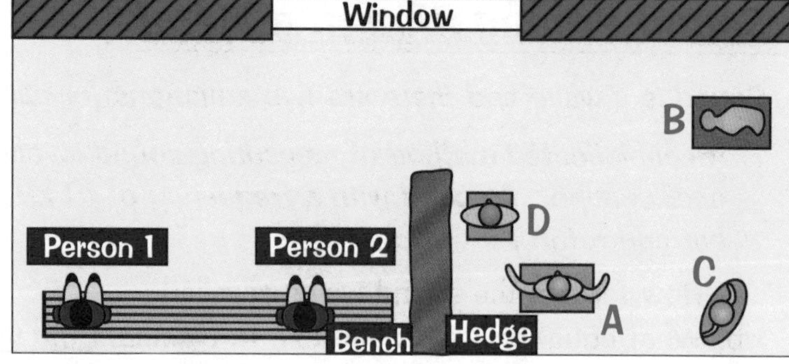

6) In the diagram opposite, rays are falling on the curved mirrors 1 and 2.

a) Draw the diagrams and complete the ray paths for the reflections.

b) Name the shapes of the two mirrors.

c) List two uses for each of the mirrors 1 and 2.

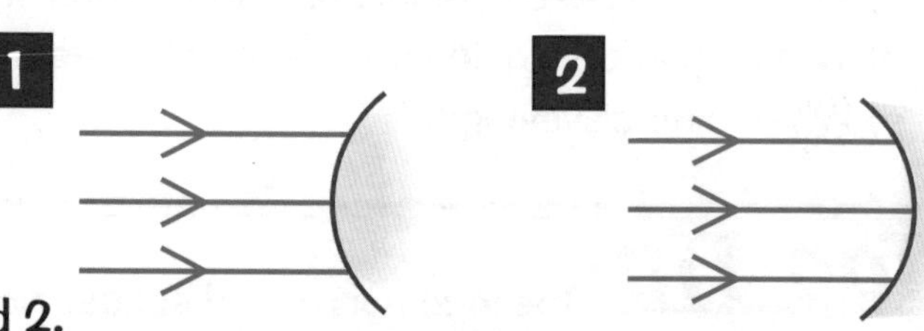

Top Tips There's quite a lot here on reflection that you really need to know. You've got to learn all the *diagrams* in question 4 and be able to *draw* them, so practise. Also, you need to be able to draw a diagram to show how an image is formed in a flat mirror. Watch out with your labels — the angles of incidence and reflection are between the ray and the *normal*, *not* the ray and the *surface*. Remember that all reflected rays obey the law of reflection.

Refraction

Rules of Refraction

1) *Fill in the gaps or choose the correct words* for the following sentences about refraction.
   a) Light travels at different __________ in different media.
   b) Light will [speed up/ slow down] when it travels from air into glass.
   c) When the light goes back into air it will [speed up/ slow down].
   d) The change of speed occurs at the ______________ of the two media.

2) What is meant by the *"normal"* to a surface?
3) Does the *frequency* of light change as it enters a different medium?

Rays in a Rectangular Block

4) *Study the rays in the two diagrams on the right.*
   a) In Diagram 1, a ray *enters* a glass block. Which ray X, Y or Z, shows how it would continue?
   b) In Diagram 2, a ray *leaves* the block. Which ray A, B or C shows its path correctly?

Diagram 1

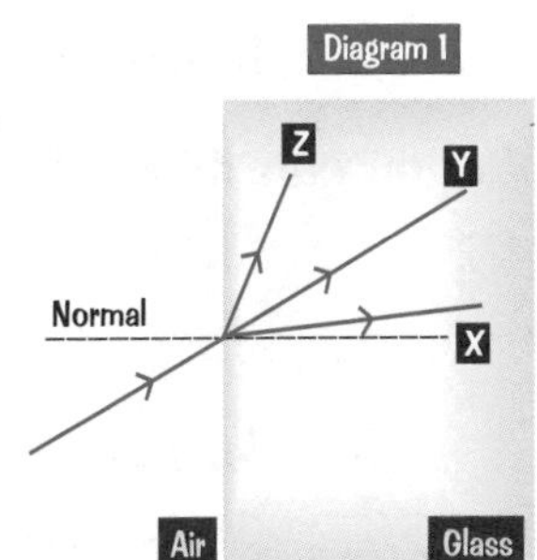

Diagram 2

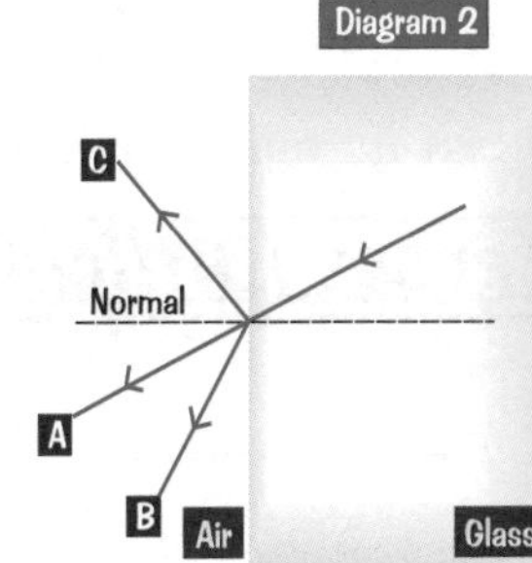

5) *Copy and complete*:

> When a ray of light enters a glass block it is bent [towards / away from] the normal.
> When a ray of light leaves the glass block it is bent [towards / away from] the normal.

Using the Idea of Wavefronts

6) *This diagram shows a ray of light entering a glass block as a wavefront.*

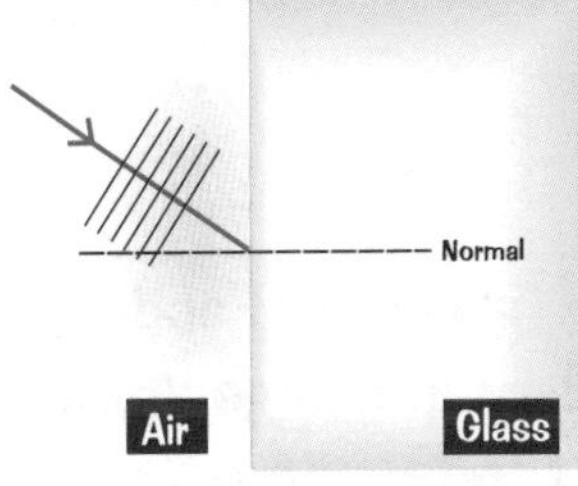

Write an explanation of the refraction of this ray in the block using the idea of a wavefront — use the *key words* opposite to help you.

KEYWORDS
angle to normal
- wavefront
- slows down
- wavelength
- direction changed
- frequency is unchanged

7) *The diagram below shows the ray of light leaving a glass block as a wavefront.*

KEYWORDS
angle to normal
- wavefront
- speeds up
- wavelength
- direction changed
- frequency is unchanged

Write an explanation of the refraction of this ray as it exits the block, using the idea of a wavefront — use the *key words* opposite to help you.

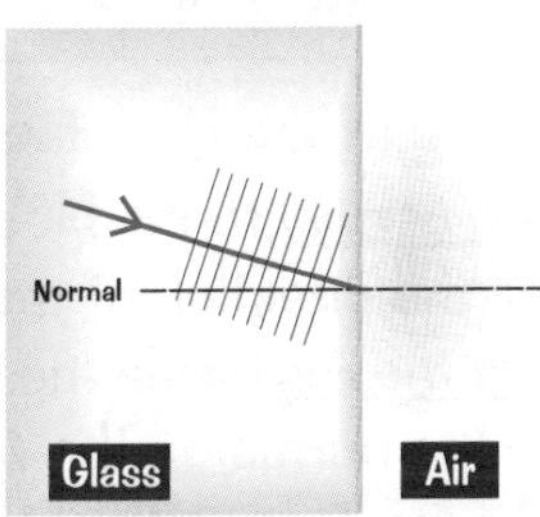

Top Tips *Refraction* and *Reflection* — the words look similar, but they're not the same. You need to know *what* refraction is and *how it happens*. Learn all the diagrams, they can ask you to draw them in the Exam. Remember that the light *won't* be bent if it enters at *exactly 90°*, but it *still slows down*. Don't forget, when you draw light rays they must be *straight lines*.

Special Cases of Refraction

Prisms

1) Make a copy of the prism opposite, with a monochromatic light ray entering it as shown.

a) Draw the *normal* to the face where the ray *enters*.
b) How will the *wavelength* and *speed* of the ray change on entering the prism?
c) Draw the ray path to the *other side* of the prism.
d) Draw the *normal* to the face where the ray leaves the prism.
e) Draw the ray *outside* the prism.
f) If the ray of light was "white" light from sunlight, what else would you see happen?

2) List as many instruments you can think of that use prisms.

Lenses (Difficult)

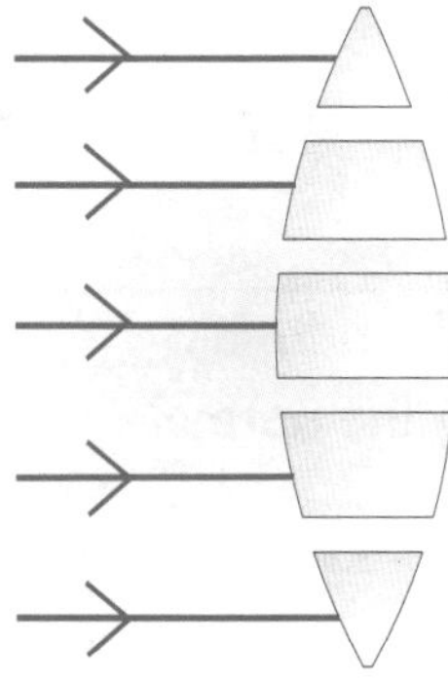

3) *A lens can be thought of as lots of separate prisms acting together. The lens on the left is split into five prisms.*

a) What *type of lens* is pictured in the diagram opposite.
b) *Draw normals* to the rays entering the top three prisms.
c) Complete the *ray paths* in the glass and leaving the glass.
d) Complete the bottom two prisms by comparing them to your answer to part c).
e) Describe the purpose of a lens this shape.

Total Internal Reflection — the inside story

4) *Copy and complete* this paragraph about total internal reflection.

"Total internal reflection happens when light is travelling in a material like [glass / air] and comes to the [edge / middle] of the block. If the light meets the boundary at a large angle to the [edge / normal], the ray is [refracted / diffracted / reflected], not [refracted / reflected]. The angle at which internal reflection begins is called the [critical / incident / normal] angle and is about [22 / 42 / 90] degrees in glass"

5) Make a copy of the glass block below, with a light ray entering it as shown.

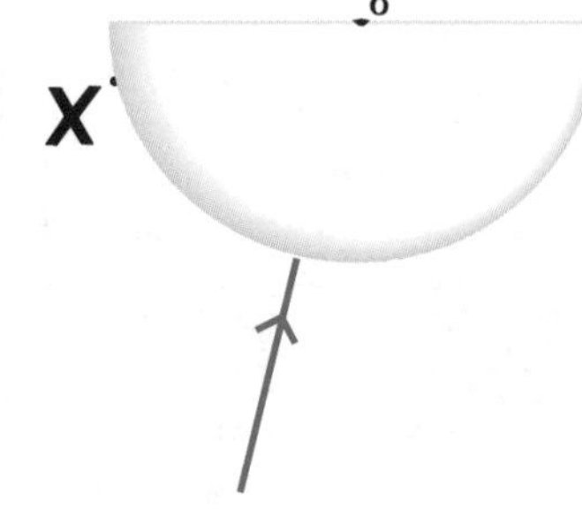

a) *Draw the normal* to the block at the point where the ray enters.
b) How will the direction of the ray *change* on entering? Why is this?
c) *Continue the ray* inside the block.
d) *Draw* in the normal to the face where the ray will leave the block. Draw the ray leaving the block.
e) *If the ray had come in through point X originally, the result would have been quite different.* *Draw* a ray coming in through point X directed towards o. Show its path *through* the glass and then *exiting* the block. What is the effect called that occurs on the *flat* side of the block?

Total Internal Reflection

6) *The diagram shows two identical glass blocks with a ray entering at two different angles.*

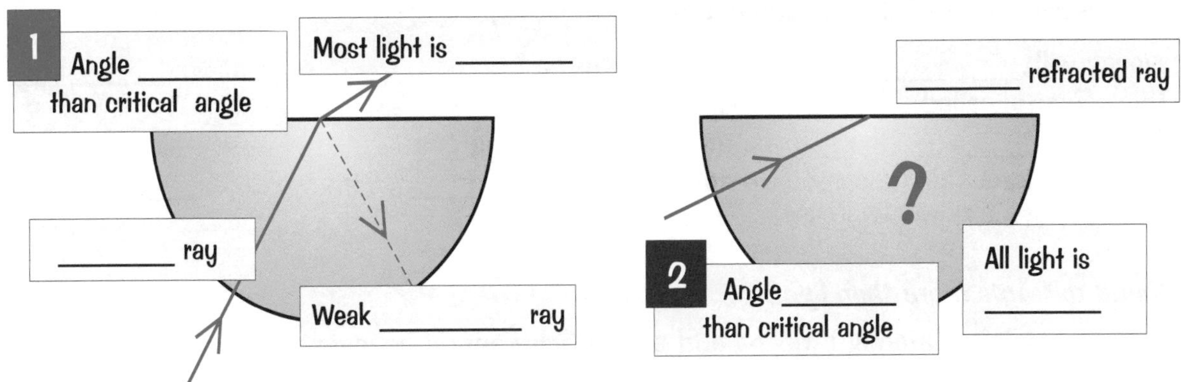

a) *Copy* Diagram 1 and *complete* the labelling.
b) *Copy* Diagram 2. *Draw* the reflected ray inside the block and *complete* the labelling.

Prisms and Optical Fibres

7) *The diagram below shows a ray of light entering a glass prism at right-angles to a surface.*

a) Why does the ray enter the prism without changing direction?
b) Copy the diagram opposite. Mark the angle of incidence and the angle of reflection, and label them.
c) What is the value of the angle of incidence at the inside surface?
d) What must be true about the angle of incidence and the angle of reflection?

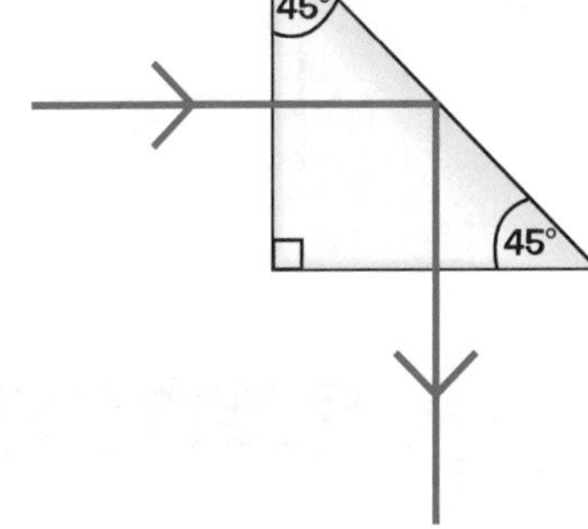

8) a) *Draw a diagram* of an optical fibre, showing:

- the layers of the fibre
- the light ray travelling along it (show 3 or 4 reflections)

Mark with arrows where total internal reflection occurs.

b) State the *advantages* of optical fibres over wires for carrying information.

9) *Describe* what an endoscope is, and give a use of an endoscope in a hospital. Can you think of one other use of total internal reflection?

Top Tip Total Internal Reflection, that sounds a bit scary... *Prisms* and *lenses* are just examples of refraction. You need to know *which way* the colours go in the rainbow from a prism — think about which colour is refracted *most* and which is refracted *least*. Remember that Total Internal Reflection is a special example of light refracting between a dense material and air. *Diagrams* to learn and remember again, this time of what happens when the *angle of incidence* is *less than*, *equal to* or *more than* the *critical angle*. Questions about total internal reflection will usually ask you to name some examples, so learn the ones on this page and two or three more.

Diffraction

Facts about Diffraction

1) *Fill in the gaps* in the following sentences...

a) Waves will __________ when they go through a ____________ or past an ___________.
b) This effect is called _____________.
c) The _____________ the gap the more diffraction there is.
d) If the gap is about the same size as the ______________ of the wave, a _____ __________ shaped wave will be produced.

2) *"Sound diffracts more than light."*
Describe what this statement means and explain why sound behaves differently.

Four Classic Cases of Diffraction

3) *The following diagrams show plane waves approaching an obstacle.*

a)
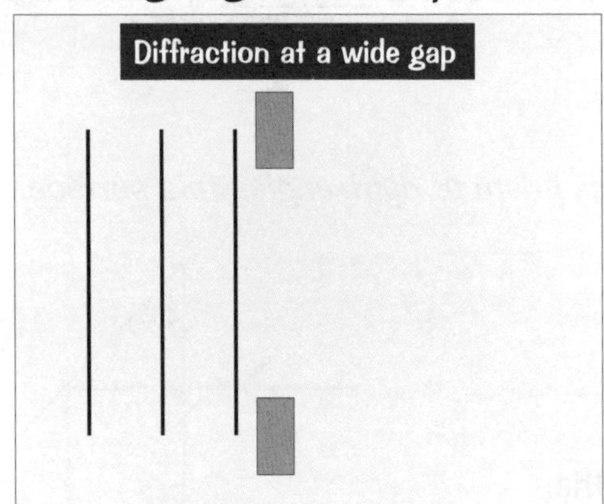

b)
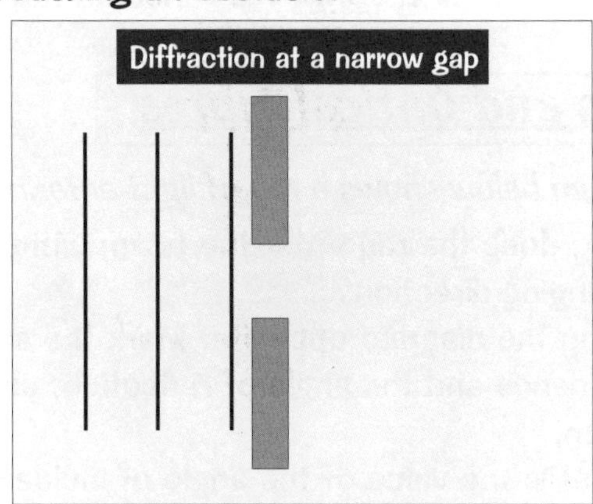

c) Diffraction at an edge

d)
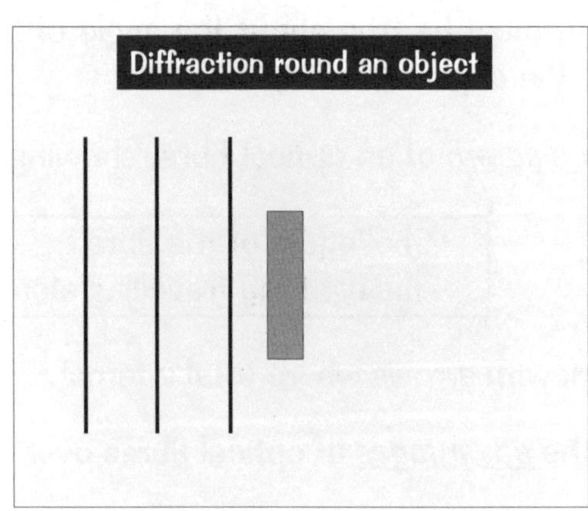

Copy the diagrams and draw the wavefronts after passing the obstacles.

Wavelength Calculations

(Speed of sound = 330m/s, speed of light = 3 x 10^8 m/s)

4) *A sound wave and visible light wave pass through a doorway 75cm wide.*

a) What *frequency of sound* has a wavelength of 75cm? Can a human *hear* this sound?
b) If the visible light wave has a frequency of 5 x 10^{14} Hz, what is its wavelength?
c) Use the results of your calculations a) and b) to *explain* why it is possible to hear around corners, but not possible to see around corners.

5) *What frequency* of electromagnetic radiation has a wavelength of 75cm?
What type EM radiation is this?

Diffraction

Diffraction of Light through a Slit

6) *This diagram shows an experiment to demonstrate the diffraction of light.*

The laser shines red light through a narrow slit. The light shows up on a white screen.

Laser
Red Light
Screen
Narrow slit

a) Why is laser light used instead of an ordinary light source?
b) How is the beam path made visible?
c) Why does the slit have to be very narrow?
d) One student looks at the screen and says, "That's just an image of the slit!" How could you show that he was wrong?
e) How would the shape of the beam change if the slit was replaced with a narrower one?
f) How would the shape of the beam change if green light was used instead of red light?

Diffraction of Sound Waves and Radio Waves

7) How can you predict whether a radiowave will show significant diffraction around an obstacle?

8) Will significant diffraction occur for the following situations, and what will be the effect?
a) A long wave radio signal of frequency 1MHz passes between 2 blocks of flats 250m apart.
b) An FM radio signal of frequency 1GHz is transmitted from the far side of a short tunnel that is 6m wide.
c) I am sitting at my desk and outside my window (50cm wide) irate drivers are blowing their horns (frequency 5000Hz).

9) The diagrams below show shortwave TV waves and longwave radiowaves approaching a hill.

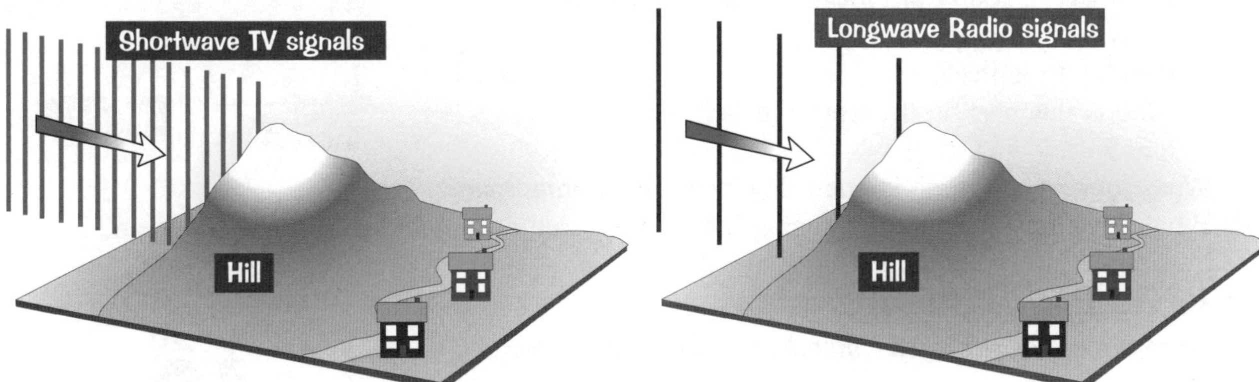

a) Copy and complete the pictures above, showing how the hill changes the direction of the EM wave.
b) Suggest a reason why people in the houses in the picture could listen to the cricket match on Test Match Special on longwave Radio 4 but not be able to watch it on the television.

Top Tip Diffraction just means the *spreading out* of waves. The thing to remember here is that waves spread out *more* going through a *narrow* gap than a *wide* gap — a narrow gap is one about the *same size* as the *wavelength*. Once again, there's diagrams to be copied and learnt — look at question 3. The important thing about diffraction of radio and light (both electromagnetic radiation, but different wavelengths) is that it is strong evidence for light being a wave.

Optical Instruments

Optical instruments all rely upon basic principles which you should know inside out.

Lenses — Converging and Diverging

1) *Copy and complete* the following sentences.

"When a ray of light moves from air into glass it bends [away from / towards] the normal.
When a ray of light moves from glass into air it bends [away from / towards] the normal."

2) *Lenses work by refracting light.*

The two lenses opposite have light rays approaching them from infinity.

Copy the diagrams and show how the light rays would be refracted by the lenses.

a)

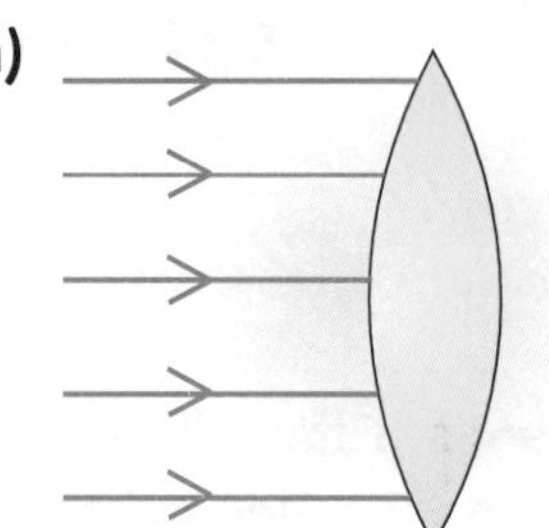

b)

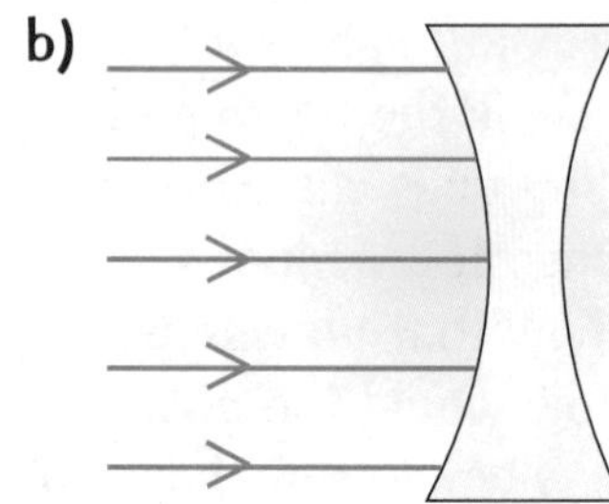

The Camera

3) *The diagram below shows a Single Lens Reflex (SLR) camera, popular with photographers.*

Which part of the camera..

a) controls the amount of light entering the camera?
b) focuses the light?
c) records the image?
d) allows the light in when the photograph is taken?

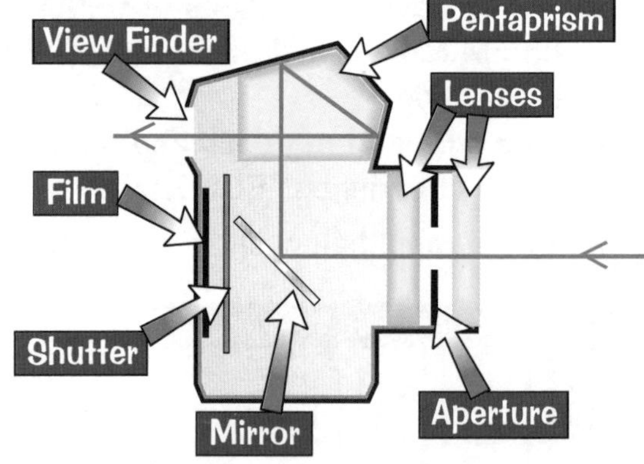

4) a) *In an SLR camera, another part has to move to allow a photograph to be taken.* Which part is this?
b) Why is this part "in the way" the rest of the time?

5) What *type of reflection* is occurring inside the pentaprism?

6) What advantages are there in using this complicated arrangement with a pentaprism?

Binoculars Use Prisms

The diagram opposite shows a standard pair of binoculars.

7) *The lens and eyepiece are offset, so that prisms are needed to bend the light through the binoculars.* What is the reason for this complicated arrangement?

8) *Complete* the light path for the other half of the binoculars.

9) *Mirrors can be used instead of prisms.* Describe one advantage of using highly reflective mirrors rather than prisms.

10) What property of the prism allows light to be 'bent' around corners?

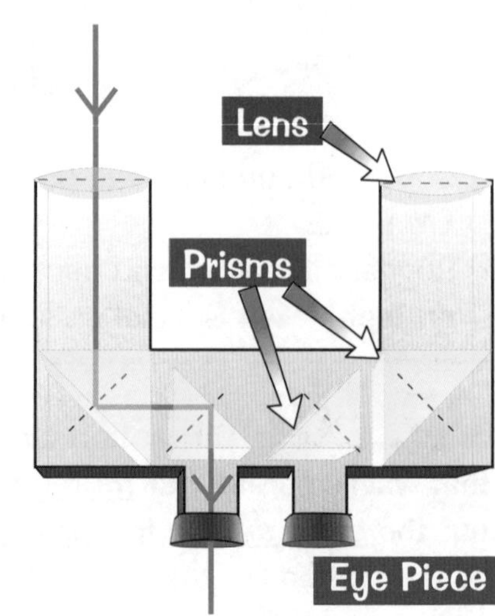

Optical Instruments

A Periscope with Prisms

11) *The diagram opposite shows light entering a* periscope.

a) Copy the diagram and *draw the light path* through the periscope.

b) How does the positioning of the prisms ensure there is no *dispersion* of the light rays when they pass through the periscope?

c) Where on the periscope would you put your eye to view a scene from a higher point?

d) What is the advantage (when looking through the periscope) of lengthening the column A-B?

12) a) Give two uses for a periscope.
b) Explain why the periscope is needed in each case.

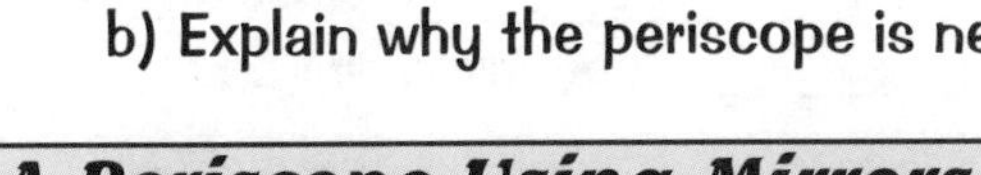

A Periscope Using Mirrors

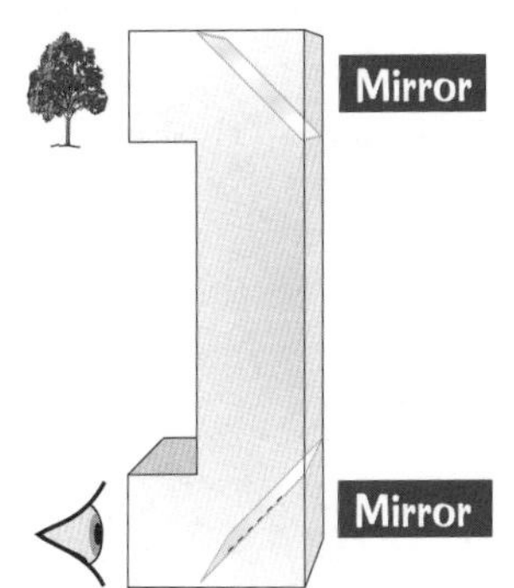

13) *This diagram shows a* mirror periscope *that has been put together* incorrectly.

a) Copy the diagram and draw the paths of two light rays travelling to the eye — one from the *top of the tree* and one from *the trunk*.

b) What *problem* can you identify with this periscope?

c) This time, *draw the periscope correctly*, with two new light rays showing how this version works as it should do.

d) List two *advantages* of using mirrors in a periscope rather than prisms.

The Bicycle Reflector

14) *The diagram below shows a light ray being reflected by a bicycle* reflector.

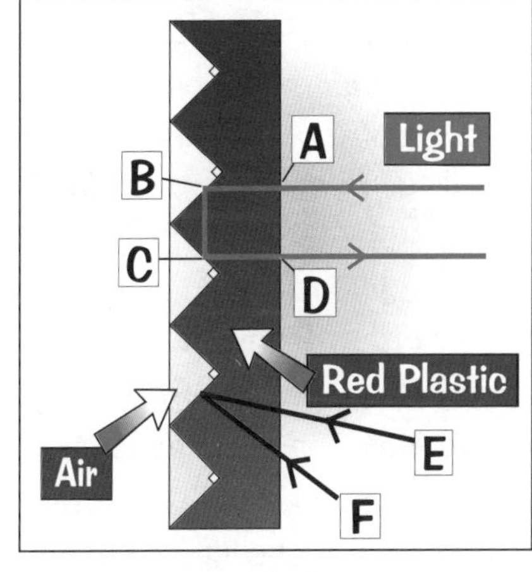

a) Explain how the incident ray is *reflected back* in the direction it came from.

This reflector will reflect light coming in from other angles too.

b) What would you expect to happen to the light ray at 'E'? (Will it be reflected back the way it came or will it leave at a different angle?)

c) What will happen to the light ray 'F'?

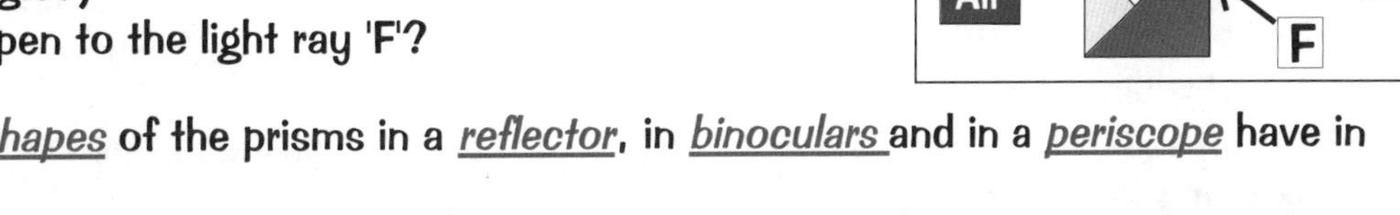

15) What do the *shapes* of the prisms in a *reflector*, in *binoculars* and in a *periscope* have in common?

Top Tip These are all smashing examples of reflection, refraction and total internal reflection. *Learn* the diagrams and *practise* drawing them, because they could ask you to fill in a partly drawn diagram of one of these instruments in the Exam. They're not difficult, but there are quite a few little details to remember.

The Electromagnetic Spectrum

Properties of Electromagnetic Waves

1) *Copy and complete the following paragraphs about electromagnetic waves.*

a) Electromagnetic (EM) waves form a continuous___________. For a given __________ all EM waves travel with roughly the same _______________. In a _____________ this_____________ is about 3×10^8 m/s. There are ____________ main types of EM wave. The correct order for these types of EM wave is (beginning with longest wavelength):
_______ ______, _______________, _______ ________, _______ ________, _______ ________, ____________ and _______ ________.

b) ______________ waves have the lowest frequency and the __________ wavelength, and _________ ________ have the highest frequency and the ______________ wavelength. Our eyes are sensitive to EM waves from the ________________ spectrum only.

2) *For each of the statements a) to j) below, state whether it is true or false, and if it is false, write down what the underlined words should be replaced with.*

a) Microwaves are used to communicate with satellites.
b) Microwaves are the same thing as heat radiation.
c) Gamma rays both cause and cure cancer.
d) Only visible light will show diffraction.
e) Radio waves can have wavelengths of many metres.
f) X-rays are used to take pictures of bones because they are relatively safe.
g) Infrared radiation causes skin cancer.
h) Microwaves are absorbed by water.
i) Long wave radiowaves are able to diffract long distances round the Earth.
j) Visible light has a wavelength of about a ten thousandth of a millimetre.

Comparing the Types of Electromagnetic Radiation

3) *The diagram shows parts of the electromagnetic spectrum and wavelengths for the different radiations. However, they are all mixed up.*

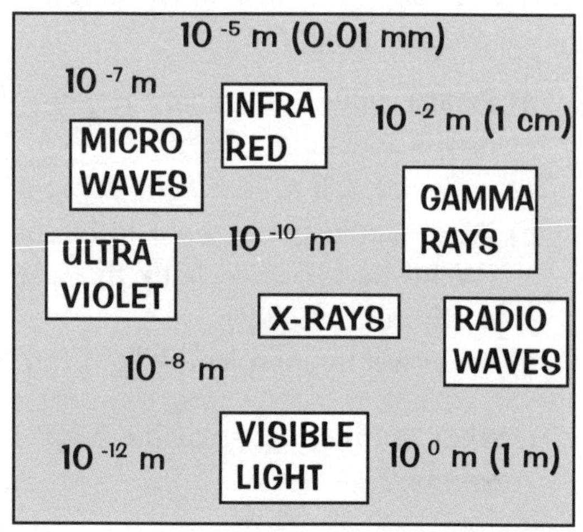

a) Draw your own diagram of a spectrum, but with the types of radiation and wavelengths in the correct order, from the shortest to the longest wavelength.
b) Calculate the frequency for each type of wave.
c) How many times longer is a typical visible light wave compared with an X-ray wave?
d) How many times longer is a microwave compared with a typical visible light wave?
e) What is the speed of an electromagnetic wave in a vacuum?

4) An electromagnetic wave is drawn on an A4 piece of paper so that one wavelength fills the page and you are told it is drawn actual size.
What two types of EM wave could the drawing represent?

5) A commonly used microwave wavelength is 3cm. What is its frequency?

The Electromagnetic Spectrum

Applications and Dangers of Electromagnetic Radiations

6) *This table is all mixed up!* Redraw the table with the information in the correct places.

Type of Radiation	Effects on Living Tissue	Uses
Gamma	• probably none	• communication • broadcasting • radar
X-Ray	• heating of water in tissues can cause "burning"	• imaging internal structures in the body • studying the atomic structure of materials
UV	• kills living cells in high doses • lower doses can cause cells to become cancerous • causes tanning	• fluorescent tubes • tanning • security marking
Visible	• kills living cells in high doses • lower doses can cause cells to become cancerous • kills cancerous cells	• kill bacteria in food • sterilise medical equipment • treat tumours
IR	• kills living cells in high doses • lower doses can cause cells to become cancerous	• radiant heaters • grills • remote controls • thermal imaging
Microwave	• causes burning of tissues	• satellite communication • cooking
Radio	• activates sensitive cells in the retina	• seeing • optical fibre • communication

"Seeing" in Astronomy

7) *Before the "Space Age" and the advent of artificial satellites, almost all astronomy was done using two particular regions of the EM spectrum.* What regions were these? *Why do astronomers now get better results utilising other regions of the EM spectrum from outer space?*

8) *The Moon would be a much better place than Earth to observe the stars and galaxies from.* Write down two reasons why it would be better to observe from the moon.

9) *Infra-red astronomy can only be done from dry, high mountain sites, from aircraft or from satellites.* Explain why this is.

White Light in a Prism

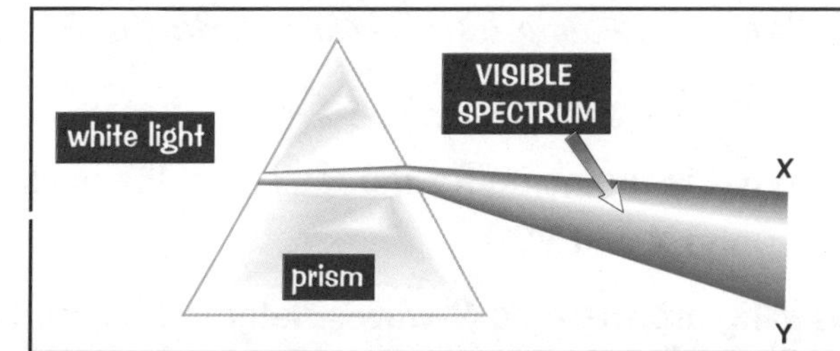

10) What coloured light would you expect to see at positions X and Y in the diagram?

11) *A rainbow is created in a similar way.* What is acting as the prism in this case?

Top Tip Lots of juicy facts on these pages. It's all important so don't skip bits. To help you learn the order of the EM spectrum you could use the following memory aid or perhaps invent a better one. Rabid Monkeys In Violet Underpants eXterminate Gibbons. Remember that the speed of light in a vacuum is constant, it's important. Learn the effects and uses of all the different types of electromagnetic radiation.

Seismic Waves

Basic Facts

Do you know the facts about seismic waves?

1) Seismic waves are caused by __________________.
2) Seismic waves start in the Earth's _______________from a point called the *focus*.
3) The point above this on the ___________________ is called the *epicentre*.
4) Seismic waves are detected using a __________________.
5) There are two types of seismic wave called _____________ waves and ____________ waves.
6) The _____________ waves are faster. They can travel through ______________ and _______________.
7) The _______________ waves are slower; they can only travel through ______________.
8) __________ waves are *longitudinal*, whereas ___________ waves are *transverse*.
9) From studying seismic waves we have learned that the Earth contains ______ layers called (from the surface inwards); the _______________, the ______________, the __________ ___________ and the ____________ ___________.
10) Both types of wave change direction inside the Earth due to the effect of _____________.
11) The waves travel in _______________ paths. This is because of changes in the ___________ of material inside the Earth.

The Earth's Layers

12) *The diagram shows the model we have developed for the Earth using information from seismic waves.*

a) *Copy* the diagram and label the different layers that make up the Earth.

b) The measurement of seismic waves can be used to learn about the interior of the Earth. Why is this a more convenient method than drilling into the earth to take measurements?

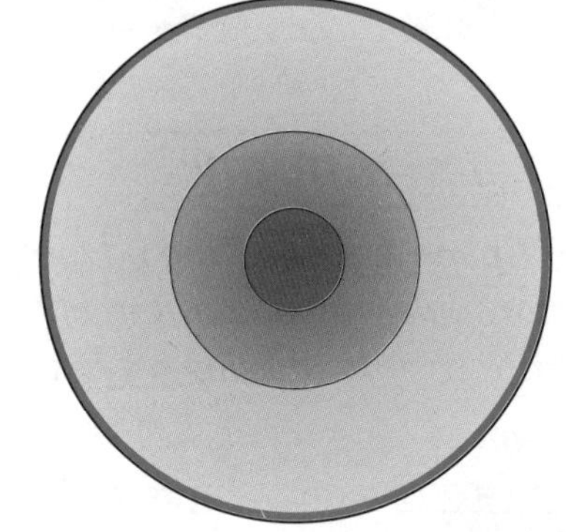

S-Waves

Study the diagram of the Earth on the right. It shows an earthquake sending four S-Waves into the Earth.

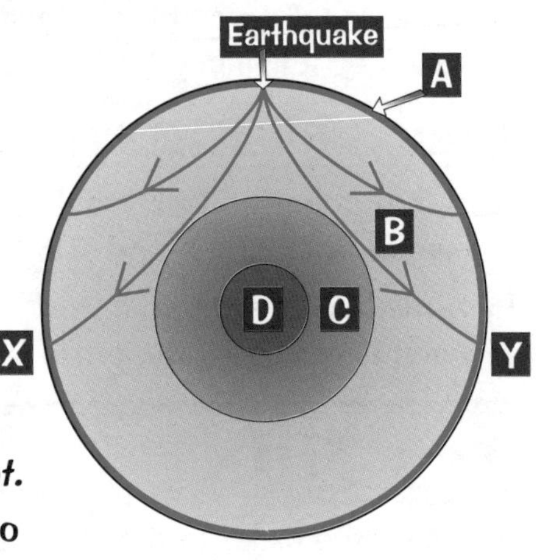

13) Describe what an "*S-Wave*" is.

14) What is the name for the region on the earth's surface beyond X and Y?

15) Why are there no S-waves detected beyond X and Y?

16) Describe the *state* of the rocks in layer B.

17) *The paths of the S-Waves travelling through layer B are bent.*

a) What property of the rock in layer B is steadily changing, to account for this observation?

b) *Now compare this effect with the refraction of light waves.* Give *two reasons* why we can say that the S-Waves in layer B are *refracted*.

Seismic Waves

P–Waves

18) Give three ways in which P–Waves are different from S–Waves.

19) *The diagram below shows the paths for some P–Waves travelling through the Earth.*

a) point D is at the boundary of which two layers?
b) *The direction of the waves at D and E changes suddenly.* Why does this happen?
c) *Detectors are placed on the Earth's surface between points P and R.* Describe where you would not expect to detect any P–Waves.
d) What property do P-waves have that allows them to reach the parts other waves cannot reach?

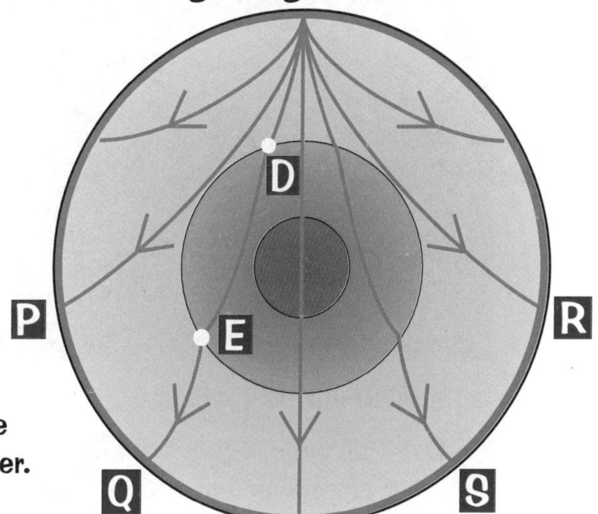

20) After an earthquake, would you expect to feel the P–Wave first, or the S–Wave? Explain your answer.

Interpreting Seismographs

The graph below shows how the velocity of a P–Wave and an S–Wave, travelling from the surface of the Earth towards the centre, changes with depth.

21) Describe and explain *the shape* of the velocity–depth curve for *a P–Wave*. Say what is happening at A, B, C, D, E and F.

22) Describe and explain the shape of the velocity–depth curve for *an S–Wave*. Say what is happening at A, B, C and D.

23) Give *two reasons* why we should want to investigate the properties of the Earth's crust.

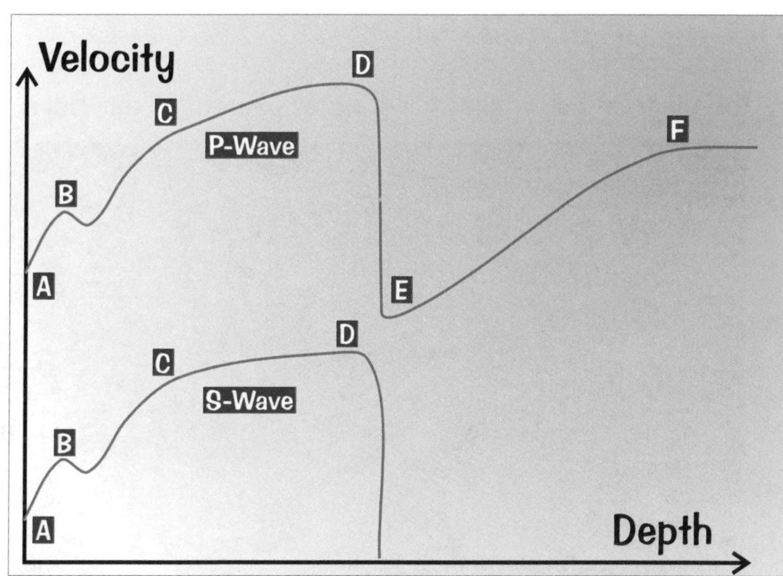

24) Why do seismometers have to be placed deep underground, especially near towns and cities?

Top Tip Exciting stuff about the inside of the Earth and what happens in earthquakes. This topic could be a bit confusing at first glance, so go through it all *step by step*. If you know the basic facts in Question 1 you won't go far wrong. There are *two* kinds of seismic wave. The really important thing to remember is that *S* waves are tran*s*verse and they only travel in *s*olids, but *P* waves are longitudinal, and they travel through solids *and* liquids. The *really exciting* thing is that you can use all the data about *how much* different parts of the earth shake during an *earthquake* to work out what's down in the centre of the Earth. Yes, I did say *really exciting*.

The Solar System

Some Facts about the Solar System

1) This question consists of a number of statements about our solar system.

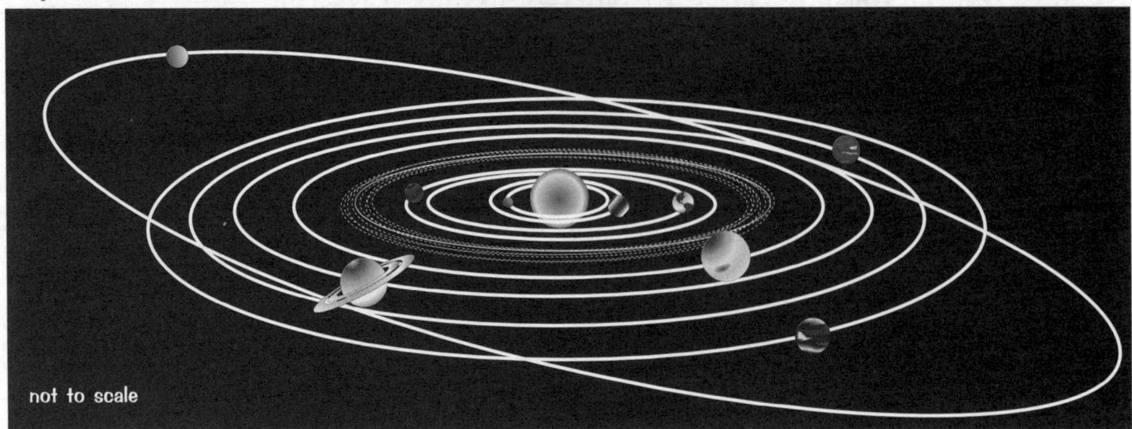

For each statement, say whether it is *true or false*, and give a *reason* for your decision.

a) The Sun makes energy by changing hydrogen gas into water.
b) The inner planets all have similar surfaces.
c) All the planets are visible because of light they produce themselves.
d) The planets in the solar system orbit around a massive object.
e) Of the planets in the outer planet group, Pluto is an odd member.
f) All planets have spherical orbits.
g) Stars in other solar systems look dim because they are smaller than the Sun.

The Outer Planets

2) The diagram below shows the outer planets of our Solar System.

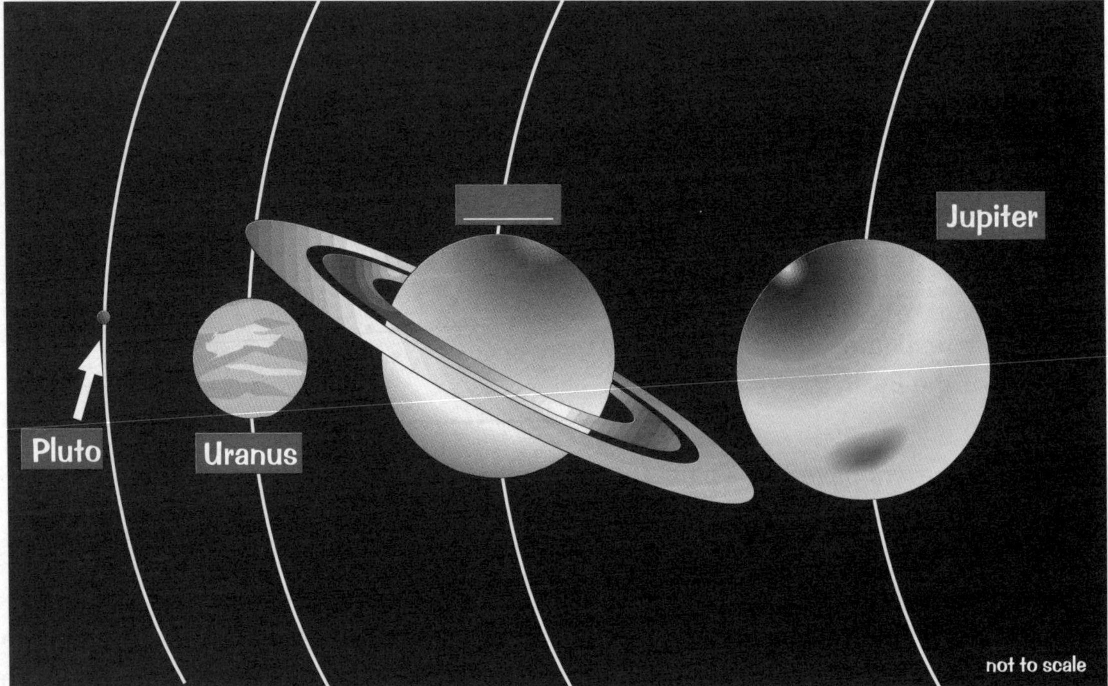

a) One planet's name has been left out. *Redraw the diagram* and add the missing name.
b) One planet has been missed from the diagram altogether. *Sketch in the orbit* on your diagram, and label it with the planet's name.

The Solar System

Jupiter and The Sun

3) Jupiter and the Sun are both members of our Solar System. The Sun is classified as a star, and Jupiter as a planet.

a) Complete the paragraph using the following words:

light, elliptical, huge, reflected, helium, heat, nuclear, planet, fusion, stars, orbit, smaller, hydrogen, star

The Sun is a _______ and produces _______ from _______ _______ reactions which turn _______ into _______. Like other _______ it is _______ and gives out a lot of _______. Jupiter, on the other hand, is a _______ hence the light we observe from it is _______. Jupiter is much _______ than the sun and follows an _______ _______ around it.

b) In your own words describe the characteristics that distinguish stars from planets.

c) Jupiter emits more heat energy than it receives from the Sun. Can you suggest why this is so?

(not to scale!)

Phases, Orbits and The Origins of the Planets

4) *Viewed from the Earth, Venus and Mercury are the only planets that show phases and appear to change shape, just like the moon does.* If we were on Saturn, which planets would show *phases*?

5) *The diagram below shows a plan view of Earth in an elliptical orbit around the Sun. The time it takes for the Earth to travel from X to Y is the same as it takes to travel from Y to Z. The area, A, "swept out" by travelling from X to Y and Y to Z is equal.*

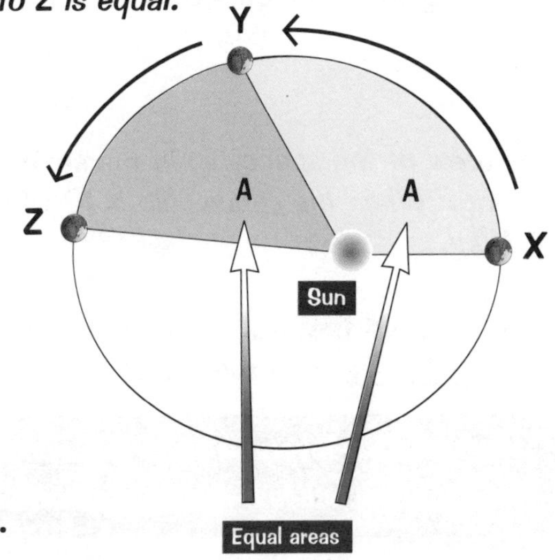

a) Use the information above and in the diagram to predict in which part of the orbit X, Y or Z the Earth travels *fastest*. *Explain* your answer.

b) Does the Earth travel faster when it is closest to the Sun, or furthest away?

6) *Current theories about the origin of the Solar System tell us that the planets were formed from the same material as the Sun.*

Explain why the planets did not become stars as well.

Top Tips

A nice jolly topic to learn, this one. You've got to learn the *order* of the planets (including the asteroids), so try a little silly sentence to help — My Very Elderly Mother etc., or something like that. The *differences* between *planets* and *stars* are pretty straightforward to learn, and a good way to some easy marks. Nothing to it, really.

The Planets

Science Fiction and Fact

1) *A science fiction series is being planned by a TV company. The authors have come up with some information about 5 planets for the series. The name of the star in the series is Grull.*

Data about Grull and its planets is given in the table below.

Name of planet	Distance from Grull (millions of km)	Surface	Atmosphere
Umblem	50	Rocky	None
Afton	100	Rocky	Thick CO_2
Sedash	150	Rocky	Thick N_2 and O_2
Clunoc	250	Rocky	Thin CO_2
Glabwell	778	Gaseous	Thick methane and ammonia

Sedash is the planet most similar to the Earth.

a) Which of the planets in the series is most similar to *Jupiter*?

b) Which planet in the series is likely to be most similar to *Venus*?

The writers are planning an episode where a spaceship travels from Afton to Umblem. One writer says that the surface temperature on Afton will be higher than that on Umblem. Another disagrees.

c) Compare Afton and Umblem with similar planets from our own solar system to explain which opinion is likely to be the correct one.

The crew of the spaceship in the series have a "Gravity Meter" that measures the force of gravity. When the space ship is 10 000 km from Umblem, the Gravity Meter shows a reading of 15 N/kg.

d) What will the Gravity Meter read when the ship is 5 000 km from the planet?

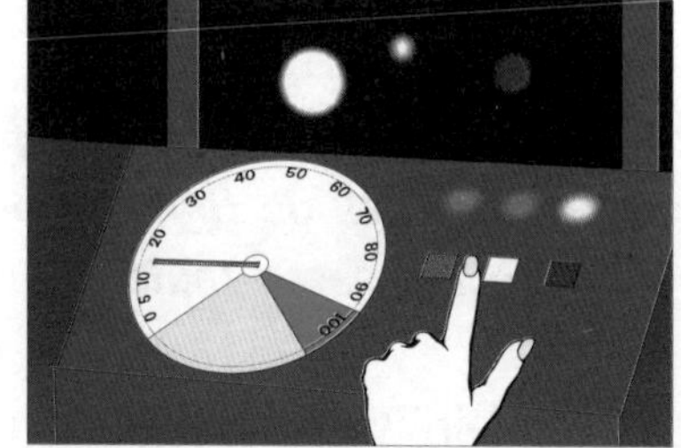

***Hint:* Use the inverse square law, which tells you that gravitational pull is inversely proportional to $(\text{distance})^2$.**

On the surface of Sedash, the Gravity Meter reads 8 N/kg. Sedash has exactly the same radius as Earth.

e) What does this reading tell you about the *density* of Sedash compared with Earth? Explain.

f) Which planet from the series will have the *shortest year*?

The Planets

Distinguishing Planets from Stars

2) *Look at the diagrams below* which represent photographs taken of a group of stars. The two photos were taken a few weeks apart.

An astronomer noticed that a planet had been captured on both photographs.

a) *Identify the planet* by putting a ring around it.
b) Why does a planet appear to cross the sky *relative* to the stars?
c) What is the *name* given to a pattern of stars that look fixed relative to one another?

Kepler's Law

3) *A famous scientist called Johannes Kepler studied the motion of the planets and discovered a number of laws for their motion. One was that the cube of a planet's mean distance from the Sun, R, is proportional to the square of its period, T.*

i.e $R^3 / T^2 = \text{Constant}$

The table below shows some data about the inner planets.

Name of planet	Mean distance from Sun, R (millions of km)	Period, T (Earth days)	R^3/T^2
Mercury	58	88	
Venus		225	
Earth	150	365	
Mars	228	687	

a) Calculate the value of R^3/T^2 for Mercury, Earth and Mars.
b) Assuming the Kepler's Law constant is the same for all bodies here, calculate the mean distance from Venus to the Sun.
c) Now calculate the likely distance from the Sun of an asteroid with a period of 1200 Earth days.

Top Tips

Planets are great — rocky ones, gassy ones, big ones, small ones... Now, you do need to have a *good idea* of which ones are biggest, which are furthest out, how long it takes them to orbit the sun, etc. — luckily you don't need to learn all the figures off by heart. Remember that gravity is pretty *strong* stuff up *close* but it weakens very *quickly* with *distance* — that's what the Inverse Square Law is about . Don't forget, it's gravity that keeps a planet in its orbit, so a planet *closer* to the sun has to move *faster* to balance the *stronger* gravity. Neat.

Moons, Meteorites, Asteroids, Comets

The Moons of Jupiter

When Galileo, a famous Italian scientist, first used his telescope to look at the planet Jupiter in 1610 AD, he soon realised that there were four "little stars" moving around Jupiter. These were soon identified as moons orbiting Jupiter. Some data about Jupiter's 4 moons appears in the table below.

Name	Diameter (km)	Mean distance from Jupiter, R (km)	Time taken to orbit Jupiter, T (days)
Io	3632	4.216×10^5	1.8
Europa	3126	6.709×10^5	
Ganymede	5276	1.070×10^6	7.2
Callisto	4820	1.883×10^6	16.7

1) If the masses of Ganymede and Callisto are similar, how will the strength of the gravitational force exerted by Jupiter on these moons compare? Give a reason for your answer.
2) Calculate the time taken for Europa to orbit Jupiter, given that the value of R^3 / T^2 is the same for all the moons of Jupiter.
3) These moons do not produce their own light. Explain why we can still see them.
4) Explain why Europa appears to change shape when seen from Callisto.

Asteroids and Meteorites

5) Most of the asteroids in the Solar System can be found between the orbits of two planets. Which two planets are these?
6) Which two main substances are the asteroids made of?
7) Some science fiction stories talk about a collision between an asteroid and the Earth. Why is this *extremely unlikely* to happen for most asteroids?
8) *An astronomer takes a timed exposure of the night sky with a camera that follows the stars.*

When she develops the film, she sees the stars as points, but there are also lines across it. These lines are not satellite or aircraft tracks, and there was no fault on the film. The photograph is shown on the right, here.

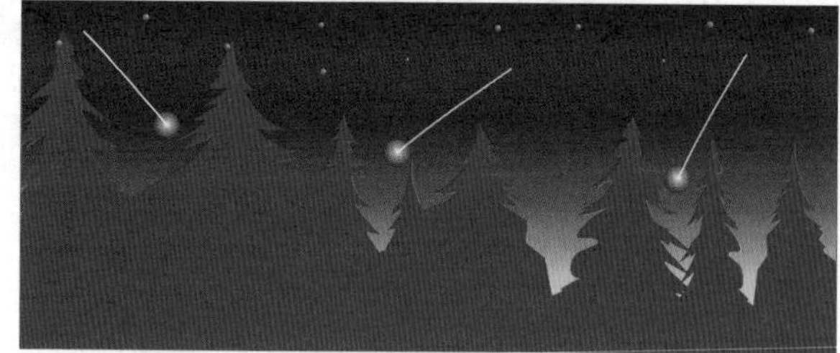

What *astronomical event* could have caused the lines?

In Arizona there is a big crater in the desert. It was not formed by a volcano, but by some other natural event.

9) How was the crater made?
10) Why are there *very few* craters like this on the Earth, but *many thousands* of them on the Moon?

Moons, Meteorites, Asteroids, Comets

Comets

Like all members of the Solar System, comets follow tracks around the Sun.

11) What name is given to the path followed by a comet?
12) Draw a diagram showing the shape of the path followed by a comet around the Sun.
13) Give the name of the shape formed by the path of a comet.
14) Explain how this shape differs from the paths followed by the planets.
15) *Comets are made from ice and rock. Their tails form as the ice melts and is left behind.* Explain why a bright comet will fade with time as it completes more and more orbits of the Sun.

Halley's Comet

It was thought that comets were part of our atmosphere. However in 1577 AD, the Danish Astronomer Tycho Brahe proved that they were celestial bodies. The famous English astronomer Edmund Halley observed a bright comet in 1682, and concluded the same comet had appeared in 1607 and 1531. He predicted that the comet would return.

16) What value did Halley find for the orbital period of the comet?
17) What year did he predict for the next appearance of the comet?

We are now in the Space Age. Several space missions were planned to Halley's comet.

18) In which year did one of these missions (Giotto) observe the comet?

Other Comets

There are some comets in the solar system that have been trapped by the gravity of the planets. They orbit the Sun with periods of between 3.3 and 9 years.

19) Which planet do you think will have had greatest gravitational effect on these comets?
20) Will these comets be as bright as those with longer orbit times? Explain your reasoning.

American space scientists have been designing missions to look at the larger asteroids, and maybe landing robots on them. If they are made from ice, then they would be a useful source of water for other space missions.

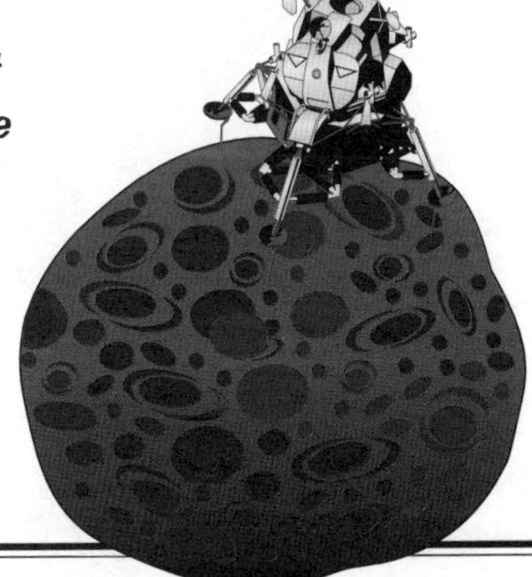

21) List the difficulties a space mission to an asteroid would suffer from, compared with a mission to a planet like Mars.

Top Tips

There's a lot more stuff in the solar system than just planets. All the things on this page are really just big chunks of rock or ice, even the cool and exciting ones like comets and shooting stars. Don't let that dull your enthusiasm, though. You need to know about moons, asteroids, meteorites and comets, because they could ask you about them in the Exam. Also, remember how the orbit of a comet is different from the orbits of the planets.

Satellites

Artificial Satellites

1) *Artificial Satellites have been used for different purposes since the first successful launch in the 1950's. Today, satellites play an important role in our lives. The following statements can describe the motion of satellites.*

> *A. a high orbit*
> *B. a low orbit*
> *C. geosynchronous*
> *D. move across the sky*
> *E. above the atmosphere*
> *F. in a polar orbit*
> *G. in an equatorial orbit*
> *H. orbits in a few hours*
> *I. orbits in 24 hours*

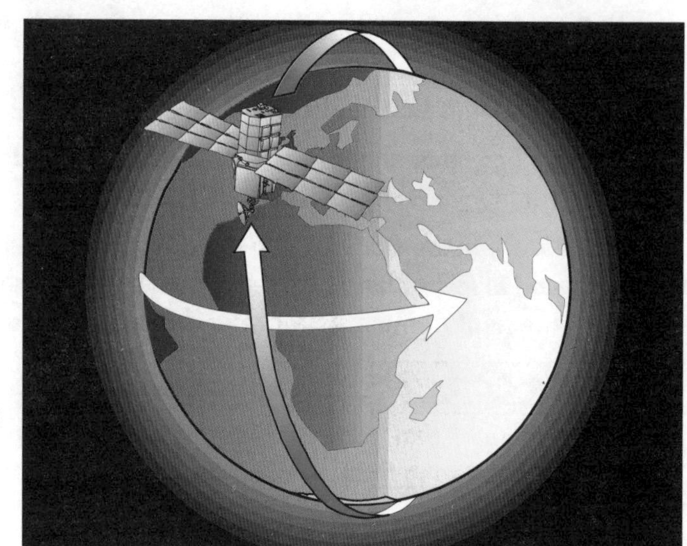

Which of the statements above will apply to:

a) communications satellites?
b) most weather satellites?
c) spy satellites?
d) satellites broadcasting TV pictures?

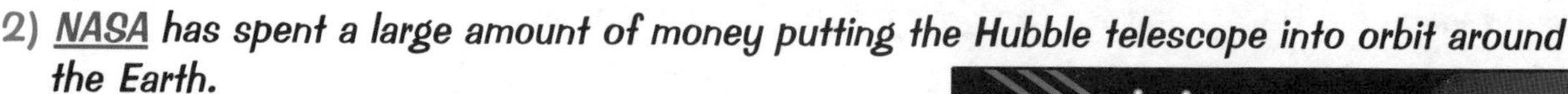

2) *NASA has spent a large amount of money putting the Hubble telescope into orbit around the Earth.*

a) What are the advantages of having the telescope in orbit?
b) Why is this helpful to the scientists?

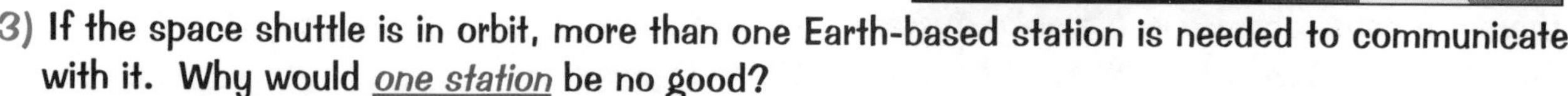

3) If the space shuttle is in orbit, more than one Earth-based station is needed to communicate with it. Why would one station be no good?

Powering Artificial Satellites

4) *Satellites use power. The first models used batteries but modern ones use fuel cells or arrays of solar cells on large panels.*

a) Why is the solar cell arrangement a good one for satellites?
b) Why do satellites generally need small rocket motors and fuel sources, even though there is no air resistance in space?
c) When Britain had a space launch program of its own, the launches took place in Australia and not Britain. Explain why.

5) *When the Voyager spacecraft was sent off to study Jupiter and Saturn, its power was generated by Radioisotope Thermoelectric Generators rather than solar cell arrays.*

a) Why do you think an alternative power source was needed?
b) Why do you think some people were concerned when Voyager was launched?
c) Although satellites and other bits of "space junk" do come back towards Earth, very little actually reaches the surface. Why is this?
d) People who design satellites spend very little time and effort making them streamlined. Why?

Satellites

Geostationary Orbits

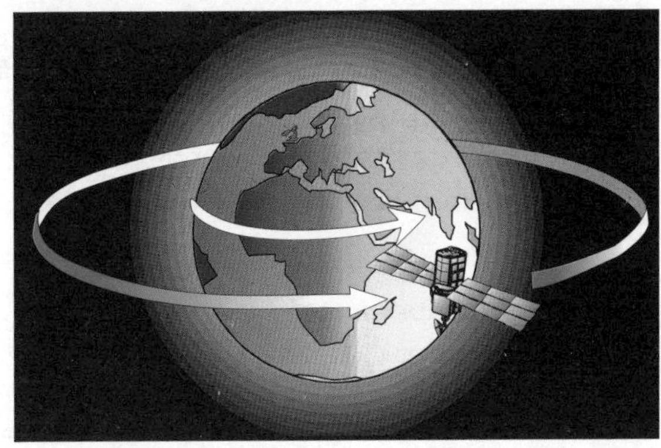

6) *A geostationary orbit is achieved by arranging that the time to complete one orbit is 24 hours. It is possible to do a bit of mathematics, and come up with an equation for any satellite in orbit.*

a) Write an expression for the speed v, of a satellite in a geostationary orbit in terms of the radius R, and the time T, to complete one orbit. *(Just use speed = distance travelled / time taken)*

Another equation for calculating the speed of a satellite in orbit is:

$$v^2 = \frac{(G \times M)}{R}$$

where: G = *gravitational constant* = (6.7×10^{-11} Nm^2/kg^2)
M = *mass of the Earth* = (6.0×10^{24} kg)
R = *radius of orbit (m)*

b) The equation obtained in a) and the expression above both contain "v". Use these two equations to eliminate v, then find the radius, R of the orbit.

c) Using the fact that the radius of the Earth is 6.4×10^6 m, calculate the height above the Earth for a geostationary orbit.

d) The speed of radio waves is 3.0×10^8 m/s. How long does it take signals to reach the satellite from the Earth?

e) How much energy is required to take a 1 kg satellite from the surface of the Earth to the required height?

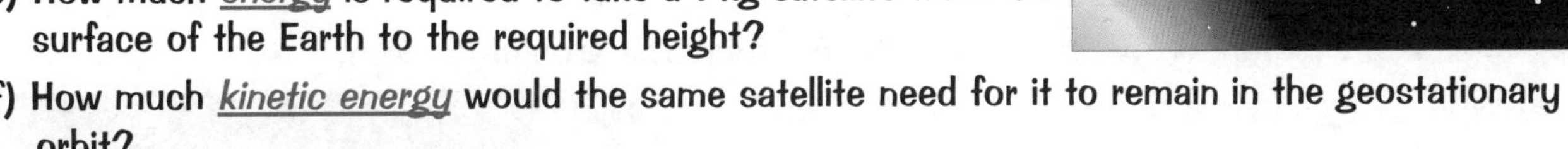

f) How much kinetic energy would the same satellite need for it to remain in the geostationary orbit?

Gravitational Forces

7) *The Moon is smaller than the Earth. Its centre is situated 3.8×10^8 metres from the centre of the Earth.*

a) Using the figures in the table below, calculate the gravitational field due to the Moon that we experience on the Earth's surface. (*Recall how gravitational strength varies with distance.*)

	Surface field (N/kg)	Radius (km)
Earth	9.8	6400
Moon	1.6	1600

b) What effect do seagoing folk experience due to this small field?

c) Consider a point on a straight line, 3.451×10^8m from Earth, between the Earth and the Moon. What is the gravitational strength due to the Earth at this point, to 2 significant figures? What is it due to the Moon? What is the overall effect of these forces?

Top Tips

More groovy space stuff, this time all man-made. First of all, you need to know why people put satellites up there in the first place. Make sure you learn the difference between geostationary and polar orbit satellites — it's important, because you have to be able to say which orbits are used for which purposes. It's all there in question 1. There's marks there to be grabbed if you learn all the little facts about satellites, and it's not too complicated.

The Causes of Days and Seasons

The Earth's Days and Seasons

1) Complete the following statements below.

a) The time taken for the Earth to rotate once is called a __________.
b) Locations along the __________ always have about 12 hours of day and 12 hours of night.
c) People experience ______________ on the side of the Earth facing the Sun.
d) On June 21st, places North of the __________ will have 24 hours of daylight.
e) The hemispheres of the Earth tilt (*away from* / *towards*) the sun during their winter.
f) The tilt of the ________ is the cause of the seasons on the Earth and other planets.
g) The average temperature in the northern hemisphere should __________ during summer.
h) The season when the days are getting shorter and the nights longer is _____________.
i) At the North Pole, the Sun never ___________ on December 21st.
j) When the northern hemisphere is experiencing spring, the season that the southern hemisphere experiences is ______________.
k) The Sun is below the horizon for __________ hours on September 21st.
l) At midsummer the Sun rises due ___________ in the U.K.
m) At midday in the southern hemisphere the Sun appears to lie in the __________.
n) The time taken for one complete orbit of the Sun by the Earth is called a _____________.

The Sun and the Earth

2) Look at the picture below that shows the Earth in orbit around the Sun.

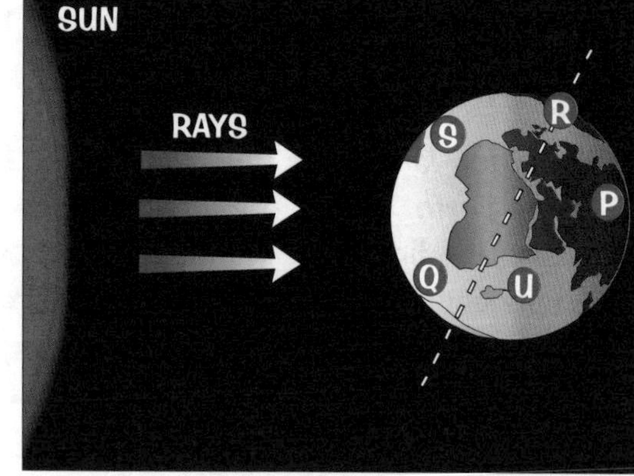

a) What *season* is it in the southern hemisphere?
b) Which letter in the picture corresponds to a location where the sun is *just setting*.
c) Which letter is positioned at the North Pole?
d) If there are no clouds, what will be seen at P?
e) If there are no clouds, what will be seen at Q?
f) Which letter is in the place you would expect 12 hours of daylight and 12 hours of night?
g) Which letter corresponds to a location with 24 hours of *darkness*.
h) If the Earth's axis was not tilted, where would the Sun be seen throughout the day from the North pole? Would it appear to move, or stay still?

Something to Think About..

3) *Everyone knows that the northern hemisphere is warmer in the summer than in the winter, but sometimes people explain this (incorrectly) by saying, " The tilt of the Earth means that the northern hemisphere is closer to the Sun than the rest of the Earth. Therefore it is warmer in the north and cooler in the south."*

How would you argue the case against this explanation given above?

The Causes of Days and Seasons

The Orbit of the Earth

4) In the table below there are a number of facts a) to l).

Fact	Rotation of the Earth	Tilt of Axis	Something Else
a) Sometimes the sky is light - at other times it is dark.			
b) In Britain, the Sun rises later throughout the month of May.			
c) The skiing season in most of France is December through April, whereas it is July through October in New Zealand.			
d) A low pressure area brings unsettled weather.			
e) A timed exposure picture of the sky taken at night shows curved tracks.			
f) A sundial can be used to tell the time on a sunny day.			
g) At midday in June, shadows are shorter than at midday in January (for the U.K.).			
h) The weather in the centre of the U.S.A. is more extreme than that near a coast.			
i) In June, daylight in Scotland lasts longer than in Wales. It is shorter in December.			
j) In Britain, shadows caused by the Sun point west in the morning, and east in the evening.			
k) In Britain, the Sun rises further north in June than in December.			
l) Lunar eclipses do not occur every month.			

Complete the table (with ticks in the appropriate column) by deciding for each of the facts whether it is due to the *rotation* of the Earth, the *tilt* of the Earth's *axis*, or *something else*.

Top Tips Isn't it brilliant how the sun rises and sets and we have winter and summer every single year. The stuff on this page does seem a bit repetitive, I admit, but you do *really* need to know *why* and *how* day and night and the seasons come about. Think about the statements in Question 1 and *explain* them in terms of the movement of the earth around the sun. (Of course, the movement of the earth only explains the seasons, not the actual weather you get)

The Universe

In the Beginning...

1) *All the stars and galaxies that we see around us in the Universe today, started off in the distant past as huge clouds of gas and dust. These clouds collapsed to form what we see today.*

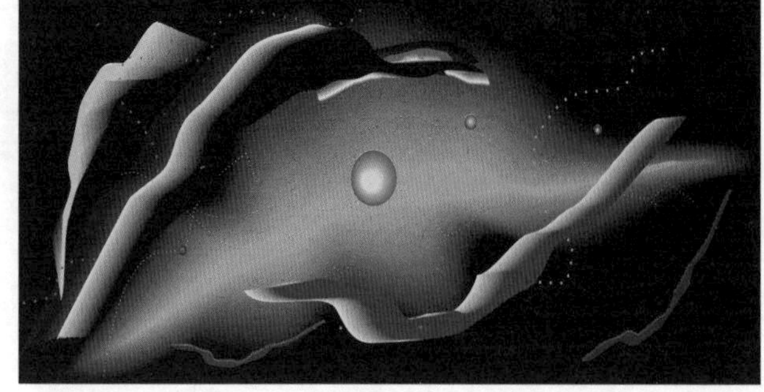

a) What caused the clouds to *collapse*?

b) *As the clouds collapsed, nuclear fusion reactions began to occur within them.* What caused these reactions to take place?

c) Explain what is believed to have happened when the nuclear reactions started.

The masses of some of the clouds were not large enough for nuclear reactions to begin when they collapsed.

d) Name *two* other things that may be formed when this occurs.

e) Why does everything we see in the Universe have a tendency *to rotate*?

The Milky Way

2) *Our Solar System is part of the Milky Way.*

a) What is the Milky Way?

b) At night time, a milky white band can be seen stretching right across the sky. What characteristic of the Milky Way gives rise to this appearance?

3) Below are some facts about our Milky Way. For each one, decide whether it is *true* or *false*.

☐ a) Neighbouring stars in the Milky Way are usually much further apart than the planets in the Solar System.

☐ b) The Milky Way is about 10,000 light years across.

☐ c) The Milky Way is at the centre of the Universe.

☐ d) There are many known solar systems in the Milky Way.

☐ e) Our Solar System is at the centre of the Milky Way.

☐ f) The Milky Way has spiral arms.

☐ g) The stars we see at night are part of the Milky Way.

☐ h) The Milky Way takes a long time to rotate.

☐ i) The Milky Way is the biggest of its kind.

☐ j) The Milky Way is separated from its neighbours by lots of empty space.

☐ k) There are still gas clouds in the Milky Way.

☐ l) No more stars will form in the Milky Way.

The Universe

The Milky Way

4) How many stars are there in the Milky Way? Choose the closest answer.

☐ HUNDREDS ☐ THOUSANDS ☐ MILLIONS ☐ TRILLIONS

Light Years

5) A Light Year *is not a period of time. It is a distance that scientists use to measure distances in the Universe.*

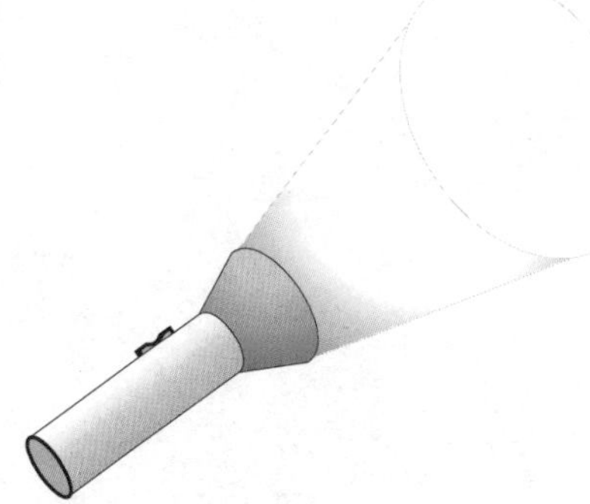

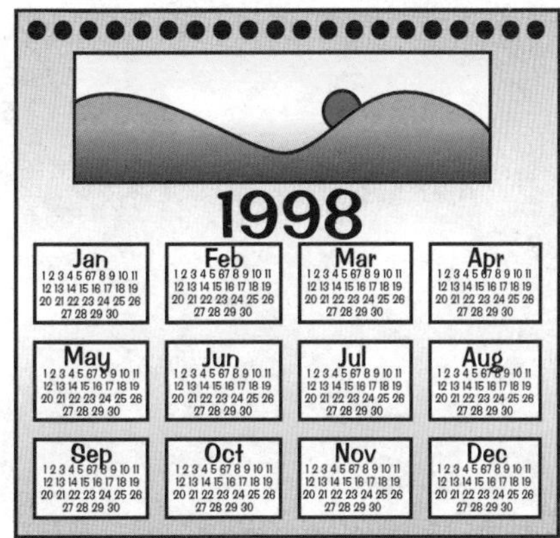

a) Why is the light year a better unit of distance to use in space than the metre or kilometre?

The table below shows some distances in light years and minutes. Light from the Sun takes about 8 minutes to reach us.

Distance from	Distance
Earth to Sun	8 light minutes
Earth to nearest star from Sun	4.2 light years
Earth to star in question	10 light years

b) If the speed of light through a vacuum is 3.0×10^8 m/s (300,000,000 m/s), calculate the distance in metres between the Sun and the Earth.

A relatively nearby star is 10 light years from the Earth.

c) Calculate the distance in metres from the Earth to this star.

The nearest star to Earth is 4.2 light years away.

d) What is the least distance there could be between this star and the star in question c) above?

e) What is the greatest possible distance between them?

Top Tips

It's big. The Universe is very, very, very, big. Think about this: Our sun is one of millions in the Milky Way galaxy, the Milky Way is 100 000 light years across and there are over a billion galaxies in the universe, all of them millions of light years apart, separated by empty space. It's enough to make your head hurt. Remember that a light year is the distance that light travels in a year — light travels very fast, so a light year is a very long way.

The Life Cycle of Stars

Astronomers have been studying groups of stars. They have used their observations to come up with an idea for how they think some of the stars evolved.

This "Life Cycle" is illustrated in the diagram below.

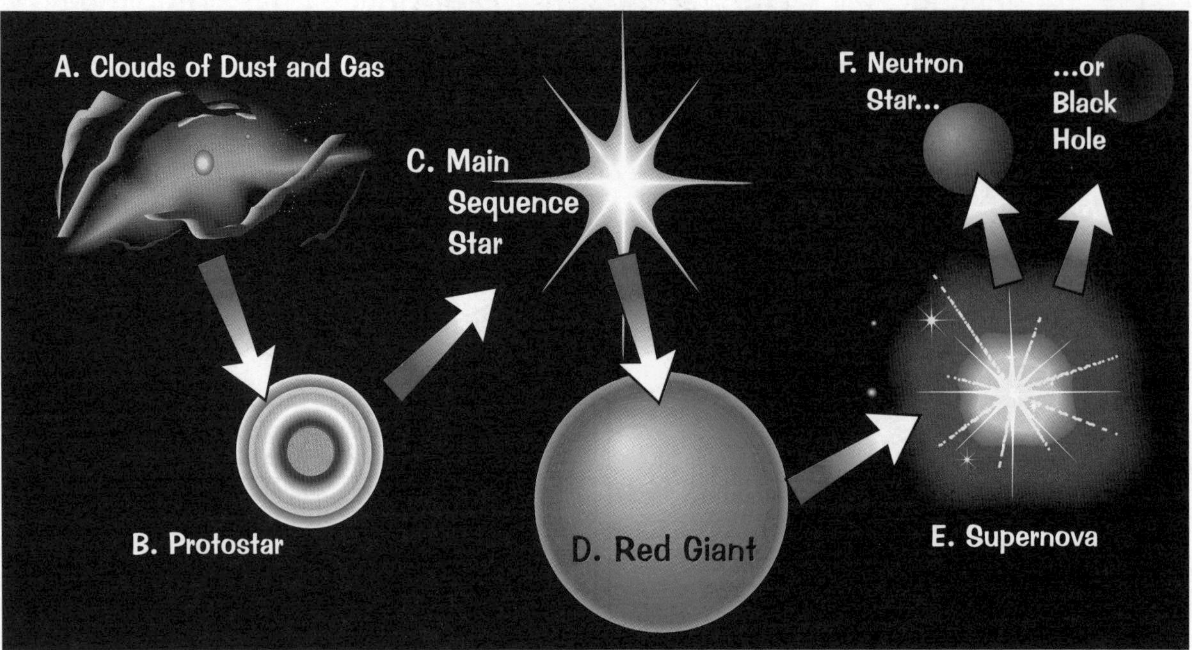

1) What *type of star* follows this life cycle?
2) Which type of star is our Sun?

From Birth to the Main Sequence

3) The scientists' ideas about stages A and B above are uncertain. Suggest why it is difficult to find *evidence* about these stages.
4) At a certain stage in the life cycle, the temperature inside a star exerts an outward force. What *causes* the inward force?
5) At which stage in the cycle do these forces balance each other?

The Final Stages

6) In the diagram above, many *heavier atoms* are made just before which stage?
7) What is happening to make the red giant star *redder* than a main sequence star?
8) How does the matter making up neutron stars and black holes *differ* from the matter we are used to on Earth?

Miscellaneous

9) *Explain why* astronomers need to study a group of stars rather than just one or two, when studying life cycles.
10) The first stars were formed from just two different elements. *Which elements are these*?
11) What is the process in which *energy* can be created when atoms are forced together?
12) Draw the life cycle for a small star (like our Sun).
13) Briefly explain how energy generation *in stars* is different from energy generation in most of the nuclear reactors on Earth.

The Life Cycle of Stars

Black Holes

14) *If a star is large enough and its nuclear fuel is used up, it may collapse to form a black hole. The density increases as the star collapses, until not even light can escape from the surface.*

> *Light can not escape if the radius of the star is less than or equal to $2GM/c^2$.*
> G = gravitational constant = 6.7×10^{-11} Nm²/kg²
> M = mass of star in kg
> c = speed of light in a vacuum = 3.0×10^8 m/s

a) Given that the mass of the Sun is 2×10^{30} kg, *calculate the radius* to which it would have to collapse to form a black hole.

b) Work out the *mass* of 1m³ of material in this black hole.

Supernova Explosions and Nebulae

15) *The Crab Nebula is the remnant of a Supernova explosion that was observed on Earth by Chinese astronomers in the year 1054 AD.*

> The famous American astronomer Edwin Hubble (remember him?) observed the light from the gas cloud around the nebula, and found that it was expanding at about 1×10^6 m/s. The nebula is about 900 light years from Earth.

a) What year (on Earth) did the explosion take place?

b) Why was the explosion not observed until 1054 AD?

c) Describe how Hubble might have measured the expansion speed of the gas cloud.

d) *Work out* the diameter of the gas cloud now (Earth Time), assuming that the expansion speed has been constant.

Clusters of Stars...

16) *When astronomers look at a compact group of stars that are in the same region of space, they assume that they have all formed at about the same time.*

Give a reason why very old groups of stars seem to contain *very few massive* stars.

> **Top Tips** Just like you, stars have a long and interesting life story, full of change and upheaval. You need to learn the story and get all the stages in the right order. Don't forget there's a *difference* between what happens to *big stars* and what happens to *small stars* after middle age (and it's not to do with whether or not they get into Who's Who or have to make do with This is Your Life). As if that's not enough, there's also a difference between *first generation* and *second generation* stars to remember. *Learn* that life story.

The Origin of the Universe

Theories on the Origin of the Universe...

1) *We know quite a lot about the Universe and how it is changing.*

Name and describe the *two main theories* that try to explain how the Universe began and continues to evolve?

2) For each fact below, state which theory it could be explained by. (*Both* theories may apply)

a) The galaxies are all moving away from each other.
b) Galaxies have red shifts.
c) There seem to be galaxies in every direction.
d) Space is filled with a low frequency radiation coming from all directions.
e) Further away galaxies are moving away from us faster.

Expansion of the Universe

3) Using the following words, *complete the paragraph* about the expansion of the Universe:
receding, larger, distant, speeds, Hubble's

"The expansion of the Universe is described by __________ Law. This says that more __________ galaxies have greater __________ than nearer ones. This means that far away galaxies are __________ faster than nearby ones. We can conclude that the Universe is getting __________ as time goes on."

4) Knowing that the Universe expands, its age can be worked out.

a) How old is the Universe?
b) How has this figure been arrived at?
c) Are all the scientists definite about this figure?
d) What is the main factor preventing an accurate estimate of the age?
e) Explain why the Universe won't expand at the same rate for ever.

Steady State Theory

5) *A lot of the observations of the Universe can be explained by the Steady State Theory, but scientists have two big problems with it.*

a) What is observed that cannot easily be explained by the theory?
b) What is the *other problem* that scientists point out with the theory?

The Origin of the Universe

Changing Frequencies

6) *When an object moves relative to an observer, the frequency of the electromagnetic radiation received by the observer changes.*

a) What is the name of this effect?
b) What happens to the observed frequency if an object is approaching?
c) What happens to the observed frequency of an object that is receding?
d) Give two examples from everyday life of this effect in action.

7) *The picture below is a representation of part of a light wave emitted by a galaxy.*

a) Copy the wave, and show how it is changed by the galaxy's movement away from us.
b) If the galaxy is replaced with a loudspeaker, describe what you would hear as it moves away with a gradually increasing velocity.
c) *This change to the light waves emitted by galaxies has been happening throughout the Universe's history, and has been happening to the background radiation as well.*

What type of radiation was the background radiation when the Universe was very, very, young?

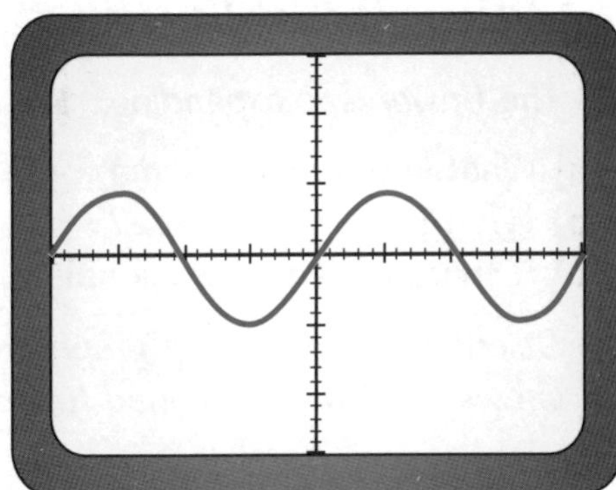

Background Radiation

8) *Some statements about the background radiation are given below. Some are true, some are false.* You have to choose which are which.

True	False	
☐	☐	a) The background radiation has a low frequency.
☐	☐	b) The background radiation is easily explained by the Steady State theory.
☐	☐	c) The background radiation is coming from all directions.
☐	☐	d) The background radiation comes from all parts of the Universe.
☐	☐	e) The background radiation is ultra violet.
☐	☐	f) The background radiation has changed since the Universe started.
☐	☐	g) The background radiation was created well after the beginning of the Universe.
☐	☐	h) The background radiation is microwave radiation.
☐	☐	i) If we travelled to another part of the Universe, the background radiation would be the same.

Top Tips How the Universe began, now there's a question to ponder. These pages concern the two main theories about the beginning of the Universe and how we know what happened in the distant past. Scientists need evidence, and there are two important factors that you need to know about — the red shift, the fact that far away galaxies are more red-shifted, and the uniform background radiation. The Big Bang theory explains most of the evidence, so it is the most popular theory.

The Future of the Universe

Factors that determine the Future of the Universe

1) Two factors help to determine how the Universe evolves.
   a) What are these two factors?
   b) One of them is easy to measure, one is a lot more difficult. Which is which?

2) *Measuring the total amount of mass in the Universe is not easy. Some matter is easy to see because it shines, and scientists can measure its mass. The rest is difficult, because we just cannot see it.* For each of the objects below, choose which are visible and which are invisible.

Supergiant Stars	Interstellar Dust	White Dwarf Stars	Black Holes
Large Planets	Black Dwarves	Main Sequence Stars	Dust between the Galaxies

Expansion of the Universe

3) *The Universe is expanding. We can be sure about this much.*
   a) What is the name of the force that could be slowing down the rate of expansion?
   b) What causes this force?
   c) If there were no forces acting, how would the Universe continue to evolve?

4) *Scientists love drawing graphs to show what is happening in the Universe. The graph below shows what has happened to the size of the Universe up to now.*

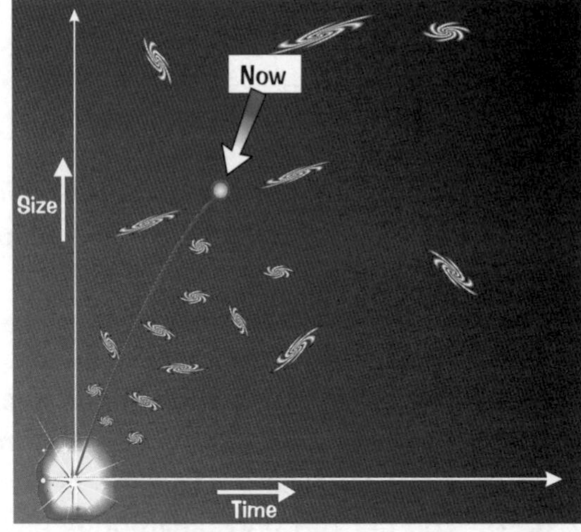

   a) The curve on the graph opposite is not a straight line but rises less and less steeply. What does this tell us about the expansion of the Universe?
   b) On two copies of this graph, sketch the two possible futures for how the Universe might evolve from now on.

5) Complete the paragraph using the following words:

Universe, Solar System, 4.5 billion years, radioactivity, Universe, 2 billion years, Moon, Earth

> The first calculations made by scientists about the age of the ________ gave an age of only ________. This result was a big surprise because previous ________ measurements on rocks from the ________(and later the ________) showed the age of the Solar System to be about ________. The ________ can't be older than the ________!!!

6) The end of the world as we know it....
   a) What is the "Big Crunch"?
   b) How long *(at least...)* have we got before it occurs? *(if it occurs...)*

7) Make another copy of the graph in Question 4. This time, extend it so that it illustrates a cyclical Universe; one that expands, then contracts, and then expands again.

The Future of the Universe

Observing The Universe

8) *We can look out into the very distant reaches of the Universe using telescopes.*
   a) Are we looking *forward* into the future, or *back* into the past?
   b) Galaxies are believed to evolve from active objects to quiescent objects. *Explain* why we do not see as many quiescent galaxies in the distant Universe compared to the nearby Universe.

9) *If there is less than a "certain critical amount" of mass in the Universe —*
   a) What would happen to the Universe in the future?
   b) Why in the very distant future will the Universe be much *darker* and *colder*.
   c) Why will there be no humans around on Earth to witness the end of the universe?

Hubble's Constant

10) *Hubble's Constant is a number that allows scientists to relate the distance to a galaxy with how fast it's moving away. This then allows them to work out how long the Universe has been expanding for, and therefore its age. Different scientists have different values for H. It is now thought that the Hubble constant lies in the range (0.5 – 1.0) x 10^{-10}/year. The age of the Universe is then just 1/H.* Using these figures *answer* the following questions:
   a) *Calculate* an *upper* and a *lower* limit for the age of the Universe.
   b) *Some old stars are reckoned to be at least 16 thousand million years old.* *What problems* does this throw up?
   c) If the value for H has been overestimated (i.e. too large), *what effect* would this have on the calculated age of the Universe?

The Composition and Density of the Universe

11) *One of the substances that astronomers look for in space is deuterium. The symbol for deuterium is* $^{2}_{1}D$*, and it can be observed by looking for the radiation it emits (wavelength 92cm). The amount of deuterium observed allows astronomers to estimate the overall mass of the visible matter in the Universe.*
   a) What is the *mass number* of deuterium?
   b) What is the *atomic number* of deuterium?
   c) How many *protons* and *neutrons* are there in an atom of deuterium?
   d) Which element is deuterium a form of?
   e) What do we call an atom such as deuterium?
   f) Which part of the electromagnetic spectrum does the light emitted by deuterium come from?

12) *When we look at the Universe now, its observable radius is approximately 1.4×10^{26}m. Astronomers are very concerned about the "critical mass density", which will tell us whether or not the Universe is open or closed. This is thought to be about 2×10^{-26} kg/m^3.*
   a) Considering the observable Universe as a sphere, *what is its volume*?
   b) If the density of the Universe is equal to the critical density, *how much mass* would there be in each cubic metre (m^3)?
   c) What would the *total mass* of the Universe be?

Top Tips The *end* of the Universe — even more mindbogglingly fascinating than the beginning of the Universe. The bottom line here is that there are *two* alternatives — the Universe could begin to collapse in on itself in a *Big Crunch*, or it could just keep on *expanding for ever*, getting more and more spread out. This would depend on the *total mass* of the Universe, compared to *how fast* the galaxies are moving apart. As you'd expect, working out the total mass of the Universe from observations is very difficult.

Energy Transfer

Types of Energy

1) What is the *significant* type of energy involved in each of the following?

a) A drawn longbow.
b) A red hot welder's rivet.
c) A mole of unstable uranium–235 atoms.
d) A piece of glowing magnesium.
e) A plate balancing on a pole.
f) A wire carrying a telephone conversation.
g) A high-calorie birthday cake.
h) A speeding bullet.

Energy Changes

2) *In each of the following examples, energy is being changed from one type into another.*
In some cases, two or more types may be produced. State what the *changes* are for:

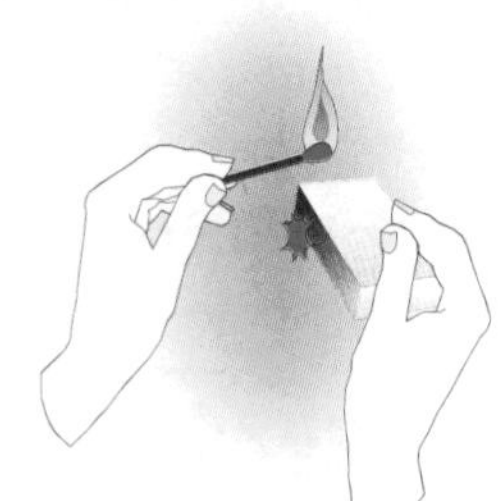

a) a descending rollercoaster car,
b) a crossbow bolt hitting a target,
c) a singer shouting into a microphone,
d) a cycle wheel spinning a dynamo,
e) a yo-yo climbing up its string,
f) a match being struck,
g) a magnifying glass concentrating the Sun's rays to burn a hole in a piece of paper,
h) a battery driving an analogue clock (one with hands),
i) a diver coming down on a springboard.

3) *In each of the following examples, energy is being changed from one type to another.* *Work out* the missing energy types (there may be more than one in each case). For each one, name another object that performs the same energy change.

a) A radio changes .... energy to .... energy.
b) A match changes .... energy to .... energy.
c) A light bulb changes .... energy to .... energy.
d) A catapult changes .... energy to .... energy.
e) A hydroelectric dam changes .... energy to .... energy.

f) An electric fire changes .... energy to .... energy.
g) An atomic bomb changes .... energy to .... energy.
h) A microphone changes .... energy to .... energy.
i) A car engine changes .... energy to .... energy.
j) A human body changes .... energy to .... energy.

Energy Transfer

A short story...

4) *The following story mentions many changes of energy from one type to another. List as many as you can, in each case giving the two types of energy involved and, if possible, another example of the same change.*

Secret Agent Serge Flambert was in big trouble. He was tied to a work bench in the evil professor's laboratory.
A candle was burning through the string holding up a sharp sword above his heart. Luckily the miniature saw fitted to his watch was cutting through his bonds. The tight elastic holding him snapped and flew across the room. Serge rolled off the workbench and on to the slippery floor. He slid across the floor and into the wall with a thump. Moments later, the candle burned through the string. The heavy sword dropped and stuck into the workbench.

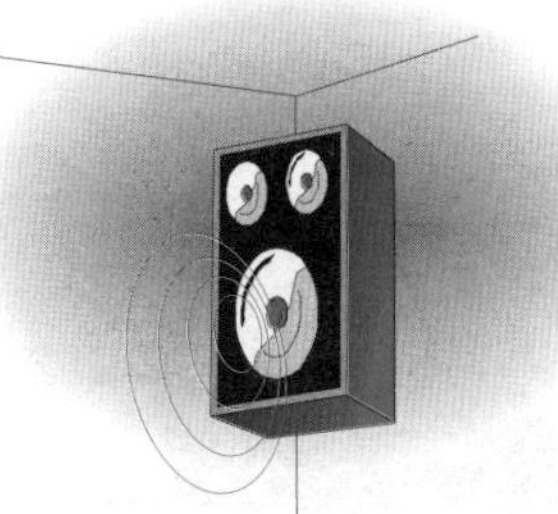

"Ahh, I see that you have escaped the first peril." The professor's voice came from a loudspeaker attached to the wall. "However, if you put your hand on the wall behind you, you will find out about the next stage of my fiendish plan."

Serge looked up and saw the CCTV camera that was obviously being used to spy on him. One shot from his revolver and the camera was history. He put his hand to the wall. It felt warm.
From his research, Serge knew that the professor had a miniature nuclear reactor in the next room. It was obviously going critical.

Serge ran to the opposite wall and removed the sole of his shoe, sticking it to the concrete. He attached his pen (detonator!) to the explosive, and retreated to the other side of the lab, unravelling the wire attached to the pen. He twisted the two ends of his tie clip so that they completed the circuit from the pen.

A controlled explosion blew out a man-sized hole in the wall, and Serge ran through it, ready to meet his next challenge.

Top Tips: You might think that all this energy transfer is complicated. But there are only *10 different types* of energy, and if you've got a good grasp of these, you won't have much trouble. Use your *imagination* — I'm sure you can come up with loads of examples.

Conservation of Energy

The Principle...

1) *Copy* and *complete* the following sentences which summarise the Principle of the Conservation of Energy:

> Energy can never be ________________ or ________________ .
> It is only ever ____________________ from one form to another.

Input Energy, Output Energy and Wasted Energy

2) *Look at the energy flow diagram shown here.* For each of the examples given below, draw an energy flow diagram. The first one has been done for you.

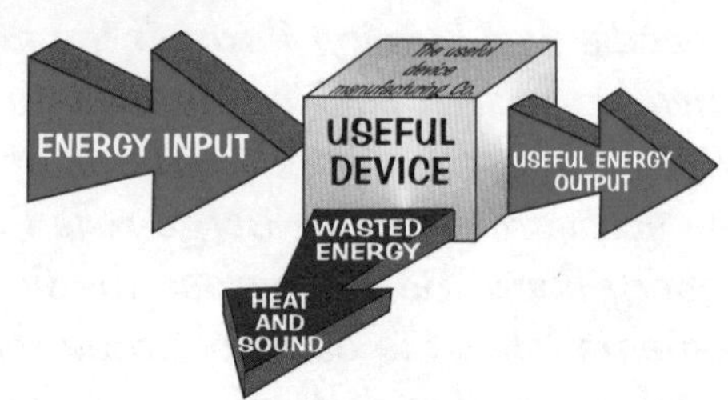

a) electric hoist.

Electric energy → HOIST → potential energy of load
↓
wasted sound and heat

b) electric light bulb.

c) electric motor.

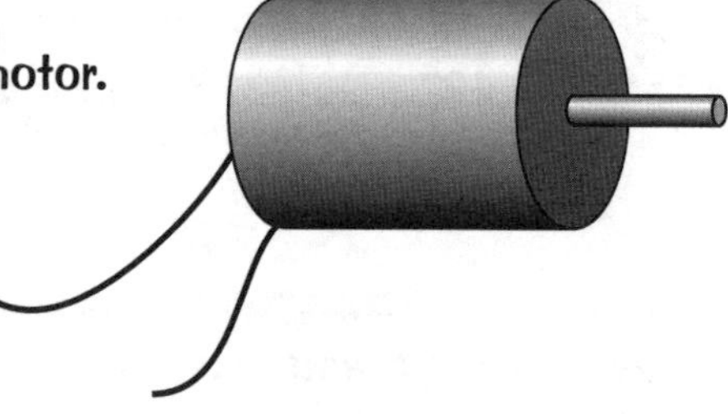

d) petrol-driven car.

e) electric kettle.

f) weightlifter lifting a weight.

g) solar cell for calculator.

h) computer monitor.

i) bicycle dynamo.

Conservation of Energy

Energy in Motor Vehicles

3) *In today's motor vehicles, lots of valuable chemical energy is changed to types of energy that are of no use to us at all.*

a) What are these useless types of energy?
b) For each type, say where in the vehicle it is wasted (there may be more than one place).

Some engineers are busy trying to overcome the particular difficulties that trains and buses have when they are starting and stopping all the time. Every time they use the brakes, energy is changed to sound and heat which is then lost. It is suggested that as an alternative, the vehicle's energy is used to power-up a flywheel to slow it down.

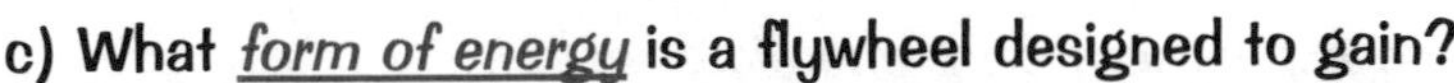

c) What form of energy is a flywheel designed to gain?
d) What will happen to the flywheel as the vehicle slows down and transfers energy to it?

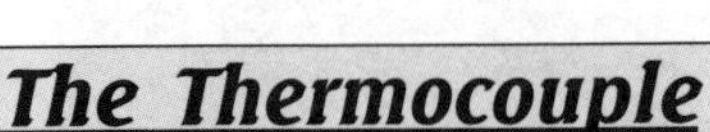

The Thermocouple

4) *Cedric has read in a book about a device called a "thermocouple". This is a device that generates electricity when one side of it is hotter than the other. Cedric thinks that this may break the Principle of the Conservation of Energy.*

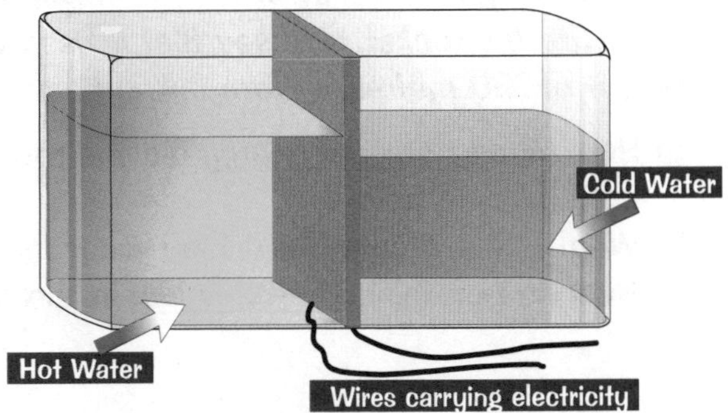

"Surely," he thinks, *"all you need to do is stick a thermocouple between a bath of water at 100°C and a bath of water at 0°C, and you'll get electricity generated for nothing."*

Explain why Cedric is wrong, and why his system doesn't break the Principle of the Conservation of Energy.

More Questions on the Conservation of Energy

5) *Some people might say that wind power and hydroelectric power are examples of getting energy for nothing.* Are they correct, and if not, where is the energy coming from?

6) *As you know, no energy transfer device is ever 100% efficient. This is because we cannot prevent the device from transforming the input energy into other, unwanted forms of energy.* What are the two most common forms of unwanted energy produced by everyday appliances?

7) *An electric heater might be 100% efficient — the exception to the rule!*

a) Explain why it can be considered to be 100% efficient. What could ruin the perfect score?
b) Is any energy wasted before it reaches the heater, and if so where?

Top Tips: When you think about all the energy wasted by motors and things like that, it's easy to forget that it all goes somewhere — it can't just disappear. The total energy *is* always conserved — you've just got to work out where it all goes. And if it doesn't add up to 100%, you've probably done something wrong.

Energy Efficiency

Some Questions involving Energy Efficiency

1) *A student wants to find out about the efficiency of a stereo system rated at 20 watts sound output. She buys some batteries, which store 400,000 joules of chemical energy. When the new batteries are put into the stereo, and the machine is switched on to play a tape, the batteries are exhausted after 5 hours.*

a) How much energy has the stereo usefully given out?
b) What is the efficiency of the tape recorder?
c) How would energy have been wasted?
d) If the stereo is used on the radio setting, would you expect the batteries to last longer? Explain your answer.

2) *A class of students are carrying out an experiment on a chemical rocket.*

The rocket has a total mass of 2kg. They load the rocket with 3000 joules worth of fuel, of negligible weight. The class fire the rocket, and see that it rises vertically to a height of 100 metres, before falling back to Earth.

a) How much potential energy did the rocket have at its highest point?
b) What is the efficiency of the rocket motor?
c) How do you think energy is lost in the system?

3) *A handyman is using an electric sander with a rechargeable battery. He charges up the sander with 2500 joules of electrical energy. It should require 20 joules of energy to sand each m^2 of surface. At the end of three hours, the rechargeable battery is exhausted. He checks his work, and finds that he has actually covered an area of $100m^2$.*

a) How much useful energy has gone into the sanding?
b) What is the efficiency of the machine?

Efficiency can change...

4) *A company is asked to study the lift in an office building. They put different loads into the lift, and then study the electrical energy that the lift consumes lifting the loads up through a distance of 20m. The results of their experiment are shown below.*

Load (N)	Energy Consumed (J)	Energy gained by load (J)	Efficiency (%)
1000	30000		
1500	34000		
2000	43400		

a) Copy and complete the table.
b) What happens to the efficiency as the load increases?
c) Explain this pattern.

Energy Efficiency

Kettles and Light Bulbs

5) *A new design of electric kettle is supposed to be 96% efficient. It needs 200,000J of energy to raise the temperature of a kettle full of water from room temperature to boiling point.*

a) How much energy will the kettle take from the mains?
b) What will the rest of the energy do?

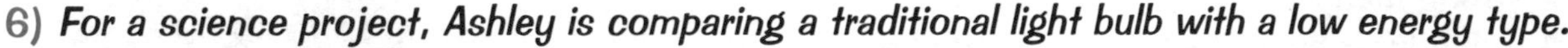

6) *For a science project, Ashley is comparing a traditional light bulb with a low energy type. Both the light bulbs give out the same amount of light.*

The traditional light bulb is rated at 100W, lasts 2000 hours and costs 50p. The low energy bulb is rated at 20W and lasts 10000 hours — but it costs £9.50.

a) How much energy does each bulb consume in 10000 hours?
b) What would this cost if electricity were charged at 2p per MJ?
c) How much would the bulbs themselves cost for this length of time?
d) Which bulb works out cheaper in the long run? Explain your answer.
e) What other considerations might you make when buying a low energy bulb?

Lifting Loads

7) *My local garage uses a pulley system to lift the engine (weight = 3000N) up 1.5 metres from my car. It uses 6000 joules to do this.*

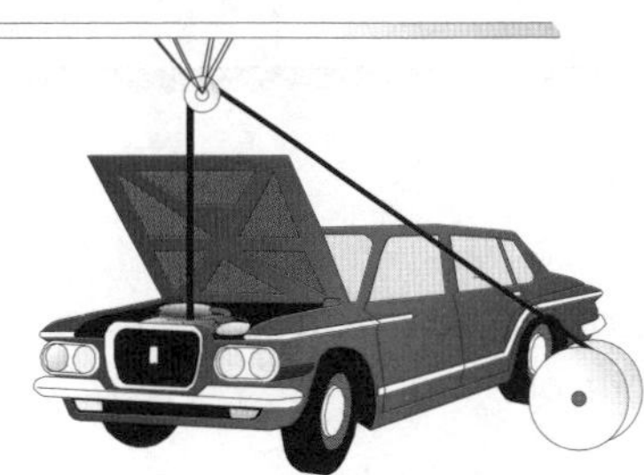

a) How much potential energy is supplied to the engine?
b) What is the efficiency of the pulley system?
c) What effect would oiling the pulley system have on its efficiency? Explain.

8) *The manufacturers claim that an electric motor is 60% efficient. In an experiment, Sandra and Joan use it to lift a mass of 5kg through a distance of 1.20 metres.*

a) How much potential energy is gained by the mass?
b) If the manufacturer's figures are correct, how much energy would you expect the motor to have used?

In fact, the motor actually consumes 110J.

c) What factors could the manufacturers say account for the discrepancy?

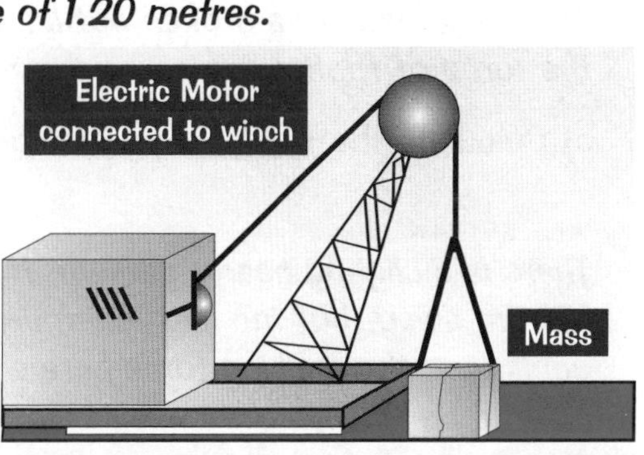

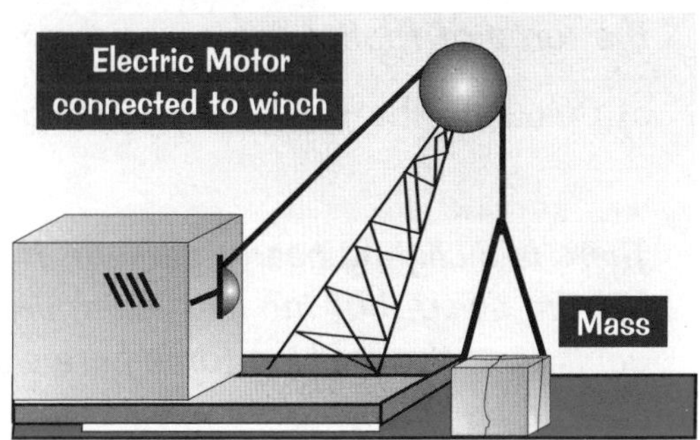

Top Tips: Energy efficiency — it's not just washing machines and light bulbs. But it is pretty simple — just one thing over another. If it comes out to more than 100% then you've probably got it upside down. If not, it's probably right. All very simple, so just hope it comes up in your Exam, and easy marks will be yours.

Work Done, Energy and Power

Work and Energy

1) Give 3 examples of everyday sources of energy that can be used to do work.

2) Which of the following involve mechanical work?

a) A shelf holding up a stack of revision books.
b) A hamster moving a treadle wheel.
c) A footpump being pushed down.
d) A strong man leaning against a brick wall.
e) A weightlifter holding 40kg above her head.
f) A railway porter carrying a passenger's two cases.
g) The railway porter holding the two cases waiting for a tip.

3) *The table shows how the force exerted by a sprinter changes with the type of training shoe worn. It also records the distance moved by the sprinter in a time of 2 seconds.*

Make a copy of the table and complete the final column showing the work done.

a) What units should be used for the work done column?
b) What force is the work mainly done against?

Brand of trainer	Force (N)	Distance (m)	Work Done
Two Stripes	4.2	1.6	
Big Cross	5.6	0.8	
Off Balance	4.8	1.2	
Obverse	5.9	1.4	
High Vest	4.5	0.9	

Pushing Cars...

4) *My old car breaks down. Luckily the road is flat. There is a garage 1500 metres away. My car manual says it needs a minimum force of 700N to push the car along a flat road.*

a) What is the minimum energy I will need to give the car to get it to the garage?

The car goes over a broken bottle, still 600m from the garage. A tyre bursts and the force of friction increases the required pushing force to 900N.

b) Calculate the total energy consumption in this case.

There is a slightly nearer garage. It is only 1300m away, but the last 100m are uphill, and the pushing force here would have to be 1150N.

c) Would I save any energy by pushing the car to this second garage, assuming that in both cases I avoid any broken bottles?

Work Done, Energy and Power

More Questions Involving Energy

5) *Scott and Sheila are waterskiing over a 400m course. When it's Scott's turn, a forcemeter on the tow rope registers a force of 475N. When Sheila has a go, the forcemeter registers 425N.*

a) Calculate the energy needed to pull each skier over the course.

b) Why would the total energy consumed by the boat be more than this in each case?

Scott now starts to show off and puts in some turns. He manages to fit in 4 turns, each of 30m, but now only travels 320m in a straight line. During each turn, the forcemeter measures 520N.

c) Calculate the energy needed to pull Scott over the course in this case.

Energy and Power

6) *A saw in a sawmill cuts wood into planks. The cutting of each plank uses up 2kJ of energy. When it is working at maximum power, the saw can divide 12 planks a minute.*

a) How much energy is used by the saw in a minute?

b) Calculate the maximum power of the saw.

7) *Karl is fitting an electric motor to his radio-controlled car. The motor is rated at 50 Watts, and it can move the car along a straight track in a time of 5 seconds.*

a) Assuming that the motor is 100% efficient, how much energy does the motor use up?

b) If Karl fitted a more powerful, 60 Watt motor to his car, how long would it now take to do the same amount of work?

8) *An electric kettle is rated at 2400 watts.*

a) How long would it take to supply 288kJ to the water in the kettle?

b) In real life, the time needed would be longer than this. Explain why.

9) *James Watt was a pioneer of the steam engine. His steam engines took over from horse and water driven machinery, and the first machines had their power given in terms of horsepower.*

Given that Watt's "standard horse" could pull with a force of 500N whilst walking at 1.5 m/s, work out the equivalent value in watts for 1 horsepower.

10) Copy and complete the following table which gives the results for some experiments carried out on a number of electric motors.

Name of Motor	Work Done (J)	Time Taken	Power (W)
Fury	150	30s	
Apollo		45s	20
Gemini	300		30
Vostok	4000	5 mins	
Soyuz		3 mins	15

Top Tips: There's lots of calculations here, but nothing demanding. Just draw and remember the energy efficiency triangle, and you're nearly there. Practice, that's the key to getting the marks. If you're still getting your energy inputs and outputs muddled — and your answers above 100% — then you need to practise some more.

Kinetic Energy and Potential Energy

In the following questions, take g, the acceleration due to gravity, as $10m/s^2$.

1) Answer these questions on the basics of kinetic energy.
 a) What is the formula for kinetic energy?
 b) What do each of the terms in the equation stand for?
 c) Give some examples of the kinds of objects that have kinetic energy?

2) Some questions on gravitational potential energy.
 a) What is the formula for gravitational potential energy?
 b) What do each of the terms stand for?
 c) Give some examples of the kinds of objects that gain or lose gravitational potential energy?

3) This question consists of a list of statements a) to h). Some are true and some are false. Write down which are true, and which are false.

a) If two objects are travelling at the same velocity, the one with the greater mass will have more kinetic energy.
b) Gravitational potential energy is the only type of potential energy in which scientists are interested.
c) Two objects of the same mass will always have the same kinetic energy.
d) If one object is double the height above ground than another with the same mass, it will have double the kinetic energy.
e) Kinetic energy is measured in joules.
f) The faster an object travels, the greater its potential energy.
g) The gravitational field strength, g, is important when working out kinetic energy.
h) If two different cans are on the same shelf, they will have the same gravitational potential energy.

4) *The table below gives some figures for a car that is standing at traffic lights, and begins to accelerate away (at time, t=0) once they have turned green.*

Time (s)	Velocity (m/s)	Kinetic Energy (J)
0.0	0	
0.5	10	
1.0	30	
1.5		2,662,875

The mass of the car is 2630kg. Copy and complete the table.

5) Which of the following has most kinetic energy?

a) A cricket ball, mass 0.4kg travelling at 40m/s.
b) An athlete of mass 70kg jogging at 5m/s.
c) A cocker spaniel of mass 15kg running at 10m/s.
d) An industrial robot of mass 1000kg moving at 0.6m/s.
e) A bullet of mass 0.005kg travelling at 250m/s.

6) *A light aircraft is taking a group of parachutists up into the air. Dressed in her parachuting gear, Amy has a mass of 90kg. The aircraft takes the group up to a height of 5000m before they jump.*

 a) How much gravitational potential energy does Amy gain?

 Amy jumps from the aircraft and free falls to a height of 3000m before opening her main parachute.

 b) How much more gravitational potential energy does she have when this happens than when she started off on the ground?

 The main parachute fails to open properly. Amy jettisons it — its mass is 5kg — and opens her reserve parachute.

 c) How much gravitational potential energy does she have when she is 1500m above the ground?

Kinetic Energy and Potential Energy

More Kinetic and Potential Energy Questions

7) *A tourist's Fiat is driving along a mountain road. The combined mass of the car and luggage is 2920kg. The car is powering uphill at 23m/s.*

a) How much kinetic energy does the car have?

At the top of the road, the car has gained a total height of 1200m.

b) Calculate the potential energy the car has gained.

As the car rounds a bend at the top of the mountain, a suitcase falls from the roof into the valley below. The suitcase has a mass of 20kg.

c) Work out the potential energy the suitcase lost when it had fallen a distance of 60m.
d) If all of this potential energy of the suitcase is converted into kinetic energy, how fast will it be travelling when it has fallen 60m?
e) Explain why it will not actually be travelling as fast as this.

8) *Some workmen are using a rope to lower a bucket full of bricks from a window. They tie off the rope when the bucket is just above the ground. As they are making their way downstairs to unload the bucket, a strong wind sets the bucket swinging.*

Draw a diagram of the path of the swinging bucket. On your diagram mark with letters A, B, C and D, the place(s):

— where the potential energy is greatest.
— where the kinetic energy is greatest.
— where the bucket is travelling fastest.
— where the bucket's velocity is zero.

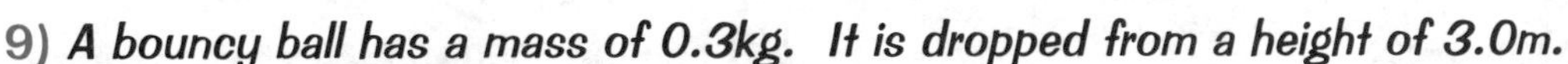

9) *A bouncy ball has a mass of 0.3kg. It is dropped from a height of 3.0m.*

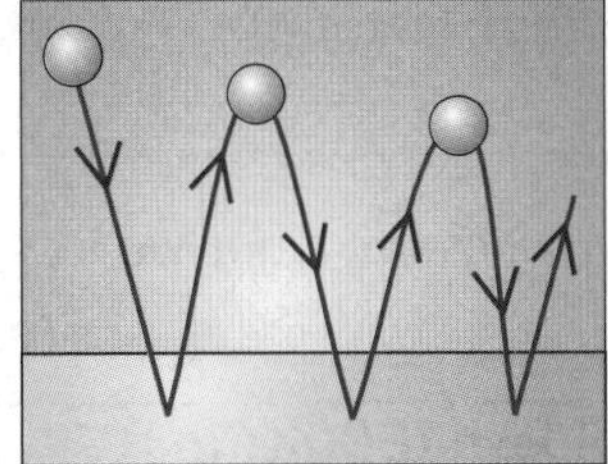

a) How much potential energy has the ball lost when it hits the ground?
b) Ignoring air resistance, how fast will the ball be travelling?

The ball rebounds vertically at a speed of 7.0m/s.

c) What kinetic energy does it now have?
d) What height will it reach on the rebound?
e) Explain what has happened to the energy that the ball has lost.

10) *Three students carry out an experiment to compare their own personal power. They measure their mass, then time how long it takes them to run up a flight of stairs 12m high.* Their results are shown in the table below. Copy and complete the table.

Name	Weight (N)	Time (s)	Potential Energy Gained (J)	Power (W)
Alex	520	14		
Billie	450	16		
Jack	600	15		

Top Tips: There's lots of maths here, but it all boils down to a couple of simple equations. They're important though — and almost bound to be in your Exams. The trickiest bit is knowing when to use them. Think about situations where both kinetic energy and potential energy are involved. For most, it's a pretty safe bet that if the PE's going down, then the KE's going up at the same rate (and vice versa).

Temperature

Heat Energy and Temperature

1) *Heat energy is supplied to a gas, a liquid and a solid.*
   a) Explain what happens to the particles when heat energy is supplied to a gas or a liquid?
   b) What happens to the particles in a solid?
   c) If there is a difference between the kinetic energy that one set of particles has, and the kinetic energy of some neighbouring particles, what will happen?
   d) When the particles in a substance move around faster, what happens to the temperature?

2) *Answer the following questions on heat and temperature.*
   a) Are heat and temperature two words for the same thing? Explain.
   b) Heat is a form of ________________ and is therefore measured in ________________.

   We use temperature as a way of comparing the energy that the particles in a substance have.
   c) If we supply a certain amount of heat energy to just a few particles, what will happen to their kinetic energy?
   d) If we supply the same amount of heat energy to a greater number of these particles, how will their individual increase in kinetic energy compare?
   e) How will the temperature rise compare for the two cases?

3) *Listed below are a number of temperatures frequently encountered in science.* Try to write down the correct temperature against each of the descriptions a) to j).

Temperatures (°C): 0, 6000, 100, 37, 1067, –39, –112, 78, –68, 357, –273

Temperature, °C	Description	Temperature, °C	Description
	a) Normal human body temperature.		b) Boiling point of pure water.
	c) Coldest land weather temperature.		d) Temperature of the surface of the Sun.
	e) Freezing point of pure water.		f) Freezing point of alcohol.
	g) Absolute Zero.		h) Melting point of gold.
	i) Boiling point of alcohol.		j) Freezing point of mercury.
	k) Boiling point of mercury.		

4) *The Absolute Temperature Scale is based on kelvin (K). A kelvin is the same size as a degree Celsius, but 0 K is actually –273°C.* Convert the following:

a) The boiling point of pure water to kelvin.	b) The melting point of lead (600K) to °C.
c) Normal body temperature (37°C) to kelvin.	d) The boiling point of propanone (330K) to °C.
e) The boiling point of O_2 (–183°C) to kelvin.	

Thermometers

5) *The thermometers found in school laboratories used to be filled with mercury.*
   a) Why do we now choose to use another liquid?
   b) What sort of liquid is now generally used?

6) *There are variations on the liquid-in-glass thermometers that are used for special purposes, and also other types of thermometer that scientists use.*
   a) Mercury thermometers are not generally any good at the North Pole. Explain why.
   b) Thermometers filled with alcohol generally cannot be used to measure such high temperatures as a mercury device. Why not?
   c) What are the special design requirements for a clinical thermometer, and how are these fulfilled?

Temperature

Calculating Temperature Rises

7) *Different substances are made up of different particles, and therefore supplying the same amount of heat energy to the same mass of particles can give a different temperature rise.*

(In all the following questions, ignore any heat losses.)

Substance	Energy needed to make the temperature of 1kg of substance increase by 1°C
Pure Water	4190
Aluminium	913
Copper	385
Ethanol	2500
Concrete	3350
Air	993

a) 4190J of heat energy are supplied to 1kg of water. How much does the temperature of the water rise?

b) *If the same amount of heat energy is supplied to 0.5kg of water, what is* the temperature rise?

c) *A refrigerator extracts 770J of heat energy from a 1kg mass of copper.* What happens to the *temperature* of the copper?

d) *If the same amount of heat energy is supplied to 1kg of ethanol, and 1kg of concrete,* which will show the bigger temperature rise?

e) *4565J of heat energy are supplied by an electrical heater to a 1kg mass of aluminium.* By how much will the temperature increase?

f) *An electric heater supplies energy to 1 kg of air. The temperature of the air rises from 30°C to 35°C.* How much energy did the heater supply?

8) *The little points of light that come shooting off firework sparklers are white hot, and usually at a temperature of over 1000°C. They can't cause a great deal of damage, but being scalded by water from a kettle at a temperature of only 90°C can give a nasty burn.* Explain the difference.

Laboratory Thermometers

9) *A standard laboratory thermometer contains a number of features which enable it to be used to measure temperatures accurately.* Match up each feature with the reason it is used.

Feature	Reason for the design
a) Large bulb and long narrow scale	Liquids expand regularly with temperature
b) Vacuum above liquid	Thermometer reacts quickly
c) The bulb is made of thin glass	The thermometer is sensitive
d) Temperature scale is regular	The liquid expands easily

Top Tips: Make sure you fully understand how temperature relates to the *motion of particles* — you definitely need to understand this for your Exams. Make sure you can convert from °Celsius to kelvin and back again. And you don't just need to know *how* designs of thermometer vary — you've got to know *why* they vary.

Expansion

Physical Effects of Heating

1) *When heat energy is supplied to substances, the particles making up the material gain more kinetic energy. This can lead to some interesting effects.* Explain the following:

a) *A round bottomed flask has a bung with a long glass tube in the top. The end of the tube is held underwater in a beaker. When a student's hands are placed around the flask, bubbles of air are seen coming out of the tube.*

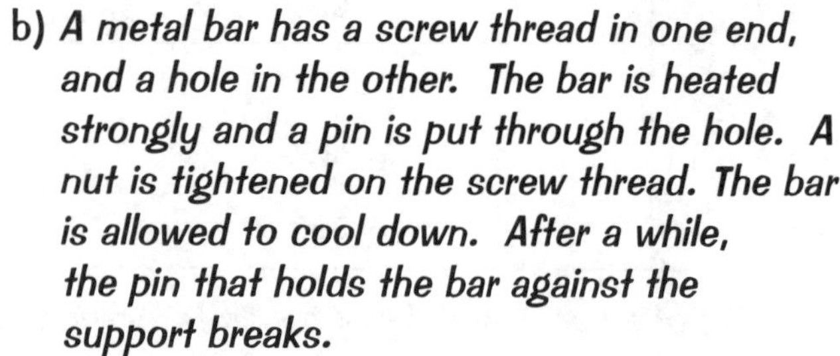

b) *A metal bar has a screw thread in one end, and a hole in the other. The bar is heated strongly and a pin is put through the hole. A nut is tightened on the screw thread. The bar is allowed to cool down. After a while, the pin that holds the bar against the support breaks.*

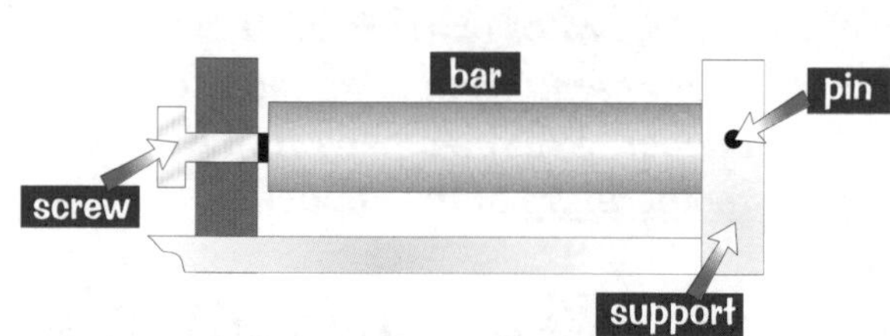

c) *A class are shown an experiment which consists of a metal ball which will just fit through a metal ring. The metal ball is heated strongly, and it will no longer fit through the ring. Then the ring is heated, and the ball will now fit through again. When both the ball and the ring have cooled down, the ball fits through again.*

Ball

Ring

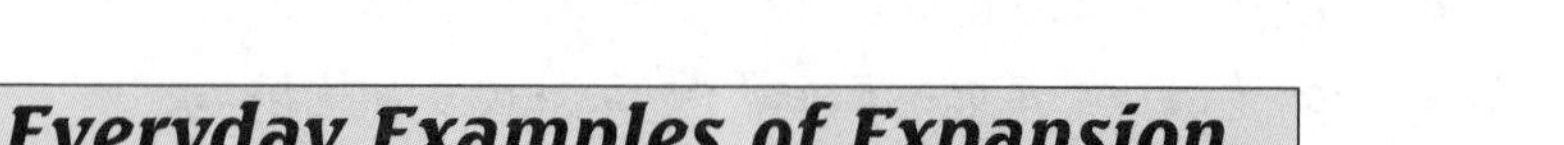

Everyday Examples of Expansion

2) *It has been a very hot day. It's now the evening, and as I have done lots of exhausting revision, I go to bed. As I lie there waiting to fall asleep, I hear the rafters and floorboards in my loft creaking.* Do I need to get up and check for burglars? Explain.

3) *Before the days of underground cables and fibre optics, telephone messages were carried in cables strung between poles (yes, some still exist!). These cables were put up in the summer during the good weather. If you were putting up these cables, would you hang them loosely or tightly? Explain your answer.*

An Expansion Calculation

4) *The amount of expansion that a substance shows depends on 3 things: the starting length of the object, the size of the temperature change, and a quantity called the linear expansivity.*

Extension = Original length × expansivity × temperature change

The Eiffel Tower is made of steel. The steel has an expansivity of 0.000012 per °C. It is 300m high at a temperature of 20°C.

a) How much higher is the top when the temperature is 30°C?
b) How much shorter is it when the temperature is 5°C?

Expansion

The Bimetallic Strip

5) *A bimetallic strip is made of two metal strips, for example one made of iron and the other made from brass. They are riveted together so that the strips cannot slide over one another. They are designed so that the strip is straight at a particular temperature. The expansivity of iron is 0.000012 per °C, and of brass is 0.000019 per °C.*

a) Which metal will expand *the most* when the two are heated?

b) Because the two strips are riveted together, what will *happen*?

c) Draw what will *happen* to the strip when it is: i) *very hot* ii) *very cold*

d) *Explain how* the strip could be used in: i) a fire alarm ii) a thermostat.

6) Try to *explain* the following:

a) The Forth Rail Bridge rests on *rollers* at either end.

b) Roads designed from concrete slabs have *gaps* between, filled with a tarry substance.

c) Rivets that hold two steel plates together are *heated* up before they are pushed through the holes and secured.

d) Metal lids to bottles and jars can be loosened by running them under the *hot tap* for a short time.

The Expansion of Water

7) *Water is quite an odd substance. It does not behave exactly as we might predict. The table below shows the volume of 1kg of water at various temperatures:*

Temperature (°C)	0	2	4	6	8	10	12
Volume (cm^3)	1003	1001	1000	1001	1002	1003	1005

a) *Sketch a graph* showing this information.

b) At what *temperature* is the volume of the water the least?

c) What does this tell you about the *density* of water at this temperature?

d) *Why does this have special significance for animals that live in ponds?*

The Expansion of Air

8) *An experiment is carried out with some air trapped in a glass tube. The tube is placed inside some beakers of water at different temperatures, and the length of the column of trapped air is measured. The readings are shown in this table:*

Temperature (°C)	20	30	50	70	90
Length (mm)	35.6	36.8	39.2	41.7	44.1

a) *Draw a graph* in which the temperature scale goes back to –300 °C, and up to 100 °C. *(The length scale must go from 0 to 45mm).*

b) What is the *value* of the length at 0 °C?

c) *When you continue the line back from 20°C so the air column goes down to zero length,* what *temperature* does this correspond to?

d) What is the *significance* of this temperature?

Top Tips: Expansion is pretty simple, but it does get more complicated when you stick two metals together that expand at different rates. Just make sure you can work out *which way* a bimetallic strip will bend when heated. And don't forget about *water* — remember it's most dense at *4°C* (just like you're most dense at 4am).

Heat Transfer

Types of Heat Transfer

1) *Below are a number of descriptions of heat transfer processes.* State whether they are concerned with conduction, convection, radiation or all three.

a) Heat flowing between two places when there is a difference in temperature.
b) Heat passing from atom to atom (most effective in solid materials).
c) Can occur through transparent substances.
d) Sets up movement currents in liquids and gases.
e) Is affected by colour and shininess.
f) Can occur through a vacuum.
g) Involves hot fluid expanding and rising.

Conduction

2) *The paragraph that follows is all about heat conduction.* You have to use the following words to fill in the gaps. The words may be used more than once or not at all:

neighbouring collide carry reflect electrons pockets vibrate close good poor solids

Conduction is the main form of heat transfer in ____________. This is because the particles are relatively ____________. Extra heat energy makes the particles ____________ more. They pass on the extra vibrational energy to ____________ particles. Metals are ____________ conductors of heat energy because they contain many free ____________ which can move through the solid and ____________ the energy. The electrons give up their energy when they ____________ with other particles.

3) Write down three insulating substances and three conducting substances, then complete this table.

Name of Substance	Conductor or Insulator	Used for

4) *This diagram shows a metal bar with a number of holes drilled into it. The holes are just big enough to fit thermometers in. Four thermometers are put into the holes, and initially read the same temperature. The bar is then heated at one end with a Bunsen burner.*

a) Redraw the diagram showing the levels recorded by the thermometers after a few minutes.
b) Explain the levels you have drawn.
c) Redraw the diagram showing the results if the same experiment was carried out using a bar of the same dimensions made from a poorer conductor.

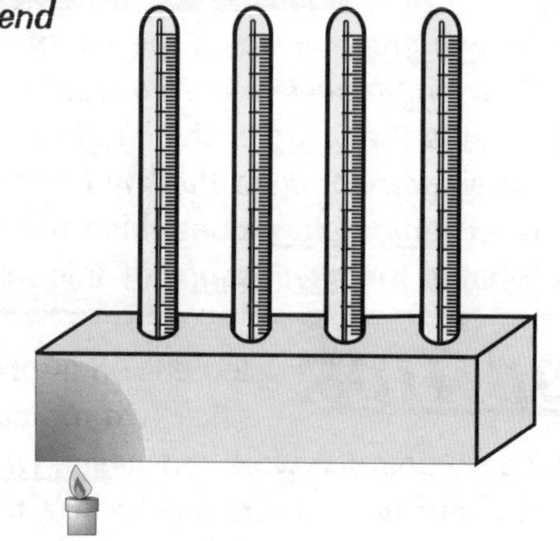

Heat Transfer

Convection

5) *A model hot air balloon is built. It contains $2m^3$ of air. The density of air at 20°C is $1.30kg/m^3$.*

a) Calculate the mass of air contained by the balloon.

The heater in the model balloon is switched on, and heats the air to a temperature of 50°C. At this temperature, the density of air is $1.25kg/m^3$.

b) Calculate the new volume of the air in the balloon.

c) Explain what will happen to the balloon, and why.

Radiation

6) *It's a hot day at the beach, and the only shelter from the Sun is behind an advertising hoarding. It is cooler where you are sitting, with your back against the hoarding, but your friend is still sweltering next to you. From your side, the board all looks the same colour.*

a) What could be causing the difference?

b) *You look out at the beach which is pretty deserted as it's so hot. You see a sunbed covered in white cloth with black plastic arms. There is a* heat haze *over the arms, but none over the cloth.* Explain why.

7) *The diagram shows beach and some land by the seaside.* Make two copies of the diagram. Draw the Sun on one to indicate daytime, and the Moon on the other to indicate night.

Decide which surface will be warmer, and therefore where the air will be forced to rise. Then draw on the air currents, and the directions of any breezes.

8) *An author is planning to write an adventure novel.*

a) *The hero of the novel has to survive in the desert Sun having been tied up, in a car, by evil villains.* Is he more likely to survive in a light coloured one or a dark coloured one?

b) *Evening brings a new torture. The desert nights can be very cold.* Which car will now be the most comfortable?

9) *Explain the following, using ideas of heat transfer.*

a) Frosty nights in winter are usually clear.

b) In a hot water tank, the heater is generally at the bottom, and the outlet is usually at the top.

c) A layer of snow can stop young plants dying in the frost.

d) A shiny teapot keeps tea hot longer than a dull one.

e) Birds try to keep warm in winter by ruffling up their feathers.

f) Holding the legs of a transistor with pliers when it is being soldered can prevent heat damage to the transistor.

Top Tips: The main thing here is to know the three methods of heat transfer. If you get this sorted out, you'll be ready for anything you meet in the Exams. You need to be able to say what's happening in each type of transfer, and recognise the situations where each is likely to occur. Don't forget, more than one type of heat transfer can happen at the same time.

Keeping Buildings Warm

Reducing Heat Loss

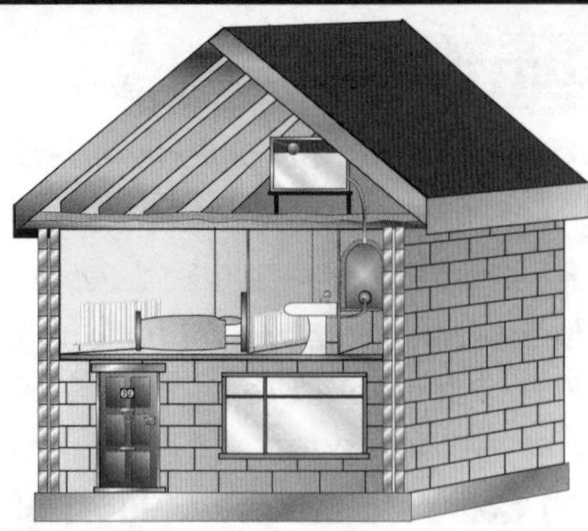

1) *Below is a list of methods of keeping heat within a house. Describe how each saves heat energy, and give the type of heat transfer that the insulation method affects.*

   a) Curtains
   b) Loft insulation
   c) Cavity wall insulation
   d) Hot water tank jacket
   e) Double glazing
   f) Draught-proofing
   g) Thermostats

Calculating How Much Money can be Saved

2) *As part of a science project, Eric investigates ways of saving energy in his grandmother's house, and finds out the cost of doing the work. Next, Eric calculates the annual saving that each piece of work would produce on his grandmother's fuel bill, as shown in the table below.*

Work needed	Annual saving (£)
Loft insulation	40
Hot water tank jacket	15
Double glazing	60
Draught proofing	65
Cavity wall insulation	70
Thermostatic controls	25

   a) Use the figures in the first table to draw a bar chart.
   b) Which method of insulation makes the greatest annual saving?
   c) Which method of insulation makes the least annual saving?

The next thing Eric does is to calculate the payback time, the time that each insulation method takes to save the money that it cost in the first place.

Work needed	Cost of work (£)
Loft insulation	250
Hot water tank jacket	15
Double glazing	3200
Draught proofing	70
Cavity wall insulation	560
Thermostatic controls	120

   d) Use Eric's figures to construct a table showing payback time for each method.
   e) Which method(s) of heat transfer pay for themselves most quickly?
   f) Which is the least effective method when looked at in this way?
   g) A double glazing salesperson calls and mentions some other benefits that double glazing would give. What might they be?

3) *A double glazing salesperson calls and gives you some figures. She says that the rate of heat loss through a single glazed window is 1.4 W/m^2 for each degree Celsius difference between the inside and outside of the pane. She claims that her double glazing can reduce that figure to 0.5 W/m^2.*
   a) *Outside your house it is 5°C. Inside it is 22°C.* How much energy is lost per second through each m^2 of single glazing? How much through each m^2 of double glazing?
   b) What is the energy loss per year in each case? Assume the temperature difference remains the same throughout the year.
   c) If you heat your house with energy costing 2p per MJ, how much would you save per m^2 in one year by changing your single glazing to double glazing?

4) *Sharon and Esme have booked a winter holiday in a log cabin. Sharon thinks that wood is a good substance to keep the holiday dwellers warm.*
   a) Do you agree?

They have a relaxing evening playing cards while it is cold and stormy outside. Esme goes up to the door. The body of the door is warm to the touch, but when she touches the brass handle, it feels very cold.
   b) Explain why this is.

Keeping Buildings Warm

Calculating Heat Loss — a hot water tank

5) *Sandra and her family have moved into a new house. They notice that the previous owners have taken away the insulating jacket surrounding the hot water tank in the airing cupboard.*

The tank is a cylinder, 1 metre high with a diameter of 0.5 m.

a) What is the *volume* of the tank?
b) What is the *surface area* of the tank?

Sandra's father suggests that instead of buying a new insulating jacket, they simply wrap the tank in shiny foil.

c) Which *method* of heat transfer will this reduce?
d) Is this likely to be effective on its own? *Explain*.

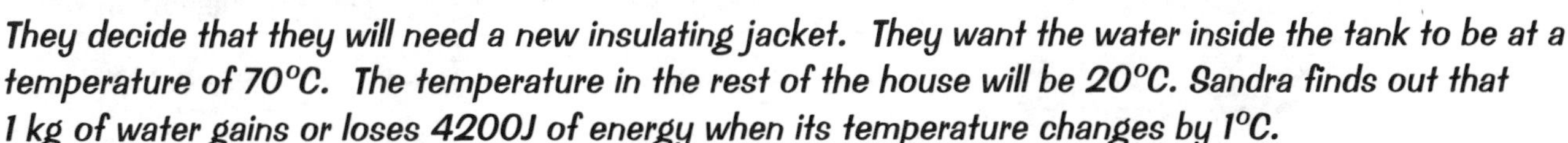

They decide that they will need a new insulating jacket. They want the water inside the tank to be at a temperature of 70°C. The temperature in the rest of the house will be 20°C. Sandra finds out that 1 kg of water gains or loses 4200J of energy when its temperature changes by 1°C.

e) Given that the density of water is 1000 kg/m^3, what *mass of water* does the tank contain?
f) How much *energy* would it take to heat up a tank full of water from 20°C to 70°C?

Sandra does an experiment on the tank. She heats the water to 70°C, and then switches off the power. An hour later the temperature is 68°C.

g) How much heat energy has the water *lost*?
h) What is the heat loss *per m^2* of tank surface?
i) What is the rate of heat loss in *watts per m^2*?

Sandra goes to buy the insulating jacket, which has a thermal conductivity of 0.01W/m^2 per °C across it.

j) If the inside of the jacket is at 70°C and the outside is at 20°C, how much *heat energy* will be conducted through the jacket in *1 hour*?
k) If this energy is extracted from the water in the tank, what will the *temperature change* be?

The Vacuum Flask

6) *The vacuum flask has a number of features which help it to insulate its contents.*

Some features are listed below. For each of them, say *which method* of heat transfer they are reducing, and *how* they do this.

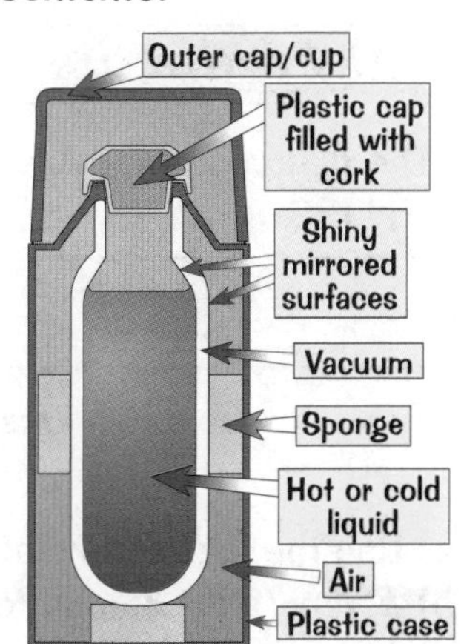

a) The cap is covered in *plastic*.
b) The cap is filled with *cork*.
c) The liquid is contained in a *glass* bottle.
d) The bottle is *double* walled.
e) There is a *vacuum* between the two walls of the glass bottle.
f) The *inside* of each glass layer is silvered.
g) The *outside* of each glass layer is silvered.
h) The bottle is surrounded by *air* inside the plastic case.
i) The bottle is supported away from the casing by insulating *foam*.

Top Tips: Examiners like asking you about these sorts of everyday things — so make sure you know the functions of all the parts of the vacuum flask, and how *all seven* of the insulation methods work. Having an idea of the cost of each would help — and you need to know how "payback time" is calculated and used.

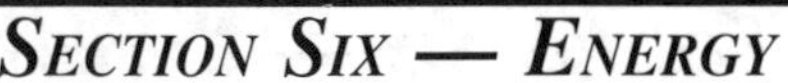

Energy Resources

Energy Chains

1) *Fill in* the energy chains from the following list of words:

Light energy, photosynthesis, plants / animals, clouds, light energy, heating sea water, heats atmosphere, rain, photosynthesis, light energy, plants / animals

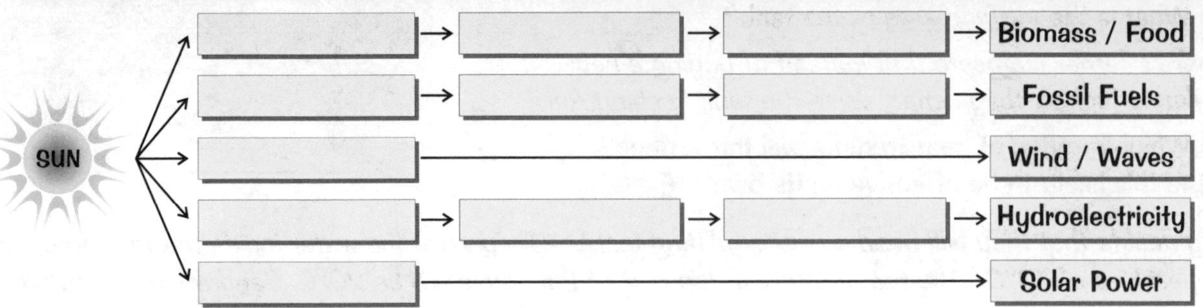

The Sun is the starting point for all of these energy chains.

a) What is the *source* of the Sun's energy?
b) *How* does the energy get from the Sun to the Earth?

2) *There are three energy sources that do not fit in with those from Qu.1.*

a) What are the *three* sources?
b) Which source uses energy emitted by the *nuclei* of some atoms?
c) Which source relies on the Earth's *gravitational attraction* to the Sun and Moon?
d) Which source relies on the *decay of radioactive atoms* within the Earth creating a source of heat?

3) *State the odd one out in each of the lists of energy resources below. Give a reason for each of your choices.*

a) Coal, Oil, Natural Gas, Nuclear
b) Wind, Wave, Geothermal, Solar
c) Tidal, Biomass, Hydroelectric, Geothermal, Nuclear
d) Food, Coal, Biomass, Hydroelectric, Oil
e) Nuclear, Coal, Geothermal, Oil
f) Solar, Biomass, Coal, Oil, Wave

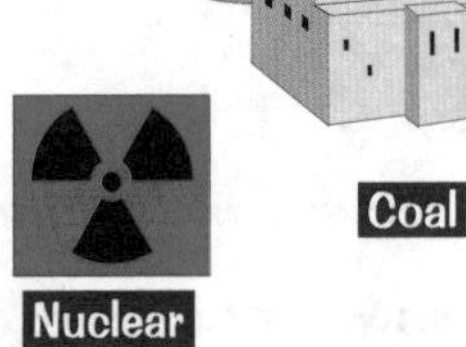

Coal Production

4) The figures in the table below show how the amount of coal used in the UK changed between 1982 and 1990.

Year	1982	1984	1986	1988	1990
Amount of Coal Produced (tonnes)	121427	49549	104645	101661	89303

a) Use the figures to plot a graph of *amount* of coal produced against year.
b) *Estimate* the amount of coal produced in 1992.
c) Can you think what might have led to the figure for *1984*?
d) Apart from 1984, what *trend* is shown by the figures?
e) What was happening to the *demand* for energy in the UK in the years shown?
f) What *conclusion* can be drawn from this?
g) Why were *alternatives* to coal being used?

Energy Resources

Nuclear Power

5) *When experiments were first carried out into nuclear power, it was thought that it would be a clean, safe and ideal energy source. However, we now know of at least 3 major disadvantages of using nuclear power to generate electricity.*

Listed below are some of the arguments <u>for</u> nuclear power. For each, list the <u>associated problems</u>, giving examples if you can.

a) Nuclear power generation is <u>clean</u>.
b) The uranium used to generate nuclear power is <u>cheap</u>.
c) We have the technology to generate nuclear power <u>safely</u>.

Non-Renewable Resources

6) Both geothermal energy and nuclear power rely on the energy locked up in the <u>nuclei of atoms</u>. What are the major <u>differences</u> in the way that they utilise this energy?

7) *There are some people who say that coal, oil and natural gas are still being created on the Earth, and that they should not be regarded as non-renewable energy resources.*
What is the main argument for still classifying them as <u>non-renewable</u>?

8) *The non-renewable energy resources are still being used to provide us with the majority of our energy. One thing that people are trying to plan for is a future when all of the non-renewable sources have been exhausted.*
What is the other <u>major disadvantage</u> with our massive use of non-renewable energy resources?

9) *Coal, oil and natural gas can release their locked-up energy by combustion. This releases heat energy, which is converted to electrical energy in a power station.*

a) What substance is needed from the atmosphere for this <u>combustion</u> to take place?
b) What two substances are <u>released</u> by the complete combustion of pure oil and natural gas?
c) Which of these substances <u>contributes</u> to the <u>Greenhouse Effect</u>?
d) What do scientists think the Greenhouse Effect could lead to?
e) Where else in the <u>solar system</u> is a large Greenhouse Effect seen?
f) Coal and oil also contain <u>impurities</u>. What emissions can these give rise to when the fuels are burned?
g) What effects can this have on the <u>environment</u>?

Growth in Energy Use

10) a) What is the <u>missing label</u> in the pie chart for 1945?

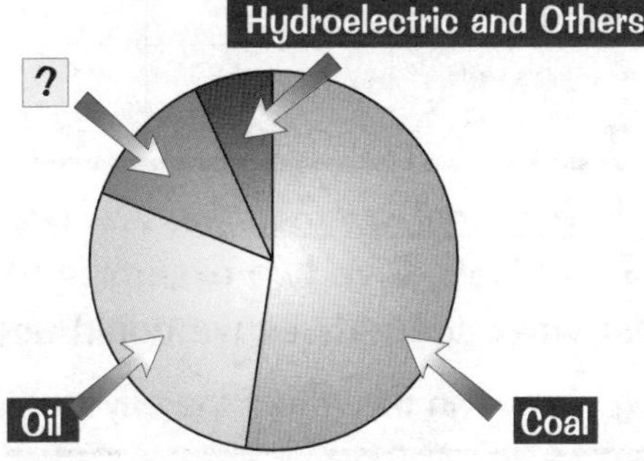

b) By 1985, the picture had changed somewhat. Once again the same label has been missed off. This time there is another section. What is the <u>other</u> section?

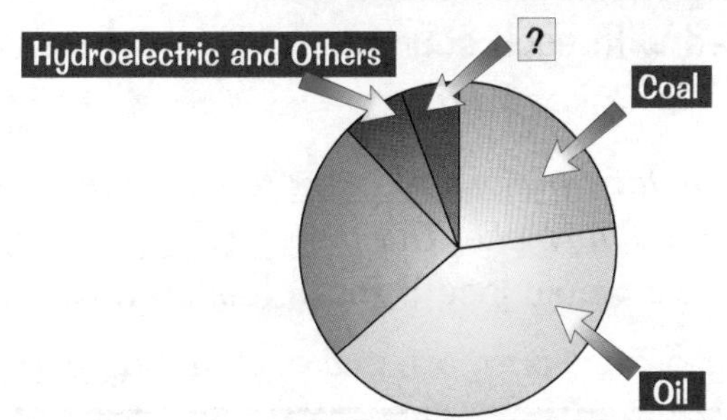

Top Tips: There's 12 resources to learn your way around. You need to know for each whether it's <u>renewable</u> or <u>non-renewable</u> — and make sure you know why. Also think about the <u>ultimate</u> source of the energy — like whether it comes from the Sun or not.

Power Stations

How They Work

1) *Despite scientific research into alternative sources of energy, most of the electricity that we use today is generated from 4 non-renewable energy sources.*
   a) Give the *names* of these 4 sources.

A traditional power station relies on the combustion of 3 of these sources.
   b) Which are the three that are *burned*?
   c) Draw one simple *block diagram* to show the general structure of all 3 types of *traditional* power station.
   d) Where will the *chemical* energy be changed into *heat* energy?
   e) Where is the *heat* energy changed into *kinetic* energy?
   f) Where is the *kinetic* energy changed into energy of *rotation*?
   g) Where is the energy of *rotation* changed into *electrical* energy?
   h) How does the electrical energy get *from* the power station *to* the users?
   i) What happens to *produce* the kinetic energy from the heat energy?
   j) *Draw* an energy chain showing how the energy types *change*.

2) *Look at this diagram of a nuclear reactor and boiler. The labels have been replaced by letters.* *State* which label corresponds to which letter.

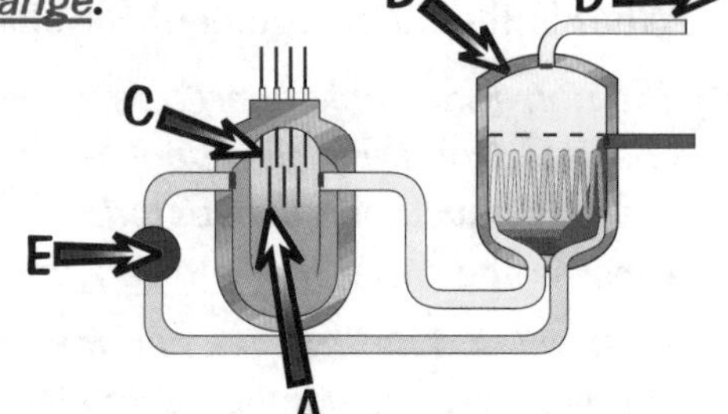

control rods	*coolant pump*	*fuel rods*
steam generator	*to turbine*	

3) *Many coal-fired power stations have vast stockpiles of coal outside.* Why are large stocks not necessary with a nuclear power station?

4) *The control rods are made of a substance that can slow down the nuclear reactions that are producing heat.* *Why are they necessary?*

5) *Traditional power stations generally have vast cooling towers.* What is being cooled here, and why is it needed?

6) Why are all of Britain's nuclear power stations *situated on the coast*?

Environmental Problems

7) *All of the* non-renewable *energy sources have associated environmental problems.*

On a *copy* of this table, put ticks to indicate which problems are associated with each source.

Problem	Coal	Oil	Gas	Nuclear
Release of CO_2 contributing to Greenhouse Effect				
Acid rain production				
Devastation of landscape				
Environmental problems due to spillage at sea				
Expensive plant and clean-up after use				
Production of dangerous, long-lasting waste				
Danger of major catastrophe				

8) *Fossil fuels took millions of years to be formed. They are vital chemical raw materials and we just send them up in smoke. Our man-made world depends on fossil fuels.* Give two examples of materials we would lose if fossil fuels ran out and suggest what alternatives we could use.

9) Power stations are often accused of producing *thermal pollution*. How can this affect the environment?

Top Tips: It's a good idea to be well up on the environmental problems associated with each of the forms of power production, as examiners are very keen on these. Learn the energy changes taking place at the different stages, not forgetting where energy is lost — and think about how fuel stocks can be conserved.

Wind Power

How It Works

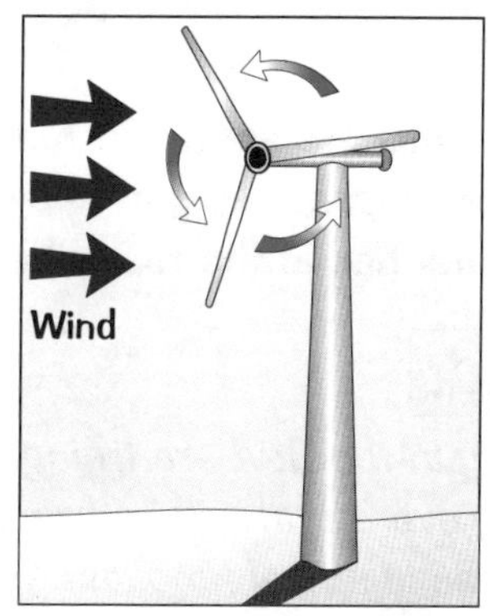

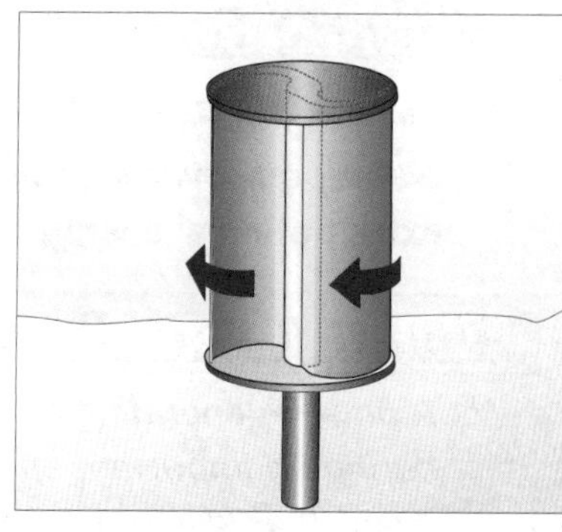

1) *There are two basic ways of collecting energy directly from wind. A traditional approach is the horizontal axis windmill. An engineer named Savonius designed a vertical axis windmill, which can also be used to extract the energy from the wind.* What advantage is there of having a windmill that operates on a vertical axis?

2) *Research in California has shown that the best radius for the sails of a horizontal axis windmill is about 30m. The best sites for wind farms have an average wind speed of 21 km/h. A typical wind turbine will generate about 200kW of power.*
   a) Convert 21 km/h to m/s.
   b) Calculate the volume of air which passes over the blades of the turbine in one second, assuming that the turbine points directly into the wind.
   c) Given that the density of air is about 1.30 kg/m^3, what mass of air does this represent?
   d) Calculate the kinetic energy of this mass of air travelling at the velocity that you calculated for part a).
   e) How efficient would the wind turbine have to be in order to generate a power of 200kW?
   f) *In California, a typical wind farm can generate a total power of 1120MW.* How many 200kW turbines would be required?
   g) Why would the kinetic energy given up by the moving air not be equal to the figure that you calculated in part d)?

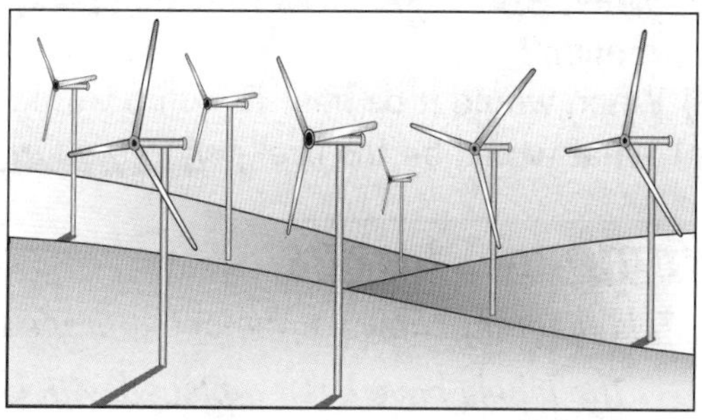

Practical Matters

3) Copy and complete the following paragraph about extracting power from the wind, using the following.

increase remote high zero 5000 windmills coasts large
wind turbines noise moors blades generator view

The energy of the wind can be extracted using devices called ____________, or more properly ____________ ____________. These can be situated in ____________ areas, such as ____________ and ____________ where there is a reliable history of wind. Each wind turbine contains its own ____________. The wind turns the ____________, providing the rotational energy used to generate the electricity. Once the wind turbine is operating there is little material pollution, but people can complain about the ____________ and the spoiling of the ____________. In order to replace one coal-fired power station it would require about ____________ turbines, and this would cover a ____________ area of ground. Problems involved with wind generated electricity include ____________ initial costs, ____________ power being generated when the wind stops, and not having any way to ____________ supply when there is extra demand.

Top Tips: Windmills are old hat, but they may be coming to a moor near you. Learn about what's needed for an effective wind farm. There are also disadvantages that you need to know: ugliness, unreliability of the wind, etc.

Hydroelectric Power

Niagara Falls

1) *The Niagara Falls in North America are about 50 metres high. It is estimated that 1×10^8 kg of water pour over the falls every second.* If you could *design* a power station to extract half of the extra potential energy the water has at the top, what *power* would be generated?

Dealing with Demand

2) *A power-generating company in the USA are trying to predict the power requirements for a city during an important sporting event that will be broadcast on TV. They are using figures from an event that was broadcast at an identical time last year.*

The figures are shown in the table.

Time	19:00	19:30	20:00	20:30	21:00	21:30	22:00	22:30
Power Usage (MW)	23	28	35	50	36	34	65	26

a) Use the figures to *sketch a graph* of the power requirements against time.
b) At about what *time* did the event *finish*?
c) When was *half time*?

The company has two choices of how to deal with the surge in demand. It can either switch on an extra boiler at their coal fired power station, or it can use their pumped storage station at the local reservoir.

d) Why would the coal-fired option be *wasteful*?
e) When would you advise the company to run water *down* through the pumped storage power station?
f) When would it be best to pump water *back up* through it?
g) What would be the likely *energy source* for the pumping operation?

Pumped Storage

3) *This diagram shows a pumped storage reservoir system.*
The labels have been replaced with letters.
You have to *match up* the letters with the labels.

Label	Letter
turbines	
upper reservoir	
generator	
pump	
lower reservoir	
direction at night	
national grid	
direction during peak demand	

P
T
Q
R
S
U
V
W

Design a Hydroelectric Power Station

4) *Put yourself in the position of a planner with a generating company, and decide which of the following points are* advantages, disadvantages *or* neither *when considering a location for a planned hydroelectric power scheme.*

a) consistent and *high rainfall*.
b) *high population* in valley.
c) steep-sided *valley*.
d) *remote* location.
e) site of a *rare* species of plant.
f) nearby *quarry*.
g) rocks showing evidence of recent *earthquake* damage.

Top Tips: Hydroelectricity relies on the *potential energy* of water. Get used to the equation, and to converting energy into power. Pumped storage systems are big with examiners. Learn about their workings, and *why* they are so useful.

Wave Power

Generator Design

1) *The most recent design of wave generator uses the energy in water waves to drive a turbine and therefore generate electricity.*

a) As waves travel towards the shore, what is the main *direction of vibration* of the water molecules?
b) How is this *motion* used to generate electricity?
c) What gives the waves this *energy*? What was its *original* source?

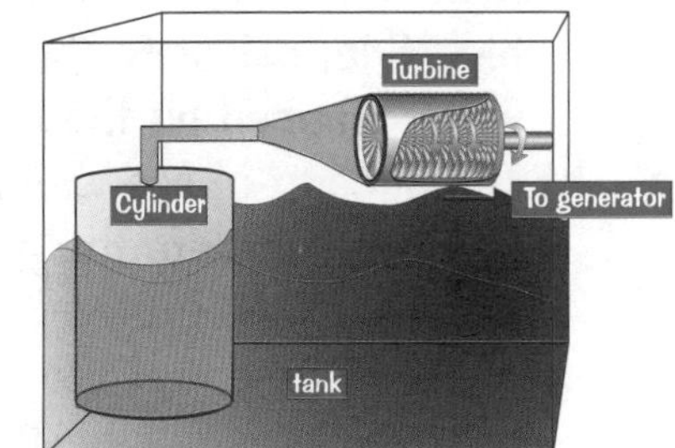

2) *A design of wave generator consists of a floating cylinder, of diameter 5m. A pipe leads from the top of the cylinder through a turbine which drives a generator. The generator is being tested in a design tank. Waves are being sent along the tank with a velocity of 2 m/s and a wavelength of 20 metres.*

a) What is the *frequency* of the waves?
The waves have an amplitude of 2.0m.
b) Sketch a diagram of the waves, showing the *amplitude* and the *wavelength*.

As the wave passes across the generator, a depth of air equal to twice the amplitude is forced through the pipe leading to the turbine, and the turbine blades are forced to spin.

c) What *volume* of air does this represent?
d) Taking the density of air as 1.3 kg/m^3, what is the *mass* of this volume of air?
e) *The air is forced out through the turbine in a time equal to half of the period of the wave.* What is this *time*?
f) The distance travelled is twice the amplitude. What is the *average speed* of the mass of air?
g) Calculate the *kinetic energy* of this mass of air.
h) If the generator can extract 10% of this energy as electricity, how much energy can *each generator* extract from each wave?
i) Calculate the power available from each generator.
j) *How many* generators would you need to provide the power equivalent of a 1000kW traditional power station?
k) What *modifications* might reduce the number of generators needed?

Locating Wave Generators

3) *The environments where these wave generators work are often quite hostile.* Give some of the *difficulties* that the designers have to cope with.

4) *Once the wave generators are in place, there is little or no pollution of a chemical nature. However, as with any large-scale development, some people will be affected.* *Who* are they and *how* are they likely to be affected?

5) *Wave generators are not very productive in very light wind conditions. They cannot therefore be counted on all the time. Researchers have suggested that the best place to put them would be where there was a long stretch of ocean over which the wind and waves can build up.*

a) Suggest an *area* where this would be the case.
b) What would be the problems of siting the generators *far offshore*?
c) What *other factors* do you think might be a problem for wave generators in deep water?

Top Tips: Make sure you know your waves as well as your wave energy — including the effect of the wind. Think about what makes a *good site* for wave power, and what things might affect this. Learn about the *disadvantages*, too. Don't get *wave* power confused with *tidal* power — at least not if you want some marks in the Exam.

Tidal Power

Tidal Barrages

1) *At Rance in France, a tidal power station was completed in 1967. When the tide is in, a pool is formed behind the barrage. This has an area of 2.2×10^6 m². The barrage across the estuary contains 24 turbines which generate electricity as the water flows out to sea.*

a) If the water behind the barrage rises an average of 8 metres after high tide, calculate the *volume* of water trapped by the barrage.

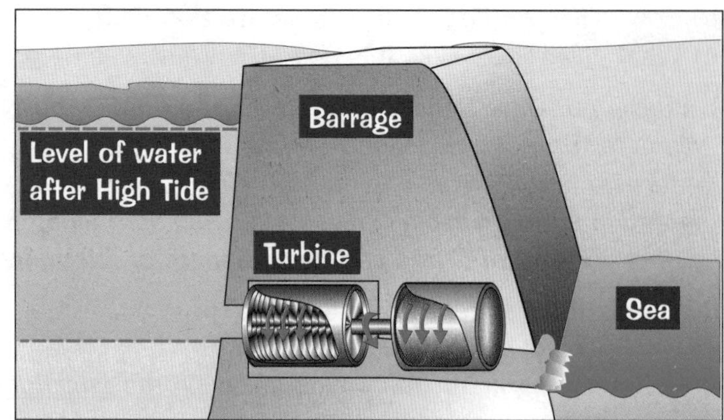

b) The density of sea water is 1200 kg/m³. Calculate the *mass* of water trapped by the barrage.

c) If we assume that the water has gained an average height above low tide level of 4.0m, calculate the *gravitational potential energy* that is represented here.

d) If this amount of energy is released over 8 hours, what *power* does this represent, assuming that the turbines are 20% efficient?

Another possible site for a tidal station is the Bay of Fundy, in Canada. What makes this site especially attractive is the greater tidal range. Here it can be up to 18m.

e) What *effect* will this have on the *generating power* of any tidal power station?

Spring and Neap Tides

2) In practice the heights of tides vary throughout the month according to the relative positions of the Sun and Moon. *'Spring'* tides are when the variation between high and low tides is the greatest, while *'neap'* tides have the smallest variation. What implications does this monthly cycle have for tidal power schemes?

Pros and Cons of Tidal Power

3) *Tidal power stations are not only suitable for generating power on a regular basis, but they can also be used to* *store energy* *for periods of high demand. Indicate roughly how you think that this could be done.*

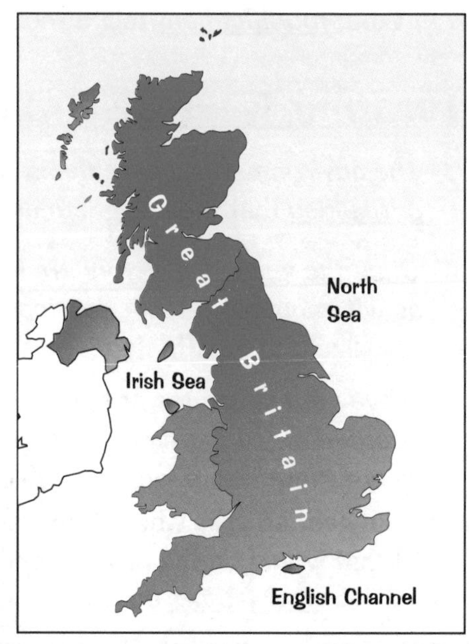

4) *Some people have said that about 100 tidal power stations, situated all around the coast of Britain, could generate the entire electricity needs of the country.* What particular *drawbacks* can you see with this plan?

5) *At first sight, it looks like tidal power could be* *energy from nothing*. Is this true? What will happen eventually?

6) *Many of the arguments against the siting of tidal power stations are concerned with their effects on people or the environment.* *List* some of these arguments.

7) Look at a map of the UK. Make a rough copy, marking some sites that might be *suitable* for a tidal barrage.

Top Tips: You've got to know the background details, like the cause of the tides. You'll need the *potential energy* equation, but don't forget that the average water rise *isn't* the difference between the tides. Think about other factors affecting tidal power — and why there are so *few* of these schemes around.

Geothermal Power

An Icelandic Saga

1) *One of the places in the world where geothermal energy is being used to contribute to the overall energy needs is Reykjavik in Iceland.*

Atlantic Ocean

a) What do you think makes Reykjavik suitable for a geothermal scheme?
Check out information on the plates that make up the Earth's surface (try P. 54 in our Chemistry Revision Guide).

b) Why are conditions this way in Iceland?

In the city of Reykjavik, water can be pumped up from underground at varying temperatures between 95°C and 135°C. This can be used for direct heating of the houses. Early Norse settlers did exactly the same thing in Iceland when they first settled there.

When the temperature of 1kg of water drops by 1°C, 4200 Joules of heat energy is removed to the surroundings. In the 1970s, 16 boreholes supplied Reykjavik with 8000kg of water every minute.

c) If the water entered the system at 130 °C, and left at a temperature of 30 °C, calculate how much energy this represents over a 24 hour period.

d) How much power would be generated if all of this energy could be converted directly into electrical energy?

e) What could the water leaving the system at 30 °C be used for?

Using Geothermal Power

2) What makes an area suitable for geothermal power production?

3) Why do geothermal sources have such a long life?

4) One problem that may occur with water and/or steam that has originated below ground at high temperatures is purity. What could be the cause and consequences of this?

5) When scientists investigate geothermal sources, they often talk about water at temperatures as high as 130 °C. How can water remain at this temperature without turning into steam?

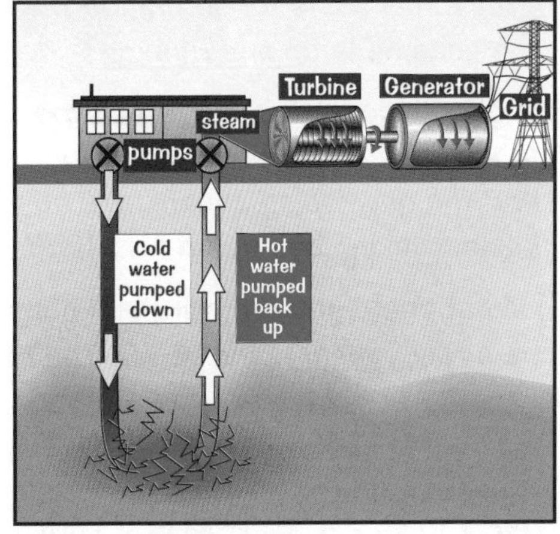

6) What is the major difficulty that scientists and engineers have to deal with when planning and constructing a geothermal energy station?

7) A site in the mountains of New Mexico, USA, was chosen by scientists. They drilled into dry rock and injected surface water. What sort of substance/structure were they hoping to find under the mountain?

Top Tips: Geothermal power sounds brilliant, but is obviously only economical in some areas — make sure you know the factors affecting this. You need to know the main drawbacks and the costs, as well as the source of the energy. And looking at some plate tectonics stuff would be a good idea to help you get it all sorted in your mind.

Biomass

Wood Burning

1) *Put* the stages in the generation of electricity from wood burning in their correct order.

harvest trees	burn in power station furnace	cultivate fast-growing trees
produce steam	chop up trees	generate electricity	power turbine

2) *Some scientists have worked out that on average, in the USA over 24 hours, the amount of radiation falling on the land is about 180 W/m².* If we take this figure, then *how much* energy falls on 1m² in ***a)*** 1 hour? ***b)*** 1 day? ***c)*** 1 year? ***d)*** 5 years?

3) *A bit of calculation can come up with the amount of energy falling on a forest of area 5km by 5km over a five year period.* *How much* energy is this?

4) *However, trees don't convert all of the incident solar energy into chemical energy. They are not 100% efficient.* Why else can't we take the figure above as the amount of *useful chemical energy* produced in the forest?

5) *A little more estimation can come up with an overall efficiency rate of 1% for the conversion of solar energy into chemical energy by trees.* How much *useful energy* does this result in over the 5 years?

6) If a wood-burning power station is 10% efficient, *how long* would a 1000 MW station take to burn the 5 years' worth of wood from our forest?

7) *How big* a forest is needed to grow 5 years' worth of fuel for the power station in 5 years?

8) What is the *main conclusion* about wood burning that these calculations show us?

Environmental Concerns

9) *An environmental group has started up a campaign against plans to run a trial with a wood burning power scheme. They claim that the main product of burning the wood will be carbon dioxide, which will add significantly to the Greenhouse Effect.* Is this a valid argument? *Explain*.

10) *The initial costs for setting up the scheme should not be too high.* What will the costs be when the scheme is *up and running*?

11) *A shady local businessman claims that he can get hold of wood much cheaper from the rainforests in a developing country. He says that as you need wood, it doesn't matter where it comes from, and the developing country will be grateful for the money.* What are the *ecological arguments* against taking him up on his offer?

12) What could you do to try and convince those who say that huge forests of identical trees would be a real *eyesore*, and use up too much of the land?

13) *The burning of wood in the furnace would still lead to some of the problems associated with burning coal in more traditional power stations.* What do you think they could be?

14) *There is another way that scientists have thought of using living organisms to harness energy from the Sun.* *Liquid or gaseous fuels*, *such as alcohol or methane, may be made.* Look at the diagram, *redraw* it and *add the labels* from the box below.

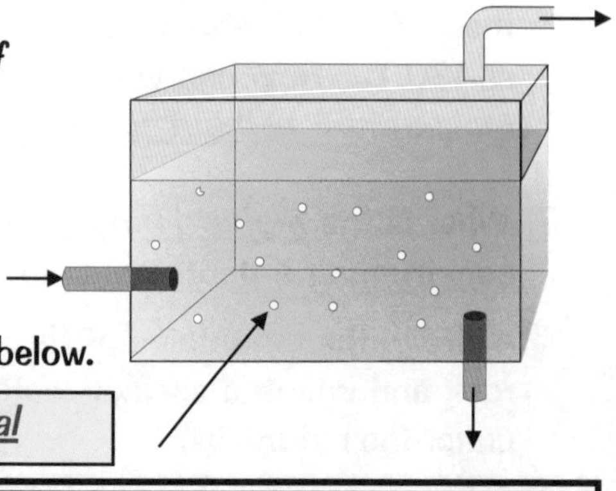

digester liquid	organic material	fuel gas	waste material

Top Tips: Having a grasp of the sorts of figures involved in biomass schemes — like the sizes of the forests — would be a big help in Exams. And you need to know about the *advantages* as well as the *problems*. Bear in mind that biomass doesn't *just* refer to the harvesting and burning of trees — you can use gas from rotting vegetation or sewage. Nice.

Solar Energy

Harnessing the Sun's Power

1) a) What are the *three* different ways of harnessing solar energy shown below?

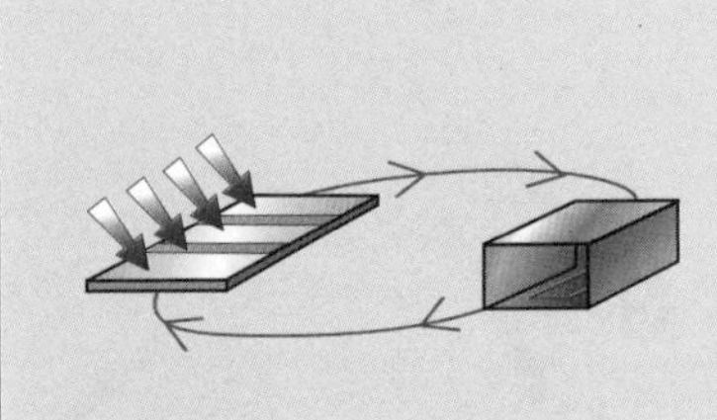
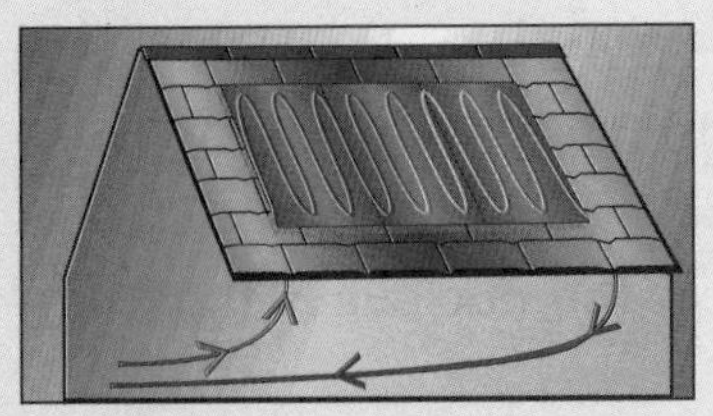

b) *Here are a number of statements about solar energy.* Decide *which* of the three methods they apply to:

i) The Sun's rays are *focused* onto one spot.
ii) *Electric currents* are produced directly.
iii) Curved mirrors *reflect* rays from the Sun.
iv) A matt black surface *absorbs* solar radiation.
v) Water is turned into *steam* to drive a turbine.
vi) *Initial costs* are very high relative to output.
vii) *Water pipes* feed in cold water and take away warmer water.
viii) Extremely *high temperatures* are produced.

Solar Cells

2) *A solar cell array is to be fitted to a satellite that is going to be launched into an orbit around the Earth. It's reckoned that the total solar energy arriving in the region of the Earth is 1350 W/m^2. A new design of solar cell is 10% efficient. When the satellite is functioning fully, its power consumption will be 3.3kW.*

a) Calculate the *area* of solar cells needed.
b) Will there be restrictions on when the satellite is able to be *fully operational*?
c) For a solar powered machine to operate at the Earth's surface, how would the area of cell array compare? *Explain*.

Heating your Home

3) *An architect is designing a house that will rely on solar panels to heat some of the water for the central heating. He wants to use a* silver material *for the panels, as this will look futuristic.* Explain why this is not a good colour for the panels, and tell him where exactly the panels should be placed.

4) A local newspaper has started a campaign to get a solar furnace built in the UK. List some of the *disadvantages* there would be to locating such a power generator here.

Top Tips: There's *three* methods of *directly* using the Sun's energy here — so in your Exam you must be sure which one you're talking about. Learn *how* each one works, and what the *disadvantages* are. Think about our weather, and what use each of the methods would be in Britain.

Atomic Structure and Isotopes

Atomic Structure

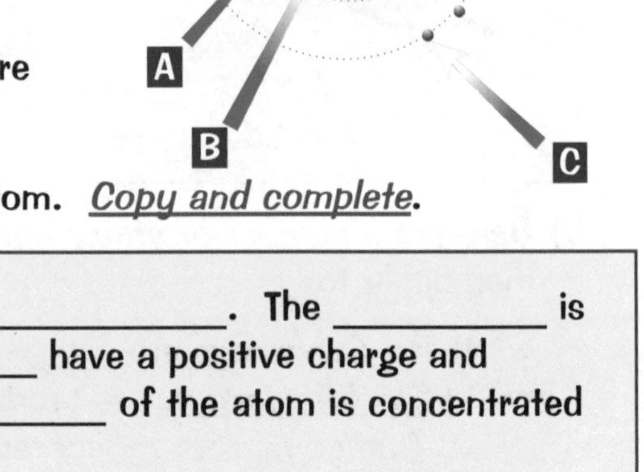

1) *The diagram opposite shows the particles that constitute an atom.*

a) *Name the particles* labelled A, B and C.

b) What stops the electrons from flying away from the nucleus?

c) How many *neutrons* are there in the nucleus if there are 16 nucleons in this atom?

2) The following paragraph describes the structure of an atom. *Copy and complete*.

All atoms consist of a __________ and a number of __________. The __________ is made up of __________ and neutrons. __________ have a positive charge and __________ are electrically neutral. Most of the __________ of the atom is concentrated here but it takes up a relatively small __________.
The __________ orbit the __________. They carry a negative charge (and are really really __________). The ratio of the mass of an electron to the mass of a proton or neutron is about __________. The masses of the __________ and the proton are almost __________.

3) *Complete the table* opposite which summarises the relative mass and electrical charges of the sub-atomic particles.

Particle	Relative Mass	Electric Charge
Proton		
Neutron		
Electron		

Rutherford's Scattering Experiment

4) *The diagram below shows the apparatus used by Lord Rutherford to probe the structure of the atom.*

a) *Name the particles* that are directed at the gold foil.

b) Why does this apparatus need to operate in a *vacuum*?

c) Which of the detectors measures the *highest* count rate?

d) Some particles are detected at Y. *Explain* this observation using your knowledge of atomic structure.

e) *Just a very small fraction of the incident particles are scattered more than 90° by the foil (some of these are detected by detector Z).*
What does this tell you about the *nuclei* of the gold atoms?

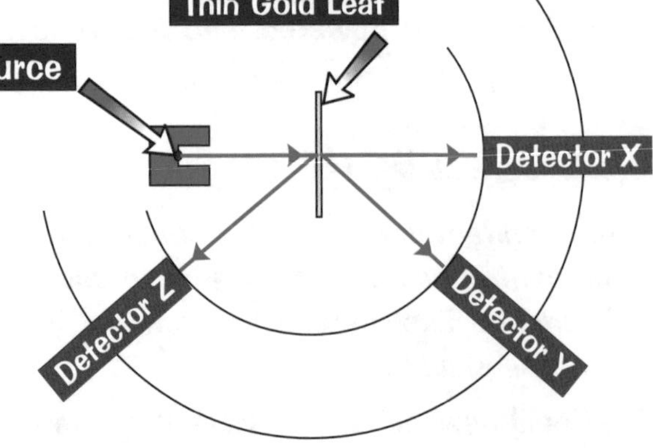

f) Gold was chosen as the target for this experiment. Give a *reason* for this choice.

g) Explain why a *gaseous* target would be unsuitable.

Atomic Structure and Isotopes

Notation for Mass Number and Atomic Number

5) *A stable atom of bismuth has a mass number of 209.*

a) Explain what is meant by "*mass number*".

The atomic number of bismuth is 83.

b) Calculate the number of neutrons in the nucleus of a *stable* bismuth atom.

c) Describe how the structure of an *unstable* atom of bismuth will be different to a *stable* atom of bismuth.

6) Copy the table opposite and *fill in the missing data*.

	Number of electrons	Number of protons	Number of neutrons	Mass Number	Symbol
oxygen-16		8			$^{16}_{8}O$
aluminium-27	13				
radium-226		88			
strontium-90	38				
hydrogen-3		1			

Isotopes

7) *Copy and complete* the following paragraph about isotopes using the given words. You may use a word more than once:

atomic mass alpha decay neutrons electrons stable beta three element energy protons

Isotopes of the same ______________ have equal numbers of ___________ and _________ but different numbers of ______________. Hence they have the same ________________ number but a different __________ number. Every ___________ has at least __________ different isotopes but usually only one or two ____________ ones. If a radioactive isotope decays, radiation is emitted. If an ____________ or a __________ particle is emitted then a different _____________ is formed.

8) Information about six atoms A, B, C, D, E and F is given below.

Atom A: 8 neutrons, mass number 16

Atom B: 3 electrons, mass number 7

Atom C: 8 protons, mass number 17

Atom D: 6 neutrons, mass number 11

Atom E: 3 neutrons, mass number 6

Atom F: 6 protons, mass number 12

For which three atoms do you not need the mass number information to identify the element?

9) *Hydrogen has three different isotopes.*

a) Write down the *common names* for these isotopes.

b) Which isotope is found in "*heavy water*"? Give a reason for the term "heavy water".

The three isotopes of hydrogen have identical chemical properties.

c) Give a reason why you might expect the *chemical properties* to be the same.

d) The boiling points of the three isotopes are different. *Explain* why.

Top Tip OK, there's quite a few numbers here. Just remember these definitions: MASS N$^{o.}$ = N$^{o.}$ OF PROTONS + N$^{o.}$ OF NEUTRONS and ATOMIC N$^{o.}$ = JUST N$^{o.}$ OF PROTONS (OR ELECTRONS). *Isotopes* of elements have *different numbers of neutrons* (so different mass N$^{o.}$) but the *same number of protons* (so same atomic N$^{o.}$). Remember that too...it's important. Strangely enough, atoms are *mostly empty space* with almost all the mass in a tiny bit in the middle — that's what Rutherford's scattering experiment is about.

Three Types of Radiation

Properties of Alpha, Beta and Gamma Radiation

1) *The diagram below shows alpha, beta and gamma radiation being fired at a line of obstacles.*

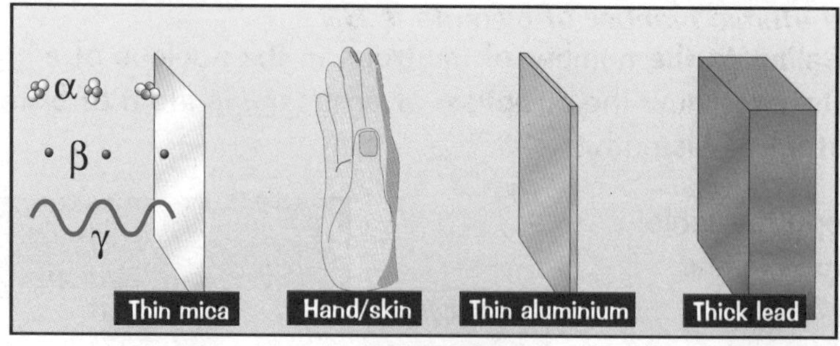

a) Copy the diagram. For each particle, draw a line to show the path it travels before it is absorbed.

b) Give a reason why alpha particles only penetrate a short distance into a material.

2) *The table lists some physical properties of alpha, beta and gamma radiation. The information has been mixed up.*

Match each to the correct radiation.

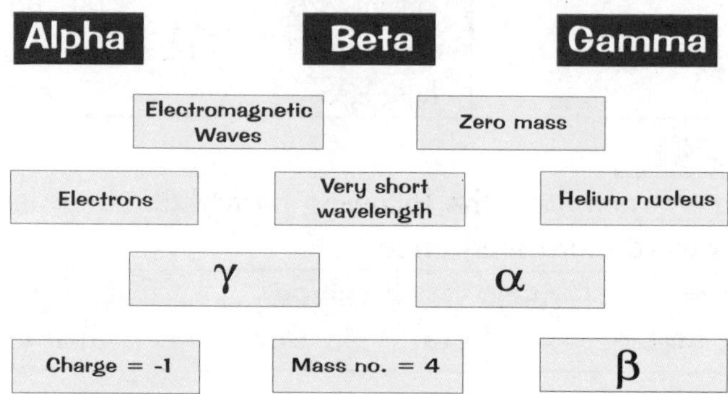

3) For each question a) to h), state which of alpha particles, beta particles and gamma radiation

a) has the largest mass?
b) travels at the speed of light?
c) causes the most ionisation?
d) has zero electrical charge?
e) is present in background radiation?
f) discharges a gold-leaf electroscope?
g) is identical to a helium nucleus?
h) is an electron travelling at high speed?

Ionising Effects of Radiation

4) *When radiation travels through matter it can cause ionisation.*

a) Explain what is meant by the term "ionisation"?

The diagram below shows a simplified drawing of an experiment to demonstrate that radiation can ionise matter.

The space between the plates is filled with argon gas at low pressure. A flow of current is measured.

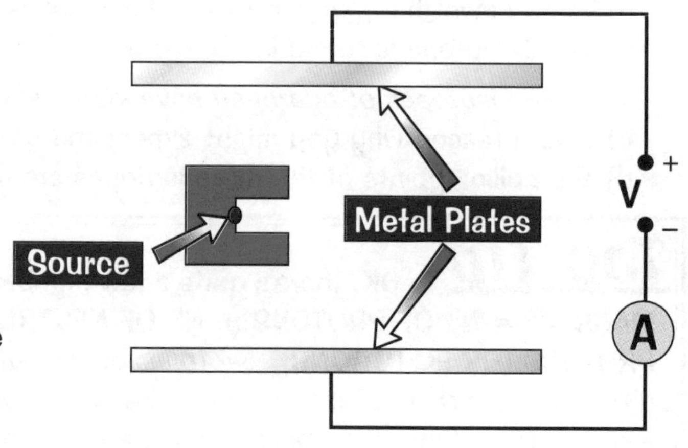

b) Name the two different particles formed when radiation from the source ionises an argon atom.

c) Describe how this leads to a current flow in the circuit.

d) The argon gas is removed from between the plates, leaving a vacuum behind. Explain why there is now no current flow.

Three Types of Radiation

Two Experiments with Radiation

5) *The diagram opposite shows a radiation source placed between two charged plates.*

The source emits alpha, beta and gamma radiation, and the radiation tracks X, Y and Z are shown.

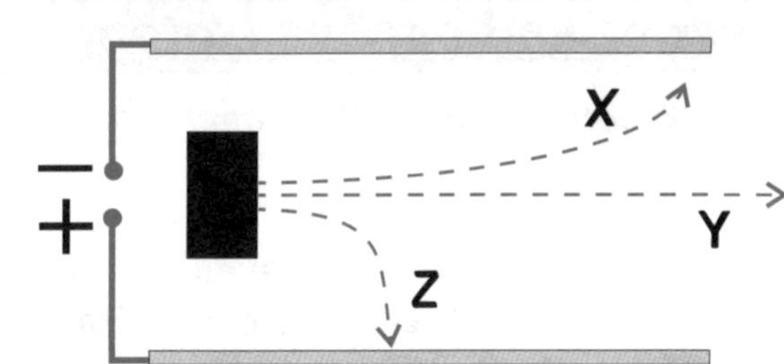

a) *Copy the diagram* and add the following labels to it.

positive plate, radiation source, power supply, negative plate

b) Which type of radiation follows track X?
c) Which type of radiation follows track Y?
d) Which type of radiation follows track Z?
e) *Explain carefully* how you identified the radiation tracks X, Y and Z.

6) *An experiment was done to identify the particles emitted from 4 different radioactive sources. These sources are named P, Q, R and S. It is known that one source emits only alpha particles, another only beta particles, another only gamma radiation, and one source gives out two types of radiation.*

The radiation count was measured for each source for the same time using a G-M tube.
Readings were taken without any obstacle present and then with different materials shielding each source.
The results are displayed in the table.

Shielding	P	Q	R	S
Nothing	20	25	20	17
Thick card	0	11	18	17
Thin aluminium sheet	0	9	0	16
2cm of lead	0	7	0	9

Use the information above to *identify the radiation* from each source P, Q, R and S.

Radioactive Decay

7) Referring to the periodic table inside the front cover, *complete the decay* for the following isotopes, writing down the *daughter atom* and the *emitted radiation*. The first has been done for you.

a) Alpha decay of Uranium-235, $^{235}_{92}U \rightarrow\ ^{231}_{90}Th + ^{4}_{2}\alpha$

b) Beta decay of Carbon-14, $^{14}_{6}C \rightarrow$

c) Beta decay of Potassium-40, $^{40}_{19}K \rightarrow$

d) Beta decay of Radium-228, $^{228}_{88}Ra \rightarrow$

e) Gamma decay of Iodine-131, $^{131}_{53}I \rightarrow$

Top Tip You MUST know the differences between the types of radiation. Learn them NOW and make life easier for yourself later.

Alpha particles are *helium nuclei* He^{2+} — stopped by *hand/skin/paper*.
Beta particles are *electrons* e^- — stopped by *thin metal*.
Gamma radiation is very short wavelength *electromagnetic waves* — stopped by *thick lead*.
All the questions on these pages are great for testing how well you know your stuff — so do them again and again.

Radioactive Materials

Uses of Radioactive Isotopes in Medicine

1) *Radioactive iodine-131 is commonly used in medicine as a tracer.*

a) Explain what you understand by the word "*tracer*".
b) Where will iodine-131 be concentrated if injected? Why is this?
c) What *type of radiation* is emitted by iodine-131?
d) Why would an alpha-emitting isotope be *unsuitable* for use in medicine as a tracer? Give *two* reasons.

2) *This question concerns the treatment of cancer using radiotherapy.*

a) High doses of gamma rays can be used to treat cancers. What effect do gamma rays have on living cells?
b) *Explain* why a patient on a course of radiotherapy feels very ill.
c) For the treatment to be a success, what *two factors* does the radiotherapist need to consider before starting the treatment?

Sterilising Food

3) Copy out the following paragraph and *fill in the gaps*.

irradiation dose surgical temperatures radioactive sterilise gamma instruments damage exposed microbes fresh safe emitter

A high dose of ________________ radiation can be used to ________________ food, keeping it ________________ for longer. The process kills harmful ________________, but does less ________________ to food, as it doesn't involve exposure to high ________________ like boiling. The food is not ________________ afterwards, so it is perfectly ________________ to eat. The isotope needs to be a very pure ________________ of gamma rays. This method can also be used to sterilise ________________ ________________.

Words and Phrases

4) After the sentences a) to g), write down the *correct word or phrase* from this list below.

Carbon-14 Heat Half-life Radioactive decay Chain reaction Uranium Electricity

a) Used as a nuclear fuel.	
b) Time taken for a sample's count rate to drop by one half.	
c) Energy is continuously generated in a nuclear fuel by a ...	
d) Useful for finding how long ago preserved plants and animals died.	
e) Radioactive decay always gives out energy in this form.	
f) Form of energy leaving a nuclear power station.	
g) Responsible for much of the heat inside the Earth.	

Radioactive Materials

Monitoring the Thickness of Materials

5) *Look at the diagram below showing how the thickness of a metal sheet is kept constant by the use of a radiation source.*

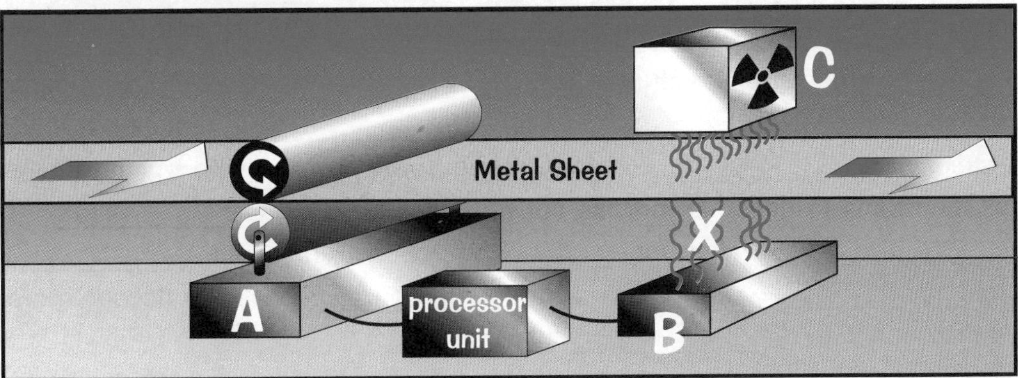

a) Name A, B and C. What type of radiation is X?
b) Suppose the thickness of the metal passing C increases. How does the system detect this change, and how does it return the thickness to its preset value?
c) The radioactive isotope used here must have a long half-life. Explain what would go wrong if the half-life was only two hours.
d) What type of radiation would you choose if you wanted to monitor the thickness of cardboard?
e) Explain why gamma radiation would be the wrong choice of radiation in d).

Leak Detection

6) *Gamma-emitting isotopes can be used to find out whether containers or pipes are leaking or not. An engineer wants to test an underground water pipe for leaks without digging up the road. It is buried one metre below the pavement.*

a) Describe what the engineer would do to carry out his test.
b) The isotope needs to have a half-life of about a week. What problems could occur if it was much longer or shorter than this?

Summary

7) Copy and complete the table summarising the uses of radioactive isotopes.

Use of radioactive isotope	Alpha, beta or gamma emitter?	Short, medium or long half-life?	Reason for choosing short, medium or long half-life
Tracers in medicine			
Tracers in industry			
Sterilisation of food			
Thickness control (paper)			
Thickness control (metal sheets)			

Top Tip You'll definitely need to know at least three examples of where each radiation source is used (like the ones on these pages) — they're seriously easy marks. And you absolutely have to remember what the half-life of the source means and why that source is chosen. It all boils down to knowing your radiation — back to p 130 if you don't.

Half-Life

The Half-Life of Radioactive Atoms

1) *Copy and complete* the following sentences about the half-life of radioactive atoms.

zero long time half atoms radioactivity gamma alpha beta short nucleus decreases decay

The ____________ of a sample always ____________ over time. Each time a decay happens ____________, ____________ or ____________ radiation is emitted. This means a radioactive ____________ has decayed. The problem with trying to measure the time for all the atoms to decay is that the activity never reaches ____________. Half-life is the ____________ taken for ____________ of the radioactive ____________ now present to ____________. An isotope with a ____________ half-life decays more quickly than an isotope with a ____________ half-life.

Count Rates

2) *Below is a table showing how the count rate decreases with time for a sample of polonium-218.*

Count rate in counts per second	390	307	240	194	156	123	96
Time in minutes	0	1	2	3	4	5	6

a) Using the data in the table, *plot a graph* of count rate (vertical axis) against time (horizontal axis).

b) Using your graph, *estimate* the half-life of polonium-218.

3) *A sample of a radioactive substance was found to be emitting 8000 beta particles a second at the beginning of an experiment. Fifteen minutes later, it was emitting 4000 beta particles a second.*

a) What is the *half-life* of the radioactive substance?

b) *How many minutes* after the start would you expect to measure a count rate of 1000 particles per second?

c) What count rate would you expect to measure after *two hours*?

d) *Background radiation from radioactive materials in the ground or in the air is about 2 counts per second.* How long would it take the count rate from the substance to fall *below this background count*?

4) *The count rate from a radioactive material was measured using a G-M tube and counter. These are the results below:*

Count rate in counts per second	95	73	55	42	32	23	18
Time in seconds	0	10	20	30	40	50	60

a) *Plot a graph* of count rate in counts / second (vertical axis) against time in seconds (horizontal axis).

b) *Find the half-life* of the material by finding how long it took the count rate to fall from 90 to 45.

c) Another material has a very low activity which makes it difficult to measure its activity above the background radiation. *Describe* how you might overcome this problem.

Half-Life

The Half-Life of Carbon

5) *The half-life of carbon-14 is 5,600 years. Carbon-14 makes up about 1 part in 10,000,000 of the carbon in air.* For each item in a) to c), calculate how long ago it was living material.

a) A fossil containing 1 part in 320,000,000 carbon-14.

b) A spear handle containing 1 part in 80,000,000 carbon-14.

c) An axe handle containing 1 part in 20,000,000 carbon-14.

6) Fill in the gaps in the paragraph below.

> Carbon-14 makes up about one ten-____________ of the carbon in the air (carbon-____________ is the main isotope of carbon). This level stays fairly ____________ in the atmosphere. The same proportion of carbon-14 is also found in ____________ things. However, when they ____________, the carbon-14 is trapped and it gradually ____________ . By simply measuring the ____________ of carbon-14 found in the artifact, you can easily calculate how ____________ ago the item was ____________ material using the ____________ of 5,600 years.

7) *Igneous rocks can be dated if you measure the ratios of uranium-238 and its decay product lead. The half-life of uranium-238 is 4.5 billion years.* Assuming no lead was present when the rocks were formed, find the ages of the rocks in a) to d) using the given ratios:

a) Uranium : lead is 1 : 1

b) Uranium : lead is 75 : 525

c) Uranium : lead is 1 : 0

d) Uranium : lead is 75 : 225

Radioactive Decay of Lead

8) *Lead-210 (atomic number 82) decays with the emission of a beta particle. Bismuth-210 is formed, which decays with the emission of a beta-particle to form polonium-210.*

a) Draw the above decay series, showing the mass and atomic numbers for all the atoms.

b) The graph opposite shows how the activity of bismuth–210 varies with time. Estimate the half-life of bismuth-210.

c) Polonium-210 decays with the emission of an α-particle. An isotope of lead is formed. What is the mass number of this isotope of lead?

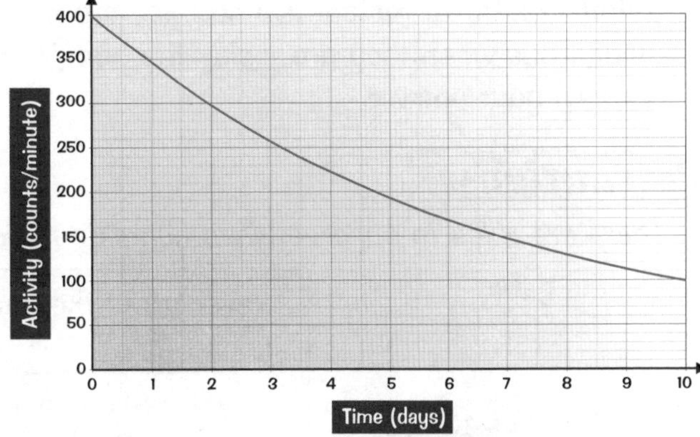

9) The table below shows how the activity of a radioactive source changes with time. The background count rate was determined to be 10 counts/min.

Time(s)	5	10	15	20	25	30	35	40	45	50	55	60	65	70	75
Activity(counts/s)	100	76	68	64	56	50	44	38	32	28	26	22	20	16	14

a) Use the data to estimate the half-life of the radioactive source.

b) The background radiation was measured over a long time. Explain why this is necessary.

Top Tips Don't forget when a nucleus decays, it can give out alpha, beta or gamma radiation. Half-life is also really important. The thing is, radioactivity never completely dies away, but just keeps on halving. The time taken for it to drop by half is the half-life. Don't worry if you find the idea of half-life confusing, the questions are pretty straightforward.

Radiation Hazards and Safety

Damage to Living Cells

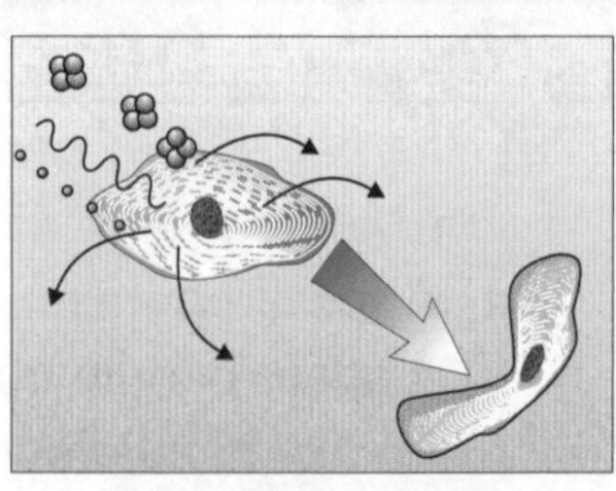

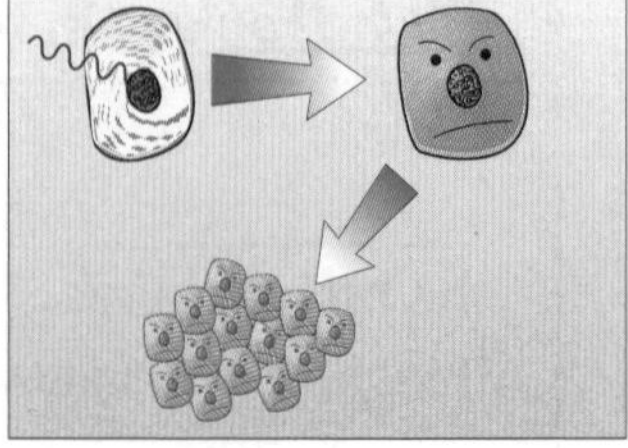

1) *Radioactive particles can be harmful to living cells.*
   a) Which *types of radiation* can do this damage?
   b) What *process* usually has to happen for damage to occur?
   c) Which part of the cell controls *cell function*?
   d) What do we call a cell that has been *slightly altered*, but not killed?
   e) Why are these cells so dangerous?
   f) What do we call the *condition* commonly caused by these cells?

2) *Different types of radiation cause varying degrees of damage to cells.*
   a) Which of an *alpha particle*, a *beta particle* or a *gamma ray* is likely to cause the *most damage* to cells?
   b) Why is this radiation more dangerous? Give *two reasons*.

Exposure to Radiation

3) *Radioactive particles can also give a person "radiation sickness".*
   a) How could a person develop radiation sickness?
   b) What happens to the body to cause radiation sickness?

4) List *at least three factors* which determine how much harm is done to a person when exposed to radiation.

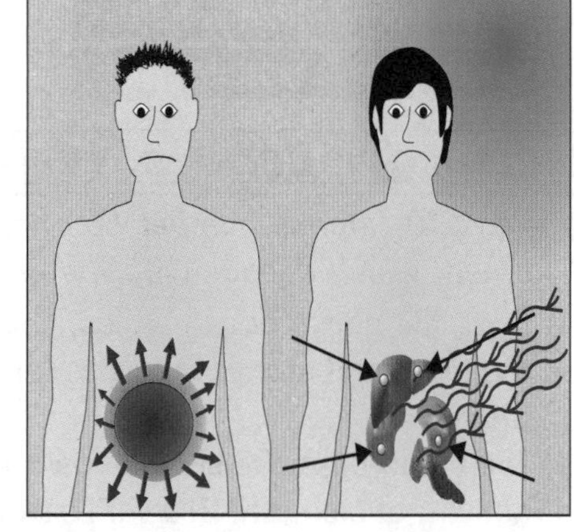

5) *Radioactive sources outside the body —*
   What type(s) of radioactivity are most dangerous when they are *outside* the body? *Explain* your answer.

6) *Radioactive sources inside the body —*
   What type(s) of radioactive sources are most dangerous when they are *inside* the body? *Explain* your answer.

Precautions

7) *There are rules to observe when handling radioactive materials in a school laboratory.*
   Fill in the gaps.

   Never allow the source to come into contact with the ______________. ______________ should always be used to handle radioactive materials. Keep the source as ______________ ______________ the body as possible. Point the source ______________ ______________ the body. Avoid looking ______________ at the source. Keep the source in a box made from ______________ . When the experiment is finished, ______________ the source as soon as possible.

8) *People who work in the nuclear industry take even greater precautions.*
   Describe precautions workers can use to protect themselves from the following risks:
   a) Tiny radioactive particles being inhaled or getting stuck on the skin.
   b) Areas highly contaminated with gamma radiation.
   c) Areas too dangerous even for the best-protected workers.

Radiation Hazards and Safety

Smoke Detectors

9) *The diagram shows a design for a smoke detector that could be fitted in a house. A weak radioactive source causes ionisation between the electrodes. The ions are attracted to one of the electrodes, and a small current flows.*

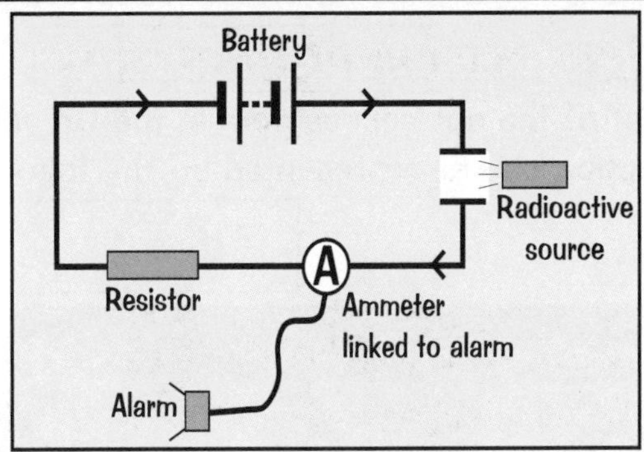

a) What *type of source* would be suitable for this application?
b) What happens when smoke enters the detector? How does this set off the alarm?
c) Some consumers might be worried about the presence of a radioactive source in the detector. How would you reassure them?

Medical Treatment

10) *In the Health Services, radiation is used in the treatment of many cancers.*

a) What *type of radiation* is generally used?
b) What does the radiation do?
c) Why does the radiation need to be *very well-targeted*?

The medical physicists who are responsible for calculating the doses need to ensure that the dose of radiation is not too low or too high.

d) What could happen if the dose is *too low*?
e) What could happen if the dose is *too high*?

Some More Questions on Hazards and Safety

11) A burn caused by radiation can look just like a normal burn, with redness and blistering around the affected area. *However, radiation burns heal a lot more slowly than normal burns.* Why do you think this is?

12) *Young children and developing embryos are particularly susceptible to the effects of radiation.* Why is this?

13) *Bone marrow is important for white blood cell production and is easily damaged by radiation.*
What effect do you think a *large dose* of radiation to the bone marrow would have on
a) white blood cell production.
b) the body as a whole.

14) *The Chernobyl power station disaster released (among other things), a cloud of radioactive iodine-131. Iodine is absorbed by the thyroid gland in the neck. People exposed to the radiation were given a course of iodine tablets.*
— What were the authorities hoping to achieve by doing this?

Top Tips More great examples of radiation, which you WILL need, so add them to your brain-file. You already know that radiation can be dangerous but you need to *learn* all the *safety precautions*. I realise they aren't all that exciting, but they can ask you to list them in the Exam for some nice easy marks. They can also ask you *how* radiation messes up your body and *which kinds* of radiation are the *most dangerous*, so learn and enjoy.

Nuclear Fission

Nuclear Fission of Uranium

1) Most of the nuclear reactors in the UK rely on the nuclear fission of uranium fuel. This reaction can be represented by the following equation.

$$^{235}_{92}U + ^{1}_{0}n \rightarrow ^{90}_{36}Kr + ^{143}_{56}Ba + 3(^{1}_{0}n)$$

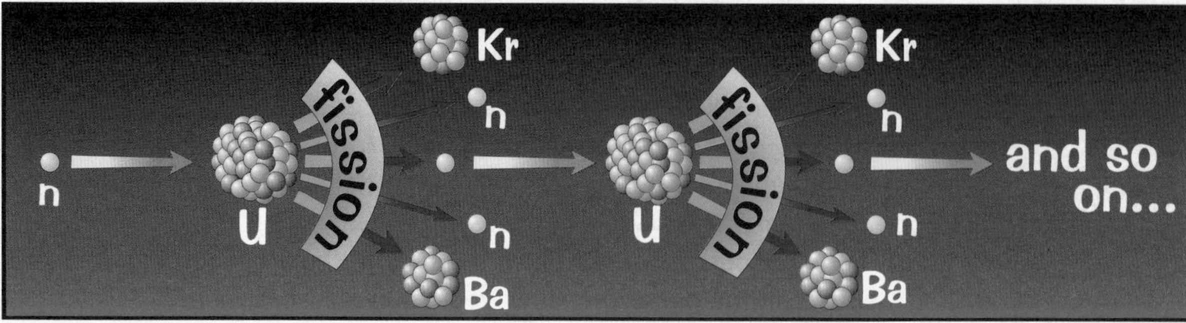

a) How many protons are there in the nucleus of the uranium atom?
b) How many neutrons are there in the nucleus of the uranium atom?
c) How many protons are there in the nucleus of the krypton atom?
d) How many neutrons are there in the nucleus of the krypton atom?
e) How many protons are there in the nucleus of the barium atom?
f) How many neutrons are there in the nucleus of the barium atom?
g) How many protons in total are there on each side?
h) How many neutrons are there in total on each side?

Energy Released by Nuclear Fission of U-235

2) *Each time a U-235 nucleus undergoes fission, 6.2×10^{-11} joules of energy is released.*

a) What is the mass of one mole of U-235?
b) How many particles is this?
c) How many particles are there in 1kg of U-235?
d) How much energy is released when 1kg of U-235 undergoes fission?

By contrast, the energy available in 1kg of natural gas is 5.6×10^{7} joules.

e) What conclusion can be drawn from this?

Chain Reactions

3) The fission of U-235 can be described by the equation: $^{235}_{92}U + ^{1}_{0}n \rightarrow ^{90}_{36}Kr + ^{143}_{56}Ba + 3(^{1}_{0}n)$

a) How many free neutrons are there to start with?
b) How many free neutrons are there after the first reaction?
c) If all these neutrons cause further fission, how many free neutrons are generated in the second stage of reactions?

d) Use a table similar to the one on the right to calculate which reaction stage first produces more than 1000 neutrons.

Stage	0	1	2	3
Number of free neutrons	1	3		

e) Explain why fission is described as a chain reaction.
f) What happens if the chain reaction is allowed to continue uncontrolled?

4) *One way of ensuring that the reaction does not run out of control is to begin with a mass of uranium less than the critical mass.* Explain why a chain reaction cannot continue in a mass of uranium less than the critical mass.

Nuclear Fission

Nuclear Bombs

5) *The scientists and engineers in charge of researching the first nuclear bombs knew about the importance of the critical mass. Why was there no danger of a nuclear explosion before the bomb was detonated?*

6) When a nuclear explosion occurs the fission products can be spread over a large area. What *name* do we give to these *radioactive products*?

Nuclear Waste

7) *The most abundant isotopes of krypton and barium are stable, these are;*

$^{84}_{36}\text{Kr}$ and $^{137}_{56}\text{Ba}$

a) *Compare* the neutron and proton numbers of these *stable* isotopes with the corresponding numbers for the krypton and barium *products in the decay* of U-235.

Isotopes that have too many neutrons generally emit beta radiation.

b) What radiation is emitted by the *unstable* barium and krypton isotopes ?

It is found that these isotopes have very long half-lives.

c) What problems does this cause the nuclear industry?

Nuclear Power Stations and Submarines

8) *Nuclear fission can be used to power nuclear reactors in either power stations or nuclear submarines.*

a) How is the heat produced in these reactors used to generate electricity?

A typical nuclear power station will generate about 800 MW of electrical power.

b) If 1 kg of uranium fuel can release about 2×10^{13} joules of energy, and a power station is 30% efficient, what *mass of fuel* will the station require in a year?

9) *The neutrons that are produced when uranium-235 splits up are actually travelling too fast to cause further fission. They have to be slowed down. In a reactor, the moderator does this.*

a) What materials are suitable for use as a *moderator*?

b) Control rods are used to control the reaction rate in a nuclear reactor. How do they work?

c) What sort of materials are suitable for use as *control rods*?

Top Tips

Nuclear fission and chain reactions — it sounds hard, but it's not. Fission is just big nuclei splitting into smaller ones, releasing *loads* of energy. Remember that *nuclear* reactions release *way more* energy than *chemical* reactions — that's why nuclear bombs are so much more powerful than ordinary bombs. Chain reaction equations are easy if you remember the mass N$^{os.}$ *and* the atomic N$^{os.}$ balance up on both sides. It's just two easy equations in one, you add up and you take away and you get the answer. The only tricky bit is remembering the mass and atomic N$^{os.}$ for the particles — look at pages 130-133, it's all there.

Nuclear Equations

Revision of the Basics

1) *Copy* the table below and complete the information about alpha, beta and gamma radiation.

Radiation	Mass Number	Atomic Number	Charge
alpha			
beta			
gamma			

2) How does the *mass number* and *atomic number* of a nucleus change, if it emits:
a) an alpha particle? b) a beta particle? c) gamma radiation?

Decay by Alpha Emission

(You may need to peek at the periodic table inside the front cover for the next two questions).

3) The alpha decay of radium-226 is illustrated here.
The following nuclei, a) to i), all decay by alpha emission.

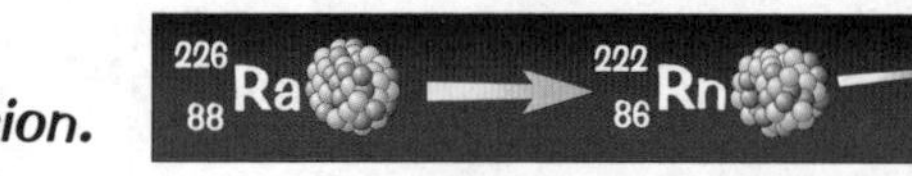

a) Radium, $^{226}_{88}Ra$	b) Thorium, $^{232}_{90}Th$	c) Thorium, $^{228}_{90}Th$
d) Radium, $^{224}_{88}Ra$	e) Polonium, $^{216}_{84}Po$	f) Radon, $^{220}_{86}Rn$
g) Bismuth, $^{212}_{83}Bi$	h) Polonium, $^{212}_{84}Po$	i) Astatine, $^{217}_{85}At$

For each decay *write down* the symbol for the *daughter* nucleus.

Decay by Beta Emission

4) The beta decay of carbon-14 is illustrated here.

The following nuclei, a) to i), all decay by beta emission.

a) Carbon, $^{14}_{6}C$	b) Uranium, $^{237}_{92}U$	c) Plutonium, $^{241}_{94}Pu$
d) Protoactinium, $^{233}_{91}Pa$	e) Bismuth, $^{213}_{83}Bi$	f) Lead, $^{209}_{82}Pb$
g) Thallium, $^{209}_{81}Tl$	h) Radium, $^{225}_{88}Ra$	i) Francium, $^{223}_{87}Fr$

For each decay write down the symbol for the *daughter* nucleus.

5) For the following isotopes a) to d), write down the *nuclear equation* representing the decay.

a) Thorium-234, $^{234}_{90}Th$, decays to form Palladium, $^{234}_{91}Pa$.

b) Thorium-230, $^{230}_{90}Th$, decays to form radium, $^{226}_{88}Ra$.

c) Palladium-234, $^{234}_{91}Pa$, decays to form uranium, $^{234}_{92}U$.

d) Thorium-232, $^{232}_{90}Th$, decays to form radium, $^{228}_{88}Ra$.

Nuclear Equations

Radon and Strontium-90

6) *Some students are carrying out (under supervision) an experiment with radon gas, $^{222}_{86}Rn$. They know that the gas is radioactive, and that it decays by emitting a heavy, positively charged particle, forming polonium, (symbol Po).* Write out the full equation for the decay.

7) *Strontium-90 is a radioactive isotope. It decays to give an isotope of Yttrium with the emission of negatively charged, high energy particles.*
Write down the complete nuclear equation for this decay.

8) a) When an isotope emits gamma rays, what happens to the atomic number and the mass number of the isotope? Explain your answer.

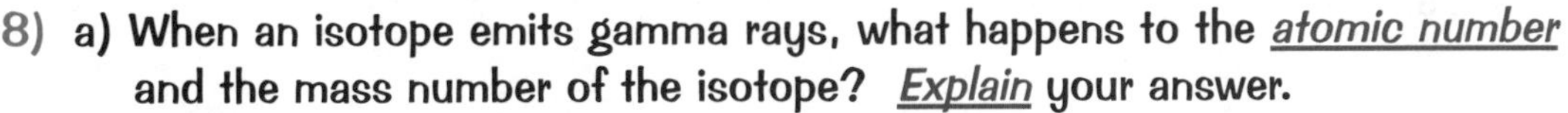

b) What are gamma rays?
c) What is happening inside the nucleus when gamma rays are emitted?

Mass and Energy

9) *One of Einstein's famous discoveries was that mass and energy are equivalent:*

$$E = mc^2$$

Study the radioactive decay below:

$$^{215}_{85}At \rightarrow \, ^{211}_{83}Bi + \, ^{4}_{2}\alpha$$

The atomic masses of these particles are:

At = 214.99866 | Bi = 210.98729 | alpha = 4.00260

a) What is the total mass before the decay?
b) What is the total mass after the decay?
c) What happened during the decay?
d) Does this mean that energy will be taken in or given out?
e) What form is the energy most likely to take?

Changes in Emissions

10) *Most GCSE courses are only concerned with the changes that occur in alpha, beta and gamma emission, but the same principles can be applied to other nuclear changes. One of Ernest Rutherford's famous experiments involved firing alpha particles at nitrogen gas. He found that some of the nitrogen atoms turned into oxygen atoms.*
Complete this nuclear equation to show what other product is formed:

$$^{14}_{7}N + \, ^{4}_{2}\alpha \rightarrow \, ^{17}_{8}O + \, ?$$

11) Complete this nuclear equation:

$$^{9}_{4}Be + \, ^{4}_{2}\alpha \rightarrow \, ? + \, ^{1}_{0}n$$

Top Tips OK, so you're not Einstein. But you don't need to be to do nuclear equations. Mass N$^{os.}$ and atomic N$^{os.}$ ALWAYS balance on both sides of the equation — know the numbers for alpha, beta and gamma emissions and all you're doing is adding up. Energy calculations are just as easy but you have to know why there's a difference in mass. To calculate the energy change use $E = mc^2$ — Einstein did the hard work, so you don't have to.

General Certificate of Secondary Education

Science: Double Award
(Co-ordinated and Modular)
Higher Paper: Trial Examination

Monday 7 June 1999 9.30 am — 11.00 am

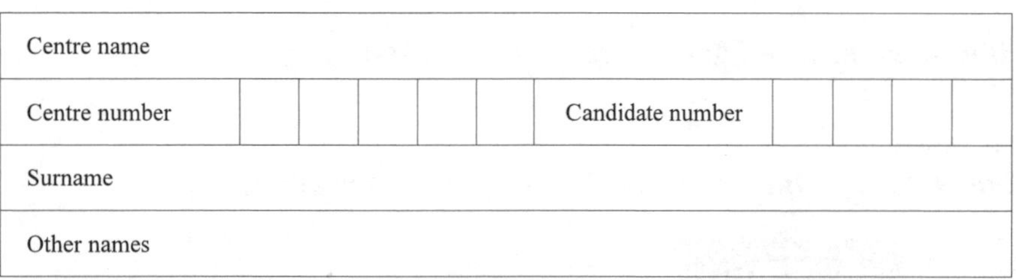

Centre name										
Centre number						Candidate number				
Surname										
Other names										

In addition to this paper you will need
- Calculator
- Pencil
- Protractor

Time
- 1 hour 30 minutes.

Instructions to candidates
- Write your name and other details in the spaces provided above.
- Answer **all** the questions in this paper.
- Write your answers in this combined question paper/answer book.
- Write your answers in blue or black ink or ballpoint pen.
- Do all rough work on the paper.

Information for candidates
- The number of marks is given in brackets at the end of each question or part-question.
- Marks will not be deducted for incorrect answers.
- You are reminded of the need for good English and clear presentation.
- In calculations show clearly how you work out your answers.

For examiner's use	
Page 145	
146	
147	
148	
149	
150	
151	
152	
153	
154	
155	
156	
Total	

1) A skier is travelling over an area where the snow is fresh and not packed down. He comes to a halt and rests. The skis stay on the top of the snow, sinking in just a bit. The skier wants to take a photograph, and not thinking very clearly, clips his boots out of the skis and steps sideways.

a) Use scientific ideas to explain what will happen.

....

....

....

....

....

....

(4 marks)

The skier continues down the slope and gets to the bottom. Here there is a lift waiting to go back up to the top. The skier has a mass of 70kg. The lift has a length of 840m, and rises through a height of 240m. The skier is taken up to the top of the slope in 2 minutes.

b) Calculate the average speed of the skier going up the lift. Show clearly how you get your answer, and give the correct unit.

....

....

....

....

(3 marks)

The formula for kinetic energy is given by:

$$KE = 0.5 \times m \times v^2$$

c) Calculate the kinetic energy of the skier as he is going up the lift.

....

....

....

(2 marks)

The formula for gravitational potential energy is:

$$GPE = m \times g \times h$$

d) Calculate the skier's gain in gravitational potential energy having travelled up the lift. *($g = 10\ m/s^2$).*

....

....

....

(2 marks)

The motor pulling up the lift has an efficiency of 45%.

e) Calculate the energy consumed by the motor pulling the skier to the top of the slope.

....

....

....

(3 marks)

2) The diagram shows an attempt to lift a heavy stone with a strong lever.
The stone has a mass of 350kg.
With the lever positioned as in the diagram, calculate the force F needed to just lift the stone. Take g = 10m/s.
(The mass of the lever is negligible)

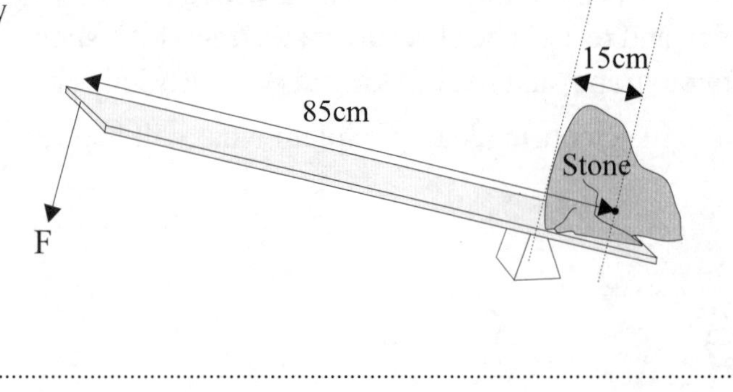

....

....

....

....
(3 marks)

3) A circuit is set up to measure the resistance of a certain component, R

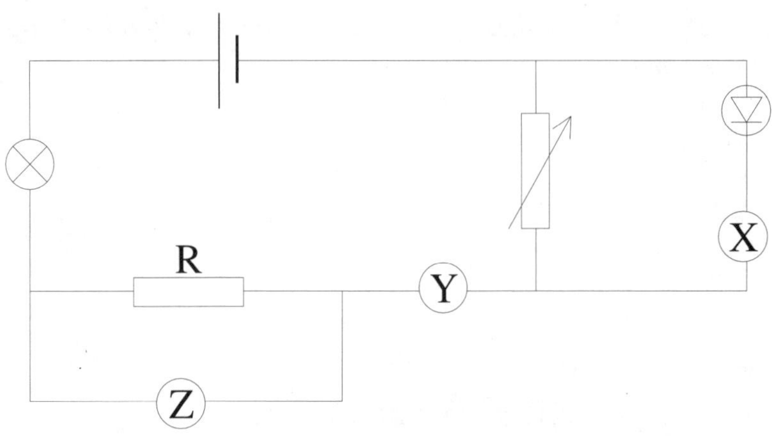

a) If you were setting up the circuit, which positions, X, Y, Z, would you choose to insert the ammeter and voltmeter?

i) Ammeter? ....
(1 mark)

ii) Voltmeter? ....
(1 mark)

b) What scientific term is used to describe the arrangement of

i) The variable resistor and diode ....
(1 mark)

ii) The variable resistor, component R and the lamp ....
(1 mark)

A set of readings of voltage and current are taken for R. They are shown in the table.

V (V)	*I (A)*
0	0
0.2	0.013
0.4	0.027
0.6	0.040
0.8	0.053
1.0	0.067

Leave margin blank

c) On the graph paper, plot a graph of V (vertical axis) against I (horizontal axis). *(4 marks)*

d) What SI units would you use to measure V and I?

i) V? ....
(1 mark)

ii) I? ....
(1 mark)

e) Use the figures or your graph to calculate the resistance of component R. Show your working, and give a unit for your answer.

....

....

....

....
(3 marks)

f) Calculate the value of I you would obtain when the value of V was 2.5 units.

....

....

....

....
(3 marks)

g) On your graph, draw a dotted line, or a line in a different colour, for a resistor having a greater resistance than R. Label it R′. *(2 marks)*

4) Kate's elder brother has gone off to university. He and some friends are living together in a house. They want to work out how much they are spending on electricity. When they moved into the house on September 1st, they wrote down the reading on their electricity meter:

4963985.3 units

They read the meter again on December 1st. This time it reads

4964739.6 units

a) What *scientific* unit do we give for the term "unit"?

....

(1 mark)

b) Calculate the number of units used.

....

....

....

(1 mark)

c) If electricity costs 6.3p per unit, calculate the cost of the electricity used.

....

....

(1 mark)

d) There is also a fixed standing charge of £7.50. What will the total bill be, excluding VAT?

....

(1 mark)

e) State, with a reason, whether you would expect the bill to be higher or lower for the period

i) December 1st to March 1st ....

Reason ....

(2 marks)

ii) June 1st to September 1st ....

Reason ....

(2 marks)

5) This graph shows how the speed of a remote controlled car varies with time.

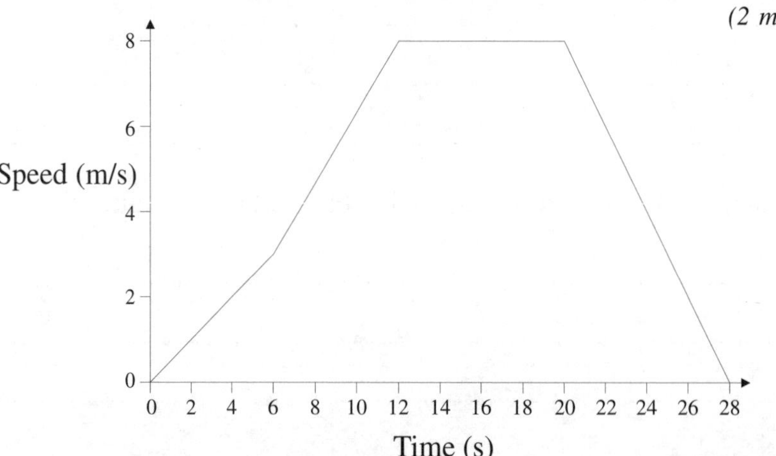

a) The speed of the car is not the same as the velocity. What other attribute of the car's motion must be displayed on the graph for it to convey information about velocity.

....

(1 mark)

b) Use the graph to calculate:

i) The acceleration of the model car in the first 6 seconds.

....
(4 marks)

ii) The distance travelled by the car in the *next* 6 seconds.

....

....

....
(4 marks)

c) The mass of the car is measured and is found to be 1.5kg. Calculate the deceleration produced by the brakes slowing down the car, and then work out the braking force.

....

....

....

....
(4 marks)

6) The diagram shows a Thermos flask (see opposite).

a) There is a narrow space between the two glass walls of the flask. What is contained here?

....
(1 mark)

b) What is the only method of heat transfer that can occur through here?

....
(1 mark)

c) Both the inner and outer walls are coated in shiny metal. What method of heat transfer is reduced by this coating?

....
(1 mark)

d) Explain your answer to part c).

....

....
(2 marks)

e) Give a suitable material for making the cap, and explain your choice.

....

....

....
(2 marks)

f) Why is a cap very important for the Thermos flask?

....
(1 mark)

7) Gerald and Cedric are planning a party. They decide that they will fill balloons with helium gas for the guests. The gas comes in a canister with a volume of 600cm³. The gas is stored at a pressure of 4 atmospheres. Each balloon will be filled with a volume of 50cm³ of gas.

a) Calculate the volume that will be occupied by the gas when it is released at atmospheric pressure.

....

....

....

(3 marks)

b) Now calculate the number of balloons that they will be able to fill with one canister of gas. (Remember that 600cm³ of gas at a pressure of 1 atmosphere will be left in the canister at the end.)

....

....

....

(3 marks)

8) The diagram below shows a ray of light travelling from one medium into another.

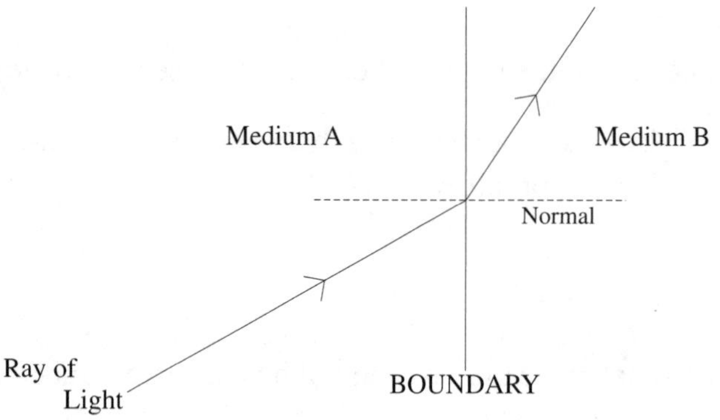

Medium A

Medium B

Normal

Ray of Light

BOUNDARY

a) On the diagram, mark the angle of incidence (i) and the angle of refraction (r).

(2 marks)

b) When the light travels from medium **A** to medium **B**, does its speed increase or decrease?

....

(1 mark)

c) Give a reason for your answer to part b).

....

....

(2 marks)

d) What do we call the process by which the direction of light changes when it goes from one medium to another?

....

(1 mark)

9) Some medical physicists are planning to use a radioactive isotope inside the body of a patient. The isotope that they have decided to use is iodine, $^{131}_{53}\text{I}$.

a) In an atom of this isotope, how many protons and neutrons are there?

i) Protons ....

ii) Neutrons ....

(2 marks)

b) This isotope decays by means of beta decay. After an atom decays, how many protons and neutrons are there?

i) Protons ....

ii) Neutrons ....

(2 marks)

c) What are the beta particles that are given off when the iodine decays?

....

(1 mark)

d) Why is a beta emitter more suitable for this use than an alpha emitter?

....

....

(2 marks)

Before administering the isotope to the patient, the physicists had to carry out an experiment to determine the half-life of the isotope. They took a series of readings of the background count, and came up with a value of 15 counts per minute. Then they took a series of readings of the activity due to a source containing the radioactive isotope.

At the start of their experiment, their reading was 14495 counts per minute. After 32 days, the recorded count rate was 920 counts per minute.

e) Use these figures to calculate a value for the half-life of the isotope.

....

....

(4 marks)

f) Give the name of the device that they could use to detect the radiation.

....

(1 mark)

g) Give three sources of background radiation.

....

....

(3 marks)

For another part of their work, they are asked to prepare a radioactive sample that can be used to treat a cancerous growth on the skin of a patient.

h) What type of radiation would you recommend for this use? Give reasons for your choice.

....

....

....

(3 marks)

10) A group of astronomers are studying a group of stars, and have taken a photograph using the Hubble Space Telescope. This is a telescope on a satellite in orbit around the Earth.

a) Give two advantages of having the telescope in orbit around the Earth.

....

....

....

(2 marks)

The astronomers use special instruments to study the light given off from the stars. They split the light up, and then they can identify the elements present in the star.

b) Name something that can be used to split light up into different colours.

....

(1 mark)

Shown here is a photograph of a group of stars, along with a table showing some information about the labelled stars A, B, C, D and E.

A
C
D
E
B

Star letter	*Mass compared to Sun*	*Stage*	*Heavy elements present?*
A	2	Main Sequence	yes
B	100	Main Sequence	yes
C	0.4	Main Sequence	no
D	0.9	Main Sequence	yes
E	4.2	Red Giant	yes

These five stars are second generation stars apart from one.

c) Which is the only star that is not a second generation star?

....

(1 mark)

d) Explain the difference between "first generation" and "second generation" when talking about stars.

....

....

....

(2 marks)

Leave margin blank

e) To which generation does our Sun belong?

....

(1 mark)

f) Which of the second generation stars is most likely to explode in a supernova explosion? Give a reason for your choice.

....

....

(2 marks)

g) Following a supernova explosion, name two objects that could be left behind.

....

(2 marks)

In a main sequence star, two forces have to balance.

h) What are the names of the two forces?

....

(2 marks)

i) What is the name of the process that stars use to generate their energy?

....

(1 mark)

11) The diagram below shows what happens when white light travels through a prism. The light is dispersed, giving a range of colours.

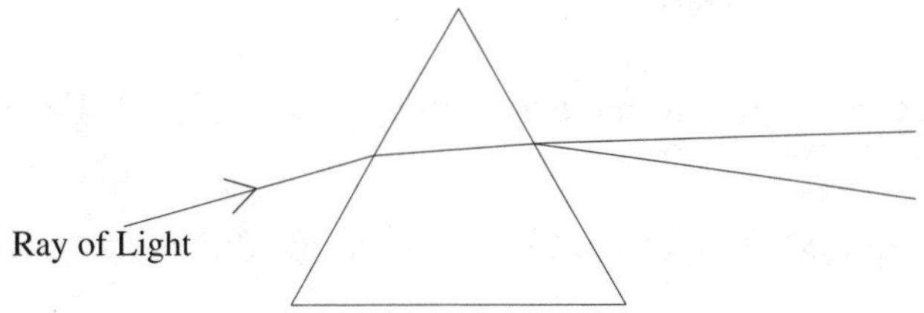

Ray of Light

a) What do we call the range of colours produced in this way?

....

(1 mark)

b) The diagram shows the position of the range of the colours. On the diagram, mark the positions of red (R) and violet (V). *(1 mark)*

c) A radio wave travels at a speed of 3×10^8 m/s. What is the wavelength of the wave if the frequency is 200kHz? Show the equation that you are using, and show all your working out.

....

....

....

....

....

(4 marks)

12) A power station is being designed to burn natural gas fuel and generate electricity.

a) Natural gas is a non-renewable fuel. Give two disadvantages of using non-renewable fuels.

....

....

....

(2 marks)

b) Give the names of two other non-renewable fuels that you know.

....

....

(3 marks)

c) What sort of energy does the natural gas fuel have?

....

(1 mark)

The power station produces electrical energy.

d) Complete the energy flow diagram below showing the basic features of the power station, and show the energy types that are involved at each stage. *(4 marks)*

Fuel → [ ] → [ ] → Generator

Chemical energy → .... energy → .... energy → Electrical energy

The power station has been designed to have an output power of 200MW. The overall efficiency of the station is 30%.

e) Calculate the energy required from the natural gas for one day's operation of the power station.

....

....

....

(5 marks)

The power station generates electricity at a voltage of 25000 volts.

f) Using the figure for the power above, and assuming that the power station only uses one generator, calculate the current flowing out through the wires of the power station.

....

....

....

(4 marks)

Before the electricity is sent to the National Grid, the voltage is stepped up to 400kV.

g) Explain why this is done.

....

....

(2 marks)

h) The primary coil on the step up transformer that transforms the voltage has 800 turns. Assuming that the transformer is 100% efficient, calculate the number of turns needed on the secondary coil.

....

....

....

(4 marks)

i) Give two reasons why the voltage is transformed back down to 240V before it comes into our houses.

....

....

(2 marks)

j) What material is used in the core of a transformer?

....

(1 mark)

13) The diagram opposite shows a coil of wire connected to a galvanometer. The north pole of a magnet is being held near the end of the coil.

When the bar magnet is moved into the coil of wire, the needle on the galvanometer moves to the left, one division.

a) Complete the rest of the table showing the results of various experiments with the coil and bar magnet. *(5 marks)*

Pole of magnet	*Direction moved*	*Speed of movement*	*Galvonometer direction*	*How far?*
North	Into coil	Slowly	Left	1 div
North	Into coil	Quickly		
North	Out of coil	Slowly		
South	Into coil	Quickly		2 div

Another bar magnet is used. This one does not have the poles marked on, but the two ends are coloured red and blue. The blue end of this magnet is moved into the coil at the same speed as the magnet in the first experiment. The galvanometer needle moves to the right, 2 divisions.

b) What can you deduce about the coloured magnet from these experiments? What colours are the North and South poles of the magnet?

....

....

(2 marks)

Leave margin blank

14) There are two types of wave produced by an earthquake. They are known as P waves and S waves.

a) Are P waves longitudinal or transverse?

....

(1 mark)

b) Are S waves longitudinal or transverse?

....

(1 mark)

c) Which type of wave travels faster through the Earth?

....

(1 mark)

Look at this graph showing how the speed of P waves varies according to the depth within the Earth.

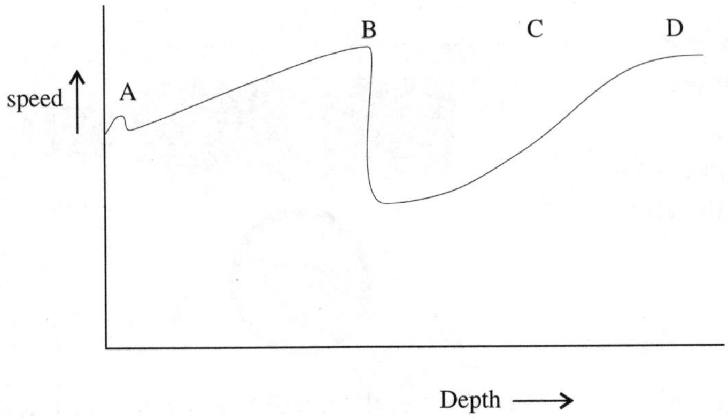

d) What letter on the graph represents the boundary between the mantle of the Earth and the outer core?

....

(2 marks)

e) Why do the waves travel faster the further down they go?

....

....

....

(2 marks)

f) Modern theories about the interior of the Earth suggest that the outer core is made from a liquid. What evidence do we have for this suggestion.

....

....

....

....

....

(3 marks)

PHW40